America's first crop
– can nothing good have endured of it?

Twenty years of farm porch-style interviews about the shade tobacco era in Gadsden Co., FL

Something Gold

Twenty years of farm porch-style interviews about the shade tobacco era in Gadsden Co., FL

by

Kay Davis Lay

Bloomington, IN Milton Keynes, UK

AuthorHouse™
1663 Liberty Drive, Suite 200
Bloomington, IN 47403
www.authorhouse.com
Phone: 1-800-839-8640

AuthorHouse™ *UK Ltd.*
500 Avebury Boulevard
Central Milton Keynes, MK9 2BE
www.authorhouse.co.uk
Phone: 08001974150

© 2007 Kay Davis Lay. All rights reserved.

No part of this book may be reproduced, stored in a retrieval system, or transmitted by any means without the written permission of the author.

First published by AuthorHouse 5/9/2007

ISBN: 978-1-4343-1004-0 (sc)

Printed in the United States of America
Bloomington, Indiana

This book is printed on acid-free paper.

Front cover: George (Sonny) Johnson behind "Duchess," returns an empty tobacco barge to the shade to be filled. Sonny also wrote the "Shade Tobacco Song" words.

Nothing Gold Can Stay

Nature's first green is gold,

Her hardest hue to hold.

Her early leaf's a flower;

But only so an hour.

Then leaf subsides to leaf.

So Eden sank to grief,

So dawn goes down to day.

Nothing gold can stay.

Robert Frost

"Nothing Gold Can Stay" from the THE POETRY OF ROBERT FROST edited by Edward Connery Lathem. Copyright 1923, 1969 by Henry Holt and Company. Copyright 1951 by Robert Frost. Reprinted by permission of Henry Holt and Company, LLC.

To Johnny and Ann

(and to ALL who stick with farming – in the dark, as well as the bright, times)

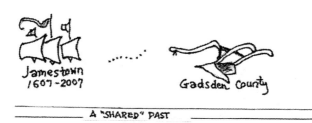

This "sewing together" of experiences from all phases of the tobacco scene in Gadsden County that could be obtained represents a "Legacy Project" to commemorate the 400th Anniversary of Jamestown, VA. (1607 –2007) Beginning in 1829, our way of life derived, in part, from tobacco seed brought here by John "Virginia" Smith that mutated, or so the story goes, with "little DuVal" (Cuban) seed being grown already by Territorial Governor William DuVal – also a Virginian by birth.

Author's Note

In my earliest line of work (stringing shade tobacco – which I started doing at age five when they put a box for me up to the table), I learned to love the simple art of spacing the leaves down a string, and the feel of the smooth, slender needle.

Turning to that familiar pattern, I have tried to thread these narratives. If I remember, a respectable stick had about 36 leaves … no blemishes or tears in any leaf. That is why there are 36 "chapters."

Alas, there will be some flaws you may readily find – it's not always easy to hear names or make sense of tapes. Some were recorded 20 years ago! Also, to keep the spontaneity of discourse, I allowed some leeway with the grammar. (Only changing if someone who checked the transcripts, and virtually each was checked, requested "adjustments." In some cases, they, or I, edited slightly to help the flow.)

Different recordings lent themselves to different formats. I hope you will be tolerant of that. (Some are cut to be essays, some are left as un-cut "interviews," and some – as in "Building A Shade" -- are just moments in time, that I chcrish.)

Mainly, please overlook that it's not always Queen's English. (Thank goodness, neither are farm folks.) They're PEOPLE. And the soul of our country.

Jamestown discovery: Seed that saved Virginia

By Mark St. John Erickson
Newport News (Va.) Daily Press

JAMES CITY, Va.

A Colonial Williamsburg archaeobotanist sifting through the muck from a 400-year-old Jamestown, Va., well has identified what could be the earliest physical evidence of tobacco cultivation in English America.

Recovered by Jamestown Rediscovery archaeologists this past summer, the muddy soil and plant samples also produced unexpected clues suggesting that the oft-maligned settlers made an impressive effort to feed themselves with the wild fruits they found in the New World.

But it was a trio of tiny half-millimeter-wide tobacco seeds that provided the first direct sign of the lucrative cash crop that saved the teetering English colony from ruin.

"To be honest, it's not a very shocking discovery. Jamestown is where you'd expect to find the earliest evidence of tobacco," archaeobotanist Steve Archer said Tuesday.

"On the other hand, it's nice to actually see it for the first time. We have a lot of tobacco pipe stems. They've recovered pipe fragments by the thousands. But this is the first evidence we have of the plant material itself."

Discovered by archaeologists in late 2005, the 15-foot-deep well dates to about 1610, the year that pioneering tobacco planter John Rolfe arrived at Jamestown. So dense and rich were the deposits of artifacts and bones found inside the 6-foot-square shaft that excavators didn't reach the layers below the water table until well into 2006.

In the oxygen-poor environment under the surface of the water, some of the seeds and leaves still showed a tinge of green — making it look as if they had been discarded only a few days earlier.

The News Herald Panama City, Florida Sunday, January 14, 2007 **3D**

There they found a substantial deposit of leaves, nuts, seeds and other plant remains that — in other conditions — would have decayed rapidly after being buried. But in the oxygen-poor environment under the surface of the water, some of the seeds and leaves still showed a tinge of green — making it look as if they had been discarded only a few days earlier.

"There is no other source for this kind of environmental data in such a preserved state," Jamestown Rediscovery director William Kelso said.

Still, the rare find might have quickly spoiled if not for the diligence of the archaeologists and the team of conservators who work at the dig's nearby lab. Knowing that some small but potentially important evidence might slip through the mesh of their one-eighth-inch screens, the scientists also made sure to take 5-liter (5.3-quart) samples of watery muck from each layer of the well they explored.

"We brought them to the lab immediately, where they were put into refrigerators," said staff archaeologist Danny Schmidt, one of the primary excavators. "That way, we knew that whatever was in there would still be preserved."

Funded by National Geographic magazine, Archer's analysis used those samples to detect the presence of scores of seeds, nuts and other plant remains, including the tiny tobacco seeds.

Measuring no larger than the dot of an "i" on a printed page, the minuscule clues first had to be sifted from the soupy soil, a task that Archer — who teaches at the College of William and Mary — accomplished by passing the samples through a series of increasingly smaller geological sieves. Then he examined the accumulated organic material under a high-definition 7,000-power optical microscope at the college's Surface Characterization Laboratory on the campus of Jefferson Lab in Newport News, Va.

"Seeds are nice because they have very specific characteristics," Archer said.

"Tobacco has this very distinctive surface that looks like the pieces of a puzzle. So when you see them, they really jump out at you."

Still to be determined is whether the seeds are specimens of harsh-tasting native tobacco or the smoother South American strain that Rolfe used to cultivate his famous sweet-scented Virginia leaf.

Though Archer attempted to compare the Jamestown examples with modern versions of the Virginia crop, the results were inconclusive. But DNA tests could still help determine the seeds' place of origin.

Additional study also could help determine the significance of the unexpectedly large number of wild berry seeds found in the well samples.

Though the English settlers wouldn't have been familiar with such fruits as persimmon and passion flower, it's clear they were eating these and other wild foods such as blueberries, huckleberries and grapes in large quantities.

"It really does appear as if they were trying to live off the land," Archer said.

Article on Tobacco and Jamestown (used with permission)

Chapters
("Strung" Leaves)

One T.W. Touchton	1
Two Byron Suber	13
Three Newton Edwards	27
Four Forrest (Johnny) Davis, Jr.	37
Five Fain Embry	45
Six Joe Cantey	53
Seven Lynn Betts	67
Eight "Barn Day 1990"	75
Nine M. D. Peavy	83
Ten Ernst and Barbara Bietenholz	93
Eleven Jim Campbell and Archie Hubbard	103
Twelve Rev. Louis Mims	113

Thirteen 　Elise (Scrap) Jackson Williams	121
Fourteen 　Vivian Allen	135
Fifteen 　Maidee Barnett	145
Sixteen 　Building a Shade	149
Seventeen 　Hal Davis	161
Eighteen 　Herschel Edwards	169
Nineteen 　Pat Carman and Barbara Bietenholz & Brigitt Bietenholz Clark	179
Twenty 　Jimmy Bowen	185
Twenty-one 　Harbert (H.C.) and Marjorie Gregory	191
Twenty-two 　Betty Davis Morrison	199
Twenty-three 　Robert and Harriett (Hattie) Parramore	207
Twenty-four 　Fount May	219
Twenty-five 　J. L. (James Louie) Barineau	227

Twenty-six Max Fletcher	245

Twenty-seven
    Trudy (Grubb) Wheeler and
    Jo-Ann (Grubb) Anderson
	259

Twenty-eight William O. (Billy) Perkins	269
Twenty-nine M. E. Smith Howell	283
Thirty Robert M. (Bobby) Hollingsworth	289
Thirty-one Bill Tappan	305
Thirty-two Katie Williams Bell	325
Thirty-three Edna Dykes White	333
Thirty-Four Nathaniel McNealy	339
Thirty-five Frances Lester Butler	347
Thirty-six Suzanne Davis Powell	355
"Loose" Leaves	359

One
T.W. Touchton
Touchton Office, Tallahasse, FL
1984

(At the time this interview was taped – the first one Bob and I did, in our starting quest to find support for preserving the shade tobacco heritage of Gadsden County – Mr. Touchton and his sons had shifted their source of livelihood from farming to construction. Their office was on White Street in Tallahassee.)

The experience I had in the tobacco business was very profitable for me in many ways, and monetarily wise. It gave me a great satisfaction in doing something I was good at. I was from Valdosta, GA., in the flue tobacco business with my father. Then after that six years in the Service, in World War II, and after I got out of the Service, I had met a girl in Havana, and married her, and later came back to buy the place that her and her mother had rented. I decided to grow three acres of tobacco in 1947 with Joe Wedeles Tobacco Company, which was a real daddy to me – Joe Wedeles was. I went in after a contract, and he didn't know me from Adam, but he saw me with my Army clothes on, and he said here's a fellow probably I can help, so he did. He helped me with the financing of it, and I delivered him some good tobacco, and I made some money. I made money the first year, and I made money each year after. I went to King Edward's, after Joe Wedeles sold to King Edward, and at that time I was growing eight acres of tobacco.

In 1952, Arthur Corry got me into the chemical business, soil treatment business. Of course, this was very profitable to me. The first year I did 35 acres in the tobacco business. The height of my chemical business was about 1600 acres a year, and I was doing only tobacco. I wouldn't do a bean shade, because there was not a lot of money that you could pay for with beans, and so the money was in the tobacco business. As I said, I started in '47 and I had a good crop in '48. In '49, I didn't have too good a crop, because on the 6th of May we had a hailstorm that completely destroyed my crop. We cut it down, made a sucker crop, and after the suckers came out, we pulled all the suckers off but one, and when I started to harvest that crop of tobacco, you couldn't tell that it wasn't the original stalk. You couldn't tell where the sucker grew from the old stalk. I had eight acres of tobacco, as I said, along in that time. I had known I would make 12 to 14 hundred pounds of tobacco per acre, and I made twelve hundred pounds that year. I had ten thousand dollars in it the day it hit me with no insurance, and I had 16 thousand dollars in the crop and year and I got (netted) $15,500 out of it, and I ate out of the crop that year, so I made money that year.

In 1959, I bought a place adjoining me, which was known as the Blackman Place. I bought it from Hugh Blackman, and later built a house on that place. It was out on Highway 12. In 1960, I bought a piece of land from May Tobacco Co. that was sandwiched in between those two farms, and I gave ten thousand dollars for the ten acres. I put a four-acre shade on it, and paid for the piece of land in two years with the four acres of tobacco. Lots of good experience in the tobacco business. In 1962, I bought 200 acres in what was known as the Mary Jean Farm. It belonged to Conrad Harold. I gave him $47,000 for the 200 acres, and I increased up to 35 to 50 acres of tobacco. Finally got it up to 70 acres. The most money I ever made on the farm in one year, on just the tobacco, was about $95,000. I never did really have a defeat any one year. As close as I ever come to having a complete disaster was in 1949 when I had the hail, but I overcome that by, as I say, cutting it down and making a sucker crop, refertilization, more irrigation. I did not put on cloth. I just pinned it up with what we called hog rings, what you put the row wire to the other wire with. I just pinned it up to get it out of the way of the mule. I didn't put the cloth back.

The tobacco business probably means as much, or did mean as much, to me as anyone in Gadsden Co. For that reason I hated to see it go out. I hated to see Central America take it away from us. Of course, we went before the International Trade Commission to try to get a tariff put on it so that we could stop some of the tobacco from coming into this country, but we were unable to do this, because the government would not heed what we were saying, and for that reason was not able to do anything with the Trade Commission, so the tobacco business went on out, and now that it is all gone, it's so sad over there in Gadsden County, because we more or less just left it up to the memory of the ones that were in the tobacco business. This is sorta sad because if we could have some kind of control on some of the plantations over there, or somewhere, that we could just hold on to the memory by doing something that we could see evidence of the tobacco business. I don't know what could be done, but I know that if we got enough people behind it, the State of Florida, maybe would get on the thing, and preserve some of the things that we worked with, and some of the things that were directly connected with the tobacco business. You could call it a museum, if you want to. I'm very interested in that name since I'm a collector of Indian relics.

I would like to go back to a time when Joe Wedeles was still my boss, and he was the man that helped me get the first money to go into tobacco. On my first crop, when he sampled the tobacco, of course, the farmer could always be present to see exactly what grade of tobacco he had, or that you had produced, so when the time came for the packer to pay you for it, the farmer, then you would know if he was somewhat in line, and he would let you look at the sample. When he was looking at my first sample, he said to me: "Touchton, this is without a doubt some of the prettiest tobacco that I've ever packed, and my dad started this Packing House and I've seen a lot of tobacco." But, he said: "This is the smoothest, silkiest tobacco I've ever seen," and I said, "Well, I had heard this once before, Mr. Wedeles, and I'm not taking any credit for it. It's the land, and not the man, that produces the tobacco. However, I will say that the man has something to do with it, but not all to do with it." We went on from there, stayed in business and we produced him a lot of good tobacco.

Now down through the years I saw needs for many changes, and one of the great changes that we had in the tobacco business was the State of Florida had an experiment station over in Quincy that produced our seed for us every year and they would sell them to us for two dollars an ounce, about what it cost the experiment station to produce the seeds. Well, they had a tobacco they called Dixie, and that was not a very good tobacco. It was brittle. It would break up when it was green and it was hard to handle, and after it was cured it had an action about it that we called in the tobacco business, "go tender." That is, when you start to put it in the machine and put it on the cigar, it would be such that it would tear up. It would not go on properly, and that is called tender tobacco. Then they crossbred some other tobaccos and got a tobacco that they called Florida-15. Florida-15 was a better, tougher tobacco, but it still would not produce the amount per pound to keep us in business with the inflation in the economy. Because we had started off growing tobacco, or I had, in 1947, at about $1100 an acre, is what it cost us to produce an acre of tobacco, that is in the field. I'm not talking about the investment in your barns and all of that. I'm talking about actual growing of the tobacco. At this time now, we're up to about 15 to 16 hundred dollars an acre, so we need a different tobacco to produce a greater amount of number one string, so that we we could make a little money or at least break even. Well, that's the farmer's hope – if he can break even every three or four years, and then one out of five years make a little profit, then he thinks he's in business. He lives on hope more than he does money.

I saw needs of other tobacco, and we were able to get a Dr. Clayton in the area, and he put up a hothouse and started the cross breeding of tobacco, which he had a lot of experience with in the bright tobacco business, which was cigarette tobacco. The area I came from, that is, bright tobacco was our meat and bread in Lowndes Co., GA. And a lot of others, in Kentucky and Tennessee, and lot of other places. Dr. Clayton had several tobaccos that were good. The first one he bred was called Gold Dust. Gold Dust would produce. I you could 800 pounds of number one string, which was the top grade of tobacco that my company wanted, you could break even with it. Well, Dr. Clayton came up with the Gold Dust that you could get about 1200 pounds of number one string. So, later in years, he had other tobacco. One he called 76.

He always had a "C" in front of these numbers. Clayton-76 or Clayton-80. C-80 was adapted to a lot of different lands, but the C-76 was the best on my land. It would produce 1800 pounds of tobacco, and I could get 1600 pounds of number one string out of it. All right, when you go from 800 pounds of Number one string to 1600 pounds, you have doubled your production. Even though, the money is still about the same thing per pound. You're doubling your income; however, you don't get up to two thousand or twenty two hundred dollars an acre to produce an acre of tobacco. Cheesecloth was a big factor. Insecticide, I guess – I spent as much for insecticide as I did any other one thing. Herbicide, and so forth. But, Dr. Clayton was the main reason we stayed in the tobacco business as long as we did. I give Dr. Clayton a lot of credit. He had this tobacco business bred up, and no one knew what the crossbreeding was except his wife, and that was for sure, nobody knew it. You could not come up with the same seed. Now, as I told you, we paid two dollars an ounce for the seed from the Experiment Station. We paid Dr. Clayton $160 an ounce, and that was the cheapest thing we bought, was Cr. Clayton's seed at $160 an ounce. Wasn't that something? Now, as I produced tobacco and lived through these years, I saw need for everything that ought to be done for tobacco. I saw a need for different types of cultivation to do away with the mules, to do it with tractors. And this is very difficult, because you got shade posts every 16 feet by 32 feet, with wire and cloth over the top, and it's hard to figure out something to do with tractors. We'd always done it with mules, and we said, well, we'll do it like daddy did it, you know. But I couldn't say that, because my daddy didn't grow shade tobacco, so I thought I ought to do something for the industry as I went along, and I made several inventions. I was not pioneering the double row. Tom Delacy was the first man that did that. But I was pioneering and adjusting the row. The post row was in the middle rather than a row of tobacco on the post row. This worked out very well with tractors, and we would do all the cultivation what you were going to do with a tractor before we put the string on it. Now, for those that would not know what I'm talking about the string on it. You tie each hill individually with a loop to the tobacco at the base of it, and you tie it to a wire overhead eight feet tall, eight feet above your head, and each week, you would go there, and what we call, wrap the tobacco. You would wrap that string around the bud as it grew upward. That was because it would be so heavy when it rained, the wind would blow it down, but the string would be able to hold it up.

There was a lot to growing shade tobacco. We fertilized tobacco after we got irrigation. We fertilized tobacco through the irrigation. I pumped water out of a homemade 12-acre pond. I would pump the fertilizer into the water as it goes up the hill, and it would be broadcast over the fields. Say I was going to pump five hours on one setting, and I would water about five acres at the setting. Taking into consideration that it takes twenty seven thousand four hundred gallons to the acre to produce one inch of rain. You could pump that many times five set-ups times five hours. You could get some reasons to how much water you were pumping out of your pond, which was about 500 gallons a minute. That's a lot of water. But, all this was involved in the tobacco business. You had to do something else with it.

I think for the type work that we had to do, we had some of the best labor in the world. I worked mostly black people, and I have nothing to say about them, but give them the highest praise, because they worked very cheap. In fact, too cheap, as I look back on it. We did not pay them enough. We had a lot of white labor that would come out of school in the summer and try to help harvest the tobacco, and their pay scale was the same. But, whoever worked in the tobacco it seemed to me, that they were underpaid. They needed more money and better housing and so forth.

Anyway, go on back to the tobacco as a whole, there was just so much about it that I could just sit here and talk for a day or two days and never tell you the same story. It would all be true, and I just hate to see it die out as the tobacco business looks like it's going to do. I would like to see the memory of it preserved, if we can't do anything else.

Now, we invented a machine that would roll up wire – row wire. I think those things ought to be preserved and set aside for our children, our children's children, to see how we made a living, and a little thing like a paint scraper that turned sidewise on a belt to cut string for the looping, for the people that looped the tobacco. Little things like that ought to be hung up there so that people could see, and know what it was. I'd like to see one of the old presses put in, the thing that we used to press the tobacco. It would be five feet tall and when we pressed it down, it would only be about 18 inches thick. It was dry enough it would stay in those bails for years to come, until the factory got ready to use it. I'd like to see a press put in there, and a stringing machine, some of the cultivating equipment.

On the last six years on the farm I did not have a mule. We put out the herbicide, the fertilize; we set the tobacco with a tobacco setter – actually, it was a celery setter. The adjustment on the wheels, you could change the spacing of it. You could put any space in it you wanted and it would set the tobacco. Two rows at the time. Four people rode on the back and dropped the plants and one person drove the tractor. I had three of those machines. Three tractors pulling them. A beautiful sight seeing it being set. These plants would come from what we called a seedbed. They would be transplanted to the field and put in the proper distance. You could not plant the seed in the field, as such. You had to plant them in a seedbed, and transplant them in the fields, because an ounce of seed at $160 an ounce, you would have about 150,000 seed to the ounce. So, you see, you could not sow those seed in the field. You had to put them on a seedbed.

I'd like to give you a rundown on what we called shades. Shades were built out of eleven foot treated posts. We used two different types of treated posts. We used one penachlophonol was put in one post and it was a longer lasting post, but more expensive. Another type post we used was wolmanized, which was a salt base. It kept bacteria out of wood so that it would not decay. Both of them were eleven feet. Put in the ground three feet deep on spacing, we had them 16 feet between the post by 32 feet check. You could look at them from any direction and they were all in line. Then we used a number four wire, which is a pretty good size wire, on top of the shade one way, that the cloth was sewed to every sixteen feet. Then we had another wire that was going the 32-foot sections that was a number six wire. Then underneath that wire, we had a number eight wire that was holding up the row wire, which were every four feet apart. The number 14 wire was there to tie the string to, as I mentioned back in the message, where you had to tie the tobacco up to keep it from falling over. We used the cheesecloth on top of that, and it was sewed on by hand. That's the only way you could do it because of the crossing of the wires, and so forth. It was like a hemstitch. It was about six inches long, the hemstitch was, and it was done with a needle about as long as an ordinary writing pencil. It had a big hold in the end that you threaded the

24-ply twine through. It was waxed twine, and you sorta looped it one, as I said, hemstitch, and that cloth would stay on there. We'd start putting it on in February. We'd get all the cloth on before we put out the fertilize, and that cloth would stay on there until the last of July to the first of August, when it would be taken down. We could use that cloth two years. It had a treatment on it also that was resistant against mildew. It would last two years, if you would take it down dry and house it properly; you could use it again next year. However, at the latter part of the tobacco industry, we had a white cloth that was put up that was a Penta Cloth that was only good for one year. We just set fire to it and burned it off. That way you didn't have to take it down and house it, but it was more expensive. It would cost you like $350 an acre for one year, whereas, if you used the treated cloth, you could get by for about $250 an acre.

O.K., keep in mind now, in 1947, the first crop I had was about $1100 an acre Now, in i973 when I ended my career in the tobacco business, because I saw the tobacco was going out, that we could no longer produce it and compete with Central America, it was costing between $5,000 and $6,000 to produce it. That was one of the reasons we went out of business, because we could not compete with those people in Central America working slave labor, really slave labor down there, for a dollar and a quarter a day, which at that time, our payroll was about $12 or $14 a day for labor, and we could not compete with them, and that's what we were trying to do with the Trade Commission, but we were not successful with it, and we lost it. However, there's a little tobacco being grown in Connecticut now, and it's grown by individual companies that use the tobacco on their own cigars. They're not selling cigars as cheaply as we were. At that time King Edward had an eight cent cigar and a ten cent cigar, and that would not produce enough money to pay better than five dollars and a half a pound. The tobacco now is probably $20 a pound. They have to put it on a seventy-five cent cigar to even come out with it. This was another thing that snagged King Edward Tobacco Co., and also Hav-A-Tampa, because they were selling the cigar too cheaply and they had done it so many years, and they didn't think they could go up on the price. They thought they would kill the sale of the cigar. That was the whole thing about the tobacco business.

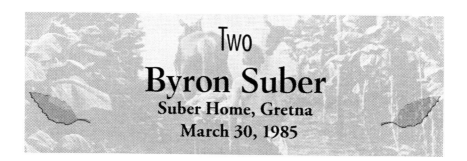

Two
Byron Suber
Suber Home, Gretna
March 30, 1985

I was involved with cigarette tobacco, sun tobacco and shade tobacco beginning when I was about six or seven years old. I worked in tobacco from about 1915 to 1968. The difference between cigarette and sun tobacco is that cigarette tobacco is what they called black tobacco and it was put in cigarettes and the sun tobacco was put in cigars ... the filler and sometimes the binder. Shade tobacco was altogether the wrapper of a cigar.

The tobacco farm was my father's place. We lived in South Sawdust. He and my grandfather Lemuel P. Suber were already growing tobacco when I came along and from the time I got big enough to remember we worked with my father. The first money I ever got out of it was about 1918. I was about nine years old. When we got through with tobacco each year, Papa put so much money in the bank for all the children, and from then on all of us worked in the tobacco, sisters, brothers and all "other help." We used to have to poison tobacco in the buds to keep the bud worms out and I did hate to do that. It didn't make any difference if I hated it or not. I had to do it.

My father was Elmer L. Suber. There was Lottie, Morris, me, Hallie, Howard and E.L. After awhile the rest of the children worked for Papa, but I was getting out working for myself.

When I got large enough, or old enough, or man enough I had to plow. Then when we started priming tobacco, I had to prime. Then we had drags pulled by mules that we hauled tobacco out of the field with and I had to drive the mule and pick up the tobacco and carry it to the barn, unload the drag and go back and get another load. I wasn't paid a salary, but when my father made some money he put some aside for each child.

Back then the average farmer didn't have but about two to three acres of tobacco and some only one acre. Five acres was a big acreage for the average farmer. I remember when my father had the first two acres of tobacco the shade was made out of lumber. There wasn't any wire on it. It was built with sawed post and then 1x3's put up there to hold them together and then 1x3's or 1x4's put across to nail the slats to. That was the first shade with slats. You nailed the slats on. After five or six years they started using wire, and then they started weaving the slats on. You had to stretch the wire so many inches or so many feet apart. You had a five foot slat that you put on. The wire that you put them on was #8, and you had a #4 running one way and your #8 running the other way on top of it and you tied that together where they crossed. Then you had what was called weaving wire. You'd start at one end and weave that same wire back and forth. You would push up put a slat in and come one way, push up put a slat in and come the over way all the way to the other end. That was a pretty good job. The slats were left up year round and would last three or four years and then you would have to rework it.

We small farmers didn't start to irrigate tobacco until the late '40s. Some of the big companies irrigated tobacco way back about 1920 or 1925. It didn't last long and then we quit irrigating altogether. We just depended on the Lord. Then after about the middle '40s a few people started irrigating and then in two or three years everybody was irrigating. When it first started you would run the water down the rows and you would have a mop or something on the end of a hoe that you could hold the water there or back it up and stop it....and that was a pretty good job. That really made tobacco grow. Tobacco is a fast growing plant anyway, but when you put some water on it would grow!

Tobacco barns were not as big then. For the little farmer the average barn would never be over 80 feet and most of them would be 60 and some 40. And instead of being 40 or 42 feet wide they would be 30 feet wide. About 1930 the average farmer started building bigger barns, but some of the bigger companies like the AST Company and Wilson Tobacco Company had bigger barns before then.

The average farmer didn't grow too much tobacco ... three, four or five acres was pretty good for the average farmer, and a lot of the little farmers didn't grow shade tobacco because it was expensive and he had to furnish everything. Later, some of the packers would furnish the money for the growers and then the tobacco business got bigger.

I grew tobacco for four or five different companies. I grew for Mr. Joe Budd and Mr. Joe Wedeles and Edmond Corry. Then finally we had a packing house of our own. Four or five of us got together and built a packing house called Southern Shade. The ones that were in it were John Allen Smith and Murray Spooner, myself and Howard (Suber) and E.L. (Suber) and Marvin (Suber), then Frank Smith. Lamar Munroe managed the packing house for us. We were tied up with Consolidated Cigar Company in New York. The packing house made money whether the farmer made any or not.

Our shade was a pretty good piece from the barn. Mules were used to bring the tobacco to the barn with a drag (a wooden sled with runners on it) when we primed it. I was only ten or twelve years old and I had two mules hitched up to a drag. Coming down a lane on the way to the barn somehow the drag got into a ditch and almost turned over and I was trying to keep it up straight and the mules didn't do just right and I fell down. I was holding on to the drag with one hand and the lines with the other and my foot got hung in the fence. I thought the mules were going to pull me into, but we finally got straight and took off for the barn.

In the earlier days, when Papa, his children and other help were growing tobacco, we didn't have a mule. You carried it to the barn on your head in something that looked like a sling. Then we started dragging it on what we called barges. After that we started building hand barges. Built a rack on the wagon and put them on the wagon. But I mostly used a mule and a drag. After we quit using the wagon the barn was closer to the shade and we got the tobacco to the barn with a mule and drag ("barge").

The more tobacco I grew the more help I had to have. I always thought I got along pretty good with my helpers, kept them satisfied and they kept me satisfied. I always tried to treat all the help I had like I'd like to be treated. I tried to make them keep the tenant house and the yards clean, tried to have plenty of water in the yards for them, although I didn't have inside water for them but water in the yard and spigots for them to have water. I didn't grow just tobacco like many others did. I grew cane, peanuts, corn and had hogs and cows. I built a smoke house for every one of my tenant houses, always killed enough hogs and put enough meat in them to last during the season. I gave them enough syrup and crib corn. They could go in the crib and get the corn and carry it to the mill and it didn't cost them anything to make a meal. I just thought I had a pretty good thing. My daddy had hired help at Sawdust and I had hired help when I farmed at Hardaway.

One year after tobacco got as high as your head there was one stalk of tobacco was a couple of feet higher than the rest of it. I kept watching it and decided to save the seed off of that stalk. You know, you top tobacco, break the tops out, well I broke them all out except for that one stalk and when the seed got dry I cut it off and got the seed out. The next year I sowed some of the seeds in one part of the plant bed and set out four or five rows and to see how it would do. Well, it did just like the first stalk and it just took off and left the other stalks. I was growing tobacco for Joe Budd and I told him about it and he came out and looked at it and he said save the seed off of it. So I saved a lot of seed off of it. The next year I didn't plant anything but that. Well I saved the seed that year too and he said save all the seed you can save, and I did. He gave seeds to 10 or 15 different people and they were all growing tobacco off that one stalk of tobacco. It had a little bit larger leaf than the other and you know tobacco leaves will turn-in when they get wet and the wind blows. It didn't turn as bad, it wasn't perfect, but it was just outstanding tobacco. This must have been about 1954. I quit growing tobacco in 1968.

I think cigar wrapper tobacco was being grown in the 1800s, maybe 1890s, but I can't say that is right. They didn't grow too much tobacco until in 1900s. My grandfather, Lemuel P. Suber, grew tobacco. Tobacco was grown in Cuba in the woods and they used the trees for shade. That's where the idea for shade tobacco came from. If you grow it under shade its leaves are thinner.

Stoney's daddy, Mr. John Walker Edwards, grew tobacco and Mr. Sam Strom, that was Maxwell's daddy, grew tobacco. Mr. Emory Dawkins grew shade tobacco. All three of these men grew tobacco in Sawdust.

The first money I got off a crop of cigarette tobacco was in 1928, but before that I had been growing a little bit of tobacco with my daddy, and a little for myself, sometimes with one of my brothers.

I was born in 1909. After I married in 1934 I was growing tobacco and grew tobacco until 1939. Then I quit and moved to Quincy. I was already in business with Morris, one of my brothers, and Durwood Johnson except I was farming and they were running it, but I was in it (Suber & Johnson Company) with them. I grew a crop in 1939 and made a little money that year, but then in 1940 my brother and I were in the tobacco business and he was running it. That year it rained so much that we didn't do so good and lost some money. It took me about five years to make enough to pay it back with growing tobacco and working in the store, too. Then in 1943, I sold my part of the store to my brother and I went back to farming for myself. In 1942 and 1943, and living in Gretna, I went back to Sawdust and Papa and I grew crops together. The three youngest children were in WWII at that time so there wasn't anything for me to do but to go down and help him. We grew three crops and made pretty good money. I made enough growing tobacco then and with what I had when I sold my part of the store to my brother I bought my first Coca-Cola stock. Then when my brothers came home I got out from helping Papa and let my brothers have it. Then Mr. Humphrey died in Aug. 1941 and Isabelle's brother Charlie was growing a crop in Hardaway. He was drinking and I had to go see about him. After that crop, I made a little money on it. He decided he didn't want to farm anymore and he was going to sell the place, so I bought it. That was in 1946 and I farmed that place until 1951 then I sold it to John Allen Smith and bought me another farm right below there and that's where I farmed until I quit in 1968. I sold the farm about 1970, and the realtor split and sold it in many small parts.

I hired a man named Charlie Eggerton from Greensboro to build some of my barns.

When we first started growing tobacco in South Sawdust at the new place about a mile away, we had a colored man that built shades and we contracted with him to build our shades, but after I started farming in Hardaway, I built my own shades with the help on the place.

Putting cheesecloth up was faster than putting up wooden slats. Putting up slats you had to have a lot of help and you would be up on those high benches with that cold wind blowing. For a while we would put the cheesecloth under the slats. Then they started making a heavier cloth and we quit using slats altogether. At one time they made a cloth called slat-cloth that was weaved with the slat. Then they made it still heavier, but on a windy day you had to tie that cloth down and go do something else until the wind quit blowing or it would pull you off if you tried to hold it. You would put that up in March, but the seed bed shade had to be up in January.

I had hail hurt the crop pretty bad a time or two, but I never did lose any money. I would have made more money if it hadn't hailed, but it wasn't a disaster, I didn't lose that crop. My father had a four acre shade one time and we were priming tobacco, we started and didn't quite get over the sand leaves when a cloud came up, it started raining and then hailing and it hailed so much it tore the crop all to pieces. There wasn't a leaf left on a stalk in the whole field.

The blue mold hurt me pretty bad one year. I'd go out there and look at the tobacco and cry a little while then come back. Finally I said I just got to plow that stuff up and set it out again because it just isn't going to do. I did that for four or five days. Then on a Saturday I told one of my workers…now Monday morning don't wait for me to say anything, when I get over there you be harrowing it up. When I got there he had the harrow at the gate. I said Ivan don't go in there yet let me go back in there one more time. I went back in and some of the spots were healing over just like it had smallpox. Finally I marked one and said I'm going to watch this another day or two. That spot finally healed completely. You couldn't even tell where it was. The green came back in it. Most of it came out of it. There would be a leaf once in a while that would have a spot -- mostly low down where it had about quit growing.

The prettiest part to me was after you got the tobacco tied up in the shade, when it got up so high and we would have a little shower, then the leaves would be sticking up and hanging out so that you could hardly see down the middle. That was a pretty thing.

One time I was in one of my barns hanging in the top, 10 or 12 spaces, four tiers and then I was firing down there. I couldn't fill up a barn in one or two days. I wilted that tobacco down good and the next day I would come back and hang four more tiers, then I'd wilt it down and the next day I'd do the same thing until I got that part full. Then I'd wilt that last down. I thought I had it in good shape. I thought I had learned something that would be worth something to me ... that's the way to do it. After I got all of it wilted down, I moved to another barn. In two or three days I went back out there and I could smell something that didn't smell right and it was rotting. I put the fire back under it and I couldn't get it doing just like I wanted it to do. So I put enough fire under there, I said well I'll just have to cook it -- I've got to do something to it or it's going to ruin. I had some tobacco sticks that had been pulled so I took a pretty good pile of them and laid them on the fire. Well it got so hot it burned a hole in that tobacco 10 feet square going up about eight or 10 tiers high. And why it didn't burn that barn down, I don't know. I reckon the fire got a little low and just went out. I was in there when that was going on and I was trying to get it out and did. Then I had one barn that there wasn't anything wrong with the way I was firing it but that was before we started firing with coal and we were still firing with wood. It caught on fire and I didn't even know it had burned until we were taking the tobacco down, getting ready to pack it and there was a hole up in there. Why it didn't burn up I don't know, I guess it just wasn't meant to be.

Mrs. Suber adds: Mr. Suber looked after his tobacco day and night. He fired it himself. He didn't leave it to somebody else to fire and he fired until midnight lot of times.

The barns were fairly close together so it didn't take you long to go from one to another. I used to fire a barn like that and I'd crack the windows or open them a little bit to make the heat go up and by the time I'd go all the way around the barn I'd said ... now I did that wrong ... and I'd go back around and let them all down ... up and down ... the temperature was so important.

This farm was sold about 1970. Besides the barn that has been made into a house, I have one barn still standing. Mr. Kurtz owns it, also in 1985.

I helped my mother make sausage and that's how I learned to make it. Many of us killed the hogs, sometimes killed as high as 75 in one day and then cut it up, salted it and get it ready to go in the cold storage. The trimmings and all were what we made the sausage with. Mama would be out there at 10:00 that night in freezing weather seasoning, grinding and stuffing 'em. I don't know how my mother lived. I'd be helping and Papa would be out there doing other things, but she was making the sausage. It's my mother's recipe that I use now.

My mother's name was Jessie Fletcher Suber and her father was Bill Fletcher. My grandfather Fletcher lived in Sycamore and we lived in Sawdust. When I was about 6 or 7 years old, that was before there were any cars, he would drive to our house in his buggy. He would carry me home with him sometimes, but then when I got up to about 8 or 10 years old Papa bought a car. Grandpa Fletcher still didn't have one so he would come down in the buggy and take me home and I'd stay for two or three days then Papa would come to Sycamore and get me. One time Grandpa came down there to get me and said, "I want you to go home with me today. I'm going to stop in Greensboro and buy you a knife." When we got to Greensboro, he stopped at Fletcher Company, went in and bought me a K-Bar knife. I was so proud of it that I wanted him to carry me back home so I could show it to all my brothers and sisters. I was probably seven or eight.

I never did do what a lots of folks did. In other words, I tried to work. Some folks would get up and tell his help what to do that day and he'd get back at dinner and say, "How'd y'all get along? Did you do what I said"? Then after dinner he would go back and tell them what to do that evening and he'd be gone again. But I didn't do that. I stayed there. I'd be working before most folks ever got up. When they knocked off in the evening, it'd be an hour before sundown, I'd work until dark. So when those folks sitting around the store talked about making a crop, I'd be in the fields trying to make one.

Mrs. Suber: When this girl that works for us at home here now (Charlene Hobbs) was a little girl she worked for us on the farm. Always the friendliest, nicest thing in the world and she worked in the tobacco. If Byron went off somewhere, or had to come home and leave them there working, if anybody didn't put the tobacco on the table or on the stick like they ought to, she would report it to Byron when he got back. We have always thought a lot of her. She has looked after us in her ways. Mr. Suber: She wouldn't tell you a story. If something was going wrong and you asked her she would tell you. They could not like it or they could, it didn't make any difference, she'd tell you how it really was.

I used to be in the barn about the time to start priming and stringing. You'd hear thunder off in the distance and directly it would be thundering right overhead, and then a puff of wind would come and directly you couldn't even see the shades for the rain and the wind and I'd be standing in the barn door praying that the tobacco didn't get torn up. Finally it would quit raining and you'd go out there and the tobacco in the shades would be leaning every which way and then you would want to cry. Then it was so wet you couldn't get there to straighten it up. Then it would dry off so you could and you'd get everybody out there pushing it up, packing around it and wrapping it trying to get it straightened back up. But when I'd stay out there so long that I couldn't stand it any longer I'd go over there in another field where the cows were and look at them. I wasn't making any money with the cows, but it gave me something else to look at.

Mrs. Suber offers: When he was growing tobacco. He fired tobacco all week long, but on Sunday during church hour, he was at church. He may go over to the farm early Sunday morning and have his fire just right, but he never missed Sunday School and church. So many people used the excuse that they had to fire their barn, but he always worked around it. I always believe that is why God blessed him the way He has. He never let growing tobacco, or anything else, interfere with his going to Sunday School and church.

Tobacco meant everything to the county. I didn't think we could live when shade tobacco went out. But it looks like there is something else going. They're growing tomatoes now, but a lot of people don't grow them. I guess if I were at the right age I might try it, but that's more risky than tobacco was. It's a little better now than when it was first started. There's so many things that can happen. The weather can be against you, or disease can be against you, or price be against you and you can't hold it. When it's ready, it's ready if you don't get it then that ends it.

Consolidated Cigar Company had four or five different brands of cigar. Dutch Masters was one. Some of them were 50 cent cigar and some were 75 cent cigar. They weren't cheap cigars. Then along came homogenized tobacco and that's what ruined it.

Three
Newton Edwards
Edwards Farmhome, Hanna Mill Pond Road
July 20, 1985

In 1905 my father started his first shade tobacco. We grew tobacco from then on until I quit in 1974. We had our ups and downs with it. He had hail and black shank and lost everything he had and started all over again. He bought two hundred acres of it back and started all over. Then it got so you could insure it from hail and they got some black shank resistant tobacco. I grew it for, I guess, thirty years and he did, too, from 1905 until he was 70 years old. We bought the farm in 1950. We'd make money on it one year, and the next year break even and maybe next year we'd go in the hole and the next maybe make a good crop and make good money for two or three years. Then maybe for two or three years have bad luck. We always managed to keep things going somehow. The farmer was the only man I know of that could live and farm on credit. They used to be able to do it year in and year out. They'd beat around the bush somehow and manage to make another crop. Mortgage a cow, or horse, or mule, or hogs or something they had, or the land. They might have three or four different mortgages on land. I never did have but one, but that was a hard one to get rid of. I finally got rid of it and I was really proud when I did, but I thought at times that I never would. I would go in the hole and it would take me two years to pay out of the hole. The last seven crops I grew were with King Edward. W.T. Laslie took over King Edward from Mr. Jack Reeves. I changed the types of tobacco that I was growing from Dixie to 80 or 80A and I made money on it for the last seven years. I had seven good crops. I paid off what I owed them and my mortgage. I got where I could walk down the street and meet most anybody and not have to dodge across the street. I quit then. Then in 1975 I sold out to my son-in-law and me and him sharecropped it for several years after that. Now the last two years I don't sharecrop anymore.

I imagine it's been in my family way over 100 years, I expect 200 years. Not growing tobacco, just farming. I remember my granddaddy used to grow a little sun tobacco, "Big Cubie" or "Little Cubie" or something like that. They first started growing sun tobacco then went to growing shade tobacco. One of the Shaws, I think it was, in Quincy grew the first shade tobacco in this county under an oak tree. He found out it would make the leaves thinner to grow it in the shade and that's what started the shade tobacco.

They'd build shades and put slats on it. Weave slats or nail them on boards and then they quit that and went to putting up wires and weaving the slats on the wire. Way back then when I was a boy they weaved it on. Before I was born they nailed them on boards and they wouldn't have over two or three acres a piece, most of the farmers. It was tough. Those shades were permanent. Later on they got to putting up just cheesecloth and we'd have to take that down every year and put it back the next year. Sometimes we used it two years and sometimes three. Three was the most we could use it. Right at the last I bought cloth that I only used one year. Then you would stick a match to it and burn it off. At one time we could take it down and sell the old cloth. It would pay us to take it down and sell it, but then it got so expenses wouldn't pay the labor to take it down so we would stick a match to it and burn it off. When I quit farming that's the way we would do it. I worked in tobacco from start to finish. I rolled cigars and everything else. I went to Daytona Beach one time with some cousins of mine, Guy and Ricardo Campbell. Stayed fourteen months, I believe, and rolled cigars. There was a little hand cigar factory down in Daytona Beach and I helped them roll cigars. A first cousin of mine, Claude Campbell, ran a factory in Deland for I don't know how long. I imagine he ran it for thirty or forty years. Then I had an uncle, my uncle Willard, had a hand made cigar factory in Bainbridge then he moved it to Americus, Georgia and that's where he died. I don't remember the name of the cigars, but I remember he use to sell a bunch to my daddy. My daddy used to distribute them for him and collect for them and send him the money.

I planted the seeds and I've even smoked cigars, but I quit that ... last April was 17 years ago. I had an operation to take my gallbladder out and I haven't wanted anything to smoke since then. I don't drink many soft drinks. Before then I would drink two or three Coca-Colas a day and smoke two or three packs of cigarettes a day.

We would get on a bench out in the tobacco and loop the tobacco, tie it to the top of the shade. Tying up tobacco they called it. I would get out of school at the first of June and come home and help loop it and tie it up. Then it was about three or four weeks after that before we'd prime it. About the 4th of July we'd just be priming good, just start to prime good. Then it got to where we would set tobacco out in March, early in March and the 12th of May we'd be priming. I've been taking the first middles off the 12th of May in the later years.

It got to where we set earlier and earlier. Then I remember one year it snowed the 28th day of March and I lacked about three acres of being through setting tobacco. It liked to tore my shades down. It weighed some of them down almost to the ground. We had to cut holes in them in some places to let the snow through to keep it from tearing down the shades. Some people's was torn down. It tore a shade down for Sidney and Dewey Johnson, I don't remember how big and tore a shade down for someone else.

Another time, a lot of people don't believe this, but its true. I don't remember what year it was, but I was farming and my daddy was still farming then. I was resetting tobacco. Down the lane I had six tenant houses and the tenants were walking up the lane, coming to work at 1:00. A whirlwind came across the field, the sun was shining. The whirlwind got under that shade and got bigger and bigger and carried that shade up in the air. You could hear those posts and the guy wires just cracking. The posts were dangling up in the air and it looked like a great big umbrella opened up. All at once it just dropped that shade back on the ground within twenty feet of where it was at to start with. A lot of people don't believe me when I tell them that. Charles Bassett was farming up there and Harry will verify it. The tobacco was about four to six inches high and they managed to straightened it up without ruining too much of the tobacco and put the shade back up. People all around come in and helped put it back and they had the shade back up in two or three days, a week anyway. I think it was a ten or fourteen acre shade. A lot of people don't believe me when I tell them the sun was shining, but it was. It was either in the last of March or first of April.

{Mrs. Edwards: It really happened. I was finishing up the dishes standing at the kitchen window looking at it. The corner post that holds the shade down with the guy wire came out of the ground and it was dangling up in the air and when it came down it came down slanty several feet away. I know of some of the hands that were here that are still living that would verify that they run out of that whirlwind. Rosie Mae Knight was one.}

I really enjoyed growing tobacco, even with its ups and downs. I enjoyed the growing of it. I've always had good health and never did have bad health up until the last it got so that I couldn't get out in it on account of the poison. It would break me out and I would have to take shots. They would spray it with a plane and I could walk down the rows where it would touch my arms and go to itching. And I had to get out of it.

Way back when we first went to growing tobacco we had a colored fellow that lived here, his name was Edwards too, Gilford Edwards. They lived here for thirty years, at least. They moved off to Tallahassee and then I moved them back here. They stayed in Tallahassee four, five or six years then I moved them back here. He had a son and way back then they blowed tobacco with hand guns and "Paris green." That "Paris green" would get on him and break him out on his neck. They had to keep his neck wrapped up or greased with some kind of ointment, but he worked in it right on. The whole family worked in tobacco ever since I could remember. In fact he was living here when he got married. They lived here and raised his whole family here. All his children were born here. He had about nine or ten children. He was a preacher and he would go off sometime and preach for a whole week and sometimes for just half a week or a weekend. Most of the time he was here farming with my daddy. At one time he was his right hand man. They finally moved off, bought them a place and built them a house, but they worked here right on for years. They did some work on other farms, Nate Johnson for three or four years, but did most of their work right here on this farm. There were others that were born and raised here. Louise Hughes was born and raised here and she did most of her farm work on this farm. She was with Bowman two or three years, then with King Edward a couple of years, but the rest of it she did it right here.

When I'd get through growing tobacco every year I would always have a fish fry for them. They'd all come and pitch in and cook and I'd clean them. Have a big time that day. They all looked forward to that every year for years. They enjoyed it and I enjoyed it too. One time they wanted a goat, so I bought them a goat to barbecue. Had a old big fat colored fella here by the name of Odis Gould. He gets on the tractor and he tells them they had to run the goat to make him tender. So he gets on the tractor and ties the goat behind the tractor and pulled him up and down the road and Murl made him stop. They took the goat then and cut his throat to bleed him, kill him. They barbecued him and it was pretty good, I ate some of it. That was funny about the goat to tender him.

{Mrs. Edwards: I heard the tractor going up and down the road so I went to the front door to see what was going on. Here was this big, fat Negro man up there running a little bitty goat tied behind a huge tractor up and down the road. I went out there and asked what was he doing. He said we're tendering the goat and I said you've tendered him enough, that's all you're going to do so I made him untie the goat.}

About every 20th of May, some of the hands here on the place would get a goat, kill it and have a picnic. I remember hearing some of their children say they'd cut the goat's throat to bleed him.

I had a lot of good times with some of them especially that one that lived here. He had two boys about my age, we went swimming together, we went opossum hunting together. We had some real good times together. One of them is dead, the other one is living in town. He's a preacher, Gilford, Jr. The older one is dead. We did a lot of hunting, bird hunting, rabbit hunting and going swimming. They were companions. Grew up with them. They moved off to Tallahassee and stayed there with the father and mother. Younger ones in the family moved back, but the older ones are scattered all around. One of them lives down here, Clara Cloud, one of the girls. Part of them are dead, but part of them live in Tampa, Tallahassee and all around. One is in Ohio, I think. One was out in Texas. He was in the Army and when he got out of the Army he married and stayed out there I think.

{Mrs. Edwards: I kept books for him, I worked in the barns, I worked in the fields, I hauled help. Did some of all of it. I wasn't raised in tobacco, I married into it. I was raised in Bainbridge, Georgia, Decatur County on a peanut and cotton farm. I was visiting a cousin of mine in Gadsden County and met Newt. We went together about six and seven months. We have one child. Our daughter is Patricia Townsend. She lives in Atlanta. One of her children is a professional model. She leaves for Paris today. Her son is in college.}

I sold tobacco to the Hav-A-Tampa Company, then I sold one crop to the Merger. Then I went to growing for Wedeles. They sold out, I don't remember what year, to King Edward. Then I left King Edward (Wedeles) and went to Greensboro for two years and growed over at Greensboro with Joe Smith and Bill Edwards again. Then I went back to King Edward and stayed with them from then on. There were a lot of times I enjoyed growing tobacco for King Edward. Course there would be times when I would feel discouraged, but I always got ready to start another crop. When I quit I almost went back a couple of times and got me a new contract to grow tobacco. It didn't last but two more years after I quit. It went out in 1976.

I grew from twelve to twenty-four acres. At one time I grew twenty to twenty-four acres. At the last I grew twelve to fifteen. The last year that I grew it I grew twelve acres and had one of the best crops I ever had in my life. And weighed one of the biggest yields I ever made. I made 2,049 pounds per acre and I cleared over $30,000 on that twelve acres of tobacco. I quit growing it then. I had everything paid up and I quit.

My father had my barns built. We had five of them. Frank Gatlin built one, Ep Clark built two of them I think. One of them was built by a fella by the name of Hiers. Mr. Forrest Davis had him build a house and a barn. I'm not sure whether he had that fella build the barn or what, but anyway he had something to do with it, I'm not sure what.

I had one on the hill that blowed down. That was my granddaddy's old barn. A small barn. It wasn't over 60 feet long and I think it was 40. It was a small barn. Then my father built one in 1905 and it blew down about five years ago. Then we had one that burned that we called the middle barn. It was a pretty old barn too. It burned when I was a boy about twelve or fourteen years old. If one was full of tobacco it was very seldom that you could put a fire out. When that tobacco was dry it was almost like gas.

I remember when that one burned. They were firing the barn one afternoon. It seems like it was on Saturday afternoon. At that time they fired with wood, then they went to firing with coal. I fired them with wood, I fired them with coal and I fired them with gas. Usually when I fired them with coal, and if I had all five barns going I'd have two men firing them, looking after two or three barns a piece. They would visit them pretty often. Then after I went to using gas I did most of the firing myself day and night. You could light that gas and there wasn't as much danger as with the coal...sparks flying. Right over the fire we would leave our holes for the fire holes we called them and build a fire right under that hole. At sometime sparks must have flew up and set some of that tobacco on fire and it burned six, eight or ten sticks of that tobacco and went out. I found it there when I was taking down the tobacco. I was doing it with coal then.

I had a barn full of tobacco and a storm come and blowed a little bit of the top off and blowed it off the blocks, but I was able to save the tobacco. Most of it was good and the insurance company paid me for what wasn't good of the sand leaves after they were raked up in the packing house. They took out what was damaged so they could weigh it up and the insurance company paid me for the damage. That was the only time I had any disaster. That was the same year that the walls of Maxwell's barns blew down. Grady Peacock had tobacco in some of them when they blew down, They had six or seven that blew down.

I learned about tobacco from my father, growing it and working in it. I grew up in it. It meant a livelihood for me and my family. We depended on tobacco mostly alone. We planted beans and corn and other stuff but we really depended on tobacco for our money crop and to pay our bills with. Usually if we had a good crop it brought good money. If we didn't have it, it didn't and that's the way it was. Pasco Strickland grew a lot of tobacco with Embry Tobacco

Company and he packed it over there. My father grew with them, and I grew two or three crops with them, too. And I worked in the sorting room with Embry Tobacco Company before I was married. When me and Murl was married I was working in the sorting room. After that I worked in the packing part in Wedeles Tobacco Company the year that they sold out to King Edward with Joe Barr. I worked one year for Weinberg in Douglas City.

My granddaddy owned an old mill, they lived on top of the hill. A cotton gin and a grits mill. I think he had a syrup mill, cane grinding mill, but I'm not sure. The cotton gin and grits mill were run by water. My father worked in the cotton gin when he was a boy. He always said his hair was gray when he was in his twenties from walking up and down that hill going to that cotton gin on the rocks bare footed. They fed it by hand. It was a hand fed cotton gin. He had some fingers cut off when he got in that gin one time. Two or three of his fingers got cut off. I've heard that my Aunt Queen Anne ran a hotel up here at Rock Comfort. They called it San Nathan. I understand that they were living there and running that when my uncle got killed. He was a deputy sheriff and a colored fella killed him. Then Steve, my first cousin, was city manager and city fire chief for years and years in Quincy. Went to work with the fire department in Quincy watering the horses. Worked himself right on up and when he died he was city manager and fire chief.

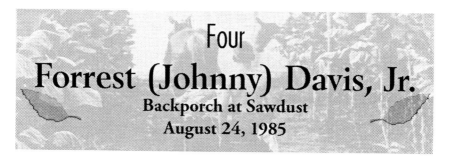

Four
Forrest (Johnny) Davis, Jr.
Backporch at Sawdust
August 24, 1985

Discussing starting a crop:

The first thing you had to do was plant the seed bed, and then take care of it. At the same time, you were preparing the shades, getting them ready. Along about February, you put out your stable fertilizer, which you needed either to broadcast or put in with a drill. The first tobacco we ever planted, we used billy-forks to put the stable fertilizer in the drill (row), using one-horse turning plows to four-furrow the rows and covering using the same process. About two weeks before planting time, we four-furrowed the beds out and put cottonseed meal and "tobacco special" fertilizer, using fertilizer bumpers pulled by mules to put this out. We would cover this the same way as for the stable fertilizer. Some of the fertilizer was used as a side-dress (fertilizer after planting).

Later, we used manure spreaders to broadcast the fertilizer and used tractors to harrow it in. Also, the cottonseed meal and commercial fertilizer were mixed together and some was used as a side-dress.

Then we would have to put up the cheesecloth which would be in the latter part of February or first of March. We'd usually try to put it up before the March winds. Wind was a big factor in trying to put up that cloth. And then we would, according to how we'd put out the stable fertilizer, make the rows and transplant.

At the first of tobacco, we didn't have any tractors – all was done by mules Now, the first tractor I used was a 1-row tractor that I cultivated just like I would with mules. And, of course, after we'd tied it up (that was putting a string around it and tying each plant up to a wire overhead), then we had to use mules to do the plowing. You couldn't get in there. But we did plow with a tractor up until the time of tying it up. And you could do so much better with a tractor. Of course, there wasn't really all that much plowing to do after the tying-up state anyway. (Just had to keep your vegetation down.)

Discussing planting:

Well, the first seed was a variety called "Rg" and was one that was used all during World War II; it was developed by the North Florida Experiment Station. Before then, which was before my time, they had the blackshank epidemic in the county that near'bout wiped out the industry. The North Florida Experiment Station developed (I believe Dr. Kincaid was the one that was working on it and came up with it) this variety that was blackshank-resistant – "Rg."

So, the "Rg" was grown for many years, and people could save their own seed if they wanted to. I didn't save mine, because at the Experiment Station they had plenty of seed. But some people, like Byron Suber and others, got to picking out some select hills and they had a little better strain of "Rg" tobacco than the others. So they grew it some years after some of the newer varieties came in.

The American Sumatra Tobacco Co. hired a fellow named Dr. Clayton (I believe it was when "Imperial Dutch" took over the American Sumatra Tobacco Co.) and he developed several varieties of tobacco that were hybrids. American Sumatra went out of business. So Dr. Clayton just got into the seed business and sold seed to the various farmers in the county. Most all the farmers, especially the ones that were growing for King Edward and Hav-A-Tampa, were more interested in his varieties (than the Experiment Station's). It was called "Gold Dust" because the seed cost so much.

The variety I liked best of the Clayton tobacco was the "80." They had one variety of Clayton – "76," which wasn't as fleck-resistant as the "80." Fleck was another problem we got into in our latter years. This was really a pollution caused by ozone coming from factories. Under certain conditions, this ozone would cause little fine specks to come on your tobacco. You had to try to gather your tobacco a little on the green side, because at maturity it was more susceptible to it.

The "80" was the one that was used more than any of the rest of it. It was a "high yielder." Your yield could go as high as 1800 lbs to a ton to the acre. These hybrid varieties that Dr. Clayton developed probably kept Gadsden Co. in the tobacco business eight or 10 years longer, because of the increase in yield. We'd only gotten 1,000 to 1500 lbs. to the acre with the "Rg" variety. So this increased yield helped farmers offset some of the increase of costs per acre and kept us in the tobacco business a little longer than we otherwise would have been.

Discussing crises in the tobacco:

Well, most all of 'em were a crisis! One of the worst disasters that I had was probably when the deep well I happened to sink down hit chloride in the water. (Now there were probably 25 deep wells in the county – just mine hit the chloride.) It was only a small amount but it was enough to make the tobacco leaf where it wouldn't burn, and I lost one crop. That was a hard loss ever to overcome during that peak time of the tobacco business.

Discussing his help:

I didn't have too many problems with my help. Some of them were housed on the place. Some we hauled in, but during the peak time, it was according to how many acres you were growing. About 20 acres was what I usually grew. And I'd probably use around 50 people during harvest time. That is, until we got into stringing machines. Now, before then, you had to have a few more, 'cause you couldn't string as much by hand as you could with a stringing machine.

Discussing his part:

Well, of course, I've done some of all of it, as far as that's concerned, because I always sorta stayed along with the labor and worked with 'em during the growing time. And then, at harvest time, I usually tried to run the field and a lot of times Ann (my wife) would run the barn. But, of course, after you put the tobacco in the barn at night you had to keep an eye on the fires and all like that in the curing process.

Mama helped with the firing and my brother and sisters helped me in tobacco, too. Later on, my children pitched in, and did a big share.

In the years I had tobacco I probably had some of as good a help as anybody – I mean as far as them really working and all. The first family I moved here was the Johnny Williams family. They didn't ever give me any problems (most of the problems I had with help were caused by drinking, and the Williams didn't drink). It was a big family of 'em and they were really the nucleus around which I grew my tobacco. Many of the others came and went, but they stayed with me all throughout.

Discussing exciting moments:

I did fall out of the tip-top of the barn (a time or two). Once, there was some tobacco that had been dry but we were trying to get it to come into case (moist where you could handle it) so we could go ahead and take it down and refill the barn. I got there early (damp time of the day) and there were a couple more people. We were getting the sticks down from up high, and the tierpole broke aloose and I fell – which, luckily, I didn't break any bones, but I was sore for quite awhile. It was about 30-40 feet to the ground.

Discussing shade tobacco's unconventional farm buildings, shaded fields and hardware:

I built most of the barges (and shades, and customized tools) – everything we used in the operation that you couldn't buy (most of it wasn't your typical farm machinery). Of course, Papa built the barn and the houses the help lived in. All the other barns he either moved in, or re-built, or we bought.

You did that kind of work in the off-season, because you had to have it ready when you went to priming tobacco. As you went along, of course, you had improvements. The first way of getting the tobacco out of the field was with a mule-drawn barge or what they called a "drag." And then they came up with a flat-hand barge with handles on 'em. You piled the tobacco up on them and you had several of 'em on a wagon. Men would tote them in to the barn.

And then we went to the "buggies." A buggy was a trailer you made from axles out of old pickup trucks and cars and things on a frame. And then you pulled them in with a tractor. You backed them in to the barn. All this was really a big saving and the best improvement we ever had in transporting tobacco (at the green tobacco stage).

Discussing various locations:

Of course, I never did have any real good, fancy tobacco dirt like a lot of others. In other words, it was just marginal type land. But I grew it on several different places and one reason was trying to find the spots that would make the best quality tobacco. The only way to find this out was to put a tobacco shade there and try it out, and of course a lot it was convenience to water and to the barn. You needed to be close to the water to irrigate.

I grew two or three crops down at what's called the Rudd Place, but most of it was grown right around here on the home farm. At that time, I also had some adjoining land we called the Brinkley Place. We considered it a part of the home farm.

Discussing firing the barns:

That was another case of improvements and advancements. First tobacco that was cured was cured with wood, usually sweet gum or some type of hardwood. Then, they came along with charcoal. There was a lot of lighter'd in the woods, especially in Liberty and Calhoun County and in that area. During World War II, they started cooking that to get the tar out of it and they had a by-product called charcoal. They would bring it up here to fire tobacco with. So for several years they used charcoal and some used the charquettes. But then they went to gas, which was the greatest improvement of all as far as curing tobacco. In the time we were growing, gas was 13 or 15 cents a gallon. Now, it'd cost so much because it's up there close to $1.00 a gallon (1985). At that time, this was probably the greatest improvement that was made in the tobacco business – being able to cure this tobacco and not having to haul coal and start fires.

Discussing irrigation:

The irrigation is something you really just about had to have to make a good quality of tobacco. Now the tobacco being grown was being grown on some better type land and the better quality could make pretty good tobacco even in a dry year. But then after you got irrigation, you could grow on almost any type land. With irrigation the tendency was you didn't know when a heavy rain was coming and you'd have the ground already wet and then get a rain and you'd run into a problem of having too much water. First irrigation was a flood type. I remember I didn't use one, but my daddy used steam. Pulpwood would burn and produce steam for the first five acres that he had, which was flood-irrigated and then we went to a tractor-drawn pump that would pump water to the field and flood-irrigate it. And then the greatest improvement that helped us in that regard was the overhead permanent type irrigation that you could put the water on there just like a rain.

Discussing harvesting:

We'd usually start about the 20th of May, along in that area, and you'd harvest for 4 or 5 weeks. Then it took, well, your lower leaves, or primings as we called 'em, would cure out faster than the other because it was thinner tobacco. The higher up the stalk, the thicker the tobacco got, the more gum it had in it; it'd take a little longer to cure it out. Now, when we started to cure tobacco, we more or less air-cured it, and put fire under it when you just had to. There at the last when gas was relatively cheap we started to running the temperature whenever we put the tobacco in – running it from 90-100 degrees or not over 105 degrees for the length of time it would take to get it cured out except for the stem. And then, you'd more or less let it dry out once a day then. And this made a smoother leaf of tobacco, although the color didn't look good at the time you were doing it. When it went through the sweating process at the packing house, it would color up and come back to the way the cigar manufacturer desired the leaf to look.

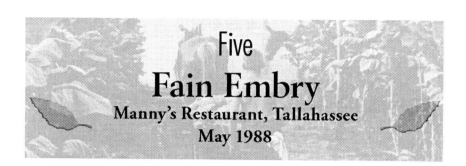

Five
Fain Embry
Manny's Restaurant, Tallahassee
May 1988

(This conversation begins with a question about Mr. Embry's niece, Julia Massey, a classmate of Kay's, at Queens College. We're having pie and coffee – Bob and Kay Lay, and Mr. Embry. Besides his recollections, he shares several classic 1906 photos of Embry kin in a Pasco County version of a slat shade.)

Julia is the daughter of my sister, Sallie Embry Massey, who was named for her grandmother and grandfather: Sallie Cooper Embry and Wallace Embry. Sallie's full name is Sallie Wallace Embry Massey. She lives in Dade City. She was born in Dade City, but she was raised in Quincy. At nineteen she married a promising young citrus operator, Herbert Massey.

Daddy was up at Kalamazoo, Michigan as a freshman in 1906 or 1907 and his father, Wallace Embry, in Dade City, got real sick and was unable to look after his tobacco crop and other agriculture products he was growing at the time. Daddy being the oldest, or next to the oldest and interested in agriculture, was forced to come back home and take over the reins of the farm.

Then he and Mr. Rosenfeld became partners or associated in the Sunnybrook Tobacco Company around 1908 until 1910 or 1911. During that period the blackshank tobacco stalk disease was so widespread over the tobacco fields and so badly infested them that there was just no way to overcome that. They didn't have enough chemicals or insecticide to fight it nor anything else. So they gave up on growing shade tobacco after about 1911.

Dad went up to Quincy where he heard there were several fellows growing shade tobacco at that time. One of those people who were particularly helpful to him was Mr. Alex Shaw of Quincy who later was involved with Shaw's Zephyr, Lincoln & Ford Company from 1923 up to his death. Two others were Fount and Fred May of the May Tobacco Company.

My daddy founded Embry Tobacco Company. His partner was Eugene Malcolm Collins from Blakely, Georgia. My mother was a Collins but there was no relation. Mr. O.J. Clayton was their lawyer and was Mama's lawyer after Daddy died. Mr. O.J. died 15 or 20 years later. He still got it mixed up in his mind that Mama and Mr. Collins were kin. He had the highest grades of any law student that had ever gone to the University of Florida up until the time that he graduated. That was 1915 or 1917. His daughter showed me his year book. She's Shellie Clayton. I don't remember what her married name is. Mr.and Mrs. Clayton had three daughters. Margie May is my age. Went to school with me first through twelfth grade. Margie May Clayton.

Mr. Collins didn't know anything about tobacco. He just knew something about fishing and he was a good bookkeeper and he was a good front man. Chamber of Commerce committee-man and Rotary, Elks that sort of stuff. Dad didn't have time for that and Dad didn't want to do that, but he liked John, knew he was honest, thought he was honest. Whenever he got the tobacco cured then he took his samples in October and went on up to New York on Water Street to see the tobacco folks up there, the manufacturers, and would sell it. Most all the companies were Hebrew.

He would be gone two or three weeks maybe. He made pretty good. It was like any agriculture deal, it was peaches and cream one week. You might have a beautiful crop of tobacco and one afternoon about 2:30 hail would come along and knock it down. Hail insurance in those days was probably so high you couldn't have thought about it.

He had a packing house down there by Love Street. The last street before you go down the hill on old US 90 where Dixon Lester used to have that big house. Where Frank McCall used to live in that Spanish looking house. One block south of there, three blocks from the Court House square. It was torn down just a few years ago. At the Leaf Theatre take a left and go one block and then take a right and go one block and there is where the building was on the corner.

Dad was a long time officer of the company and unable to participate in the active management because he was sick. He was in the hospital at Johns Hopkins for four years off and on. He had cancer, but they didn't call it cancer then

I lost a little boy in three weeks time. Died of leukemia in 1965 when he was 14 years old. I have one other boy. He is the Assistant Director of all activity of CARE in Guatemala. He has a terrific job. He was with Save the Children for seven years then he went with CARE about a year and a half ago. He graduated from Wake Forrest and went to Peace Corp for two years. He knows Africa like the back of your hand. He and his buddy, instead of letting them send them home and pay them off at the end of their duty, went to about 15 countries: Somalia, Ghana, Ivory Coast, Cameroon, Nigeria ... Then he came back and went to the University of Florida, the flag university of the state. Went there and got him a masters in Ag Economics. He sent his resume out and within 24 hours Save the Children called him up and said we haven't got the money for the funding but we're going to get it in about four months and we'll send you to Cameroon or Tanzania -- whichever you want to go to. He said I want to go to Cameroon. She said well you can go. Just let us have your phone number and where you're going to be so we can get up with you in the next four or five months. He was in Albuquerque learning about adobe building with a friend of his that was a contractor there. And they called him out there and told him to come on up here to Connecticut, we got to talk to you. Within a month he was gone to Cameroon. He was there six years. He came home 30 days every year or two. I went out there to see him in January of 1980. We had a wonderful time.

I never worked with them in the tobacco company. I worked a half a day. When I was six years old I went out there to get that lunch Mama kept packing every day in an old peach basket and I'd ride about a mile and a half and it smelled so good and I'd be so hungry. I had to wait until I got back to town to eat. I was going to be seven in October and I talked them into letting me go out there. I worked as a toter the first part of the morning and man I was about dead when noon came. I got that lunch and went back out there and worked about an hour and a half and I came flying down the road. I said, "I'm sick. I got to go home." I put those tennis shoes around my neck and walked that mile and a half on in to town.

My brothers used to have to work on Saturdays or anytime – in the rain, in the barn, on Sundays, letting up and down the windows – all that. I said, "I'm not going to work like *that*, I'm going to get me a job with Mr. James J. Love." So I got a job with J. J. Love and I worked for him for six years. When I was in college I came home for Mother's Day. My mother said, "Have you written Mr. James for your job again for this summer"? I said no. She said, "Well, you're not going to lay around here all summer." I said, "No, I'm not going to do that, but I'm going to summer school." She said, "Well, I know why you're doing that, too." I said, "Well, why"? She said, "You just don't want to work in that tobacco." I said, "You're right, Mama. For your information, I don't ever intend to go into another packing house or another tobacco shade without white shoes on in the tobacco shade and with a tie on in the packing house. I don't want to do anything but look. That's all I'm going to do and I ain't going to stay long, either." I had shirts stick to my back and I hated it.

My sisters didn't work in the tobacco. Not many girls did in those days. In fact out there on the farm none of the superintendents' daughters worked. They'd come up there and bring me some iced tea, but they didn't string or anything.

Mr. James Love had Love Leaf Tobacco Company. He was a real high powered operator. He was one of the top ones in Gadsden

County. He was worth one or two million. When I worked for him I didn't work during the gathering season. Then I spent the money at the beach and the mountains. Then after I graduated I went on in the Service almost immediately. I went to Texas and learned all they could teach me about flying in seven weeks.

My son is Richard Fain, Jr. but he goes by Rick. I have one brother left. That's Edwin. He was the youngest of the eight children ... two girls eleven months apart and then they had six little brothers and Ed was the last. I was supposed to be the last apparently. There is more distance between him and me than all the rest. He and I are very close, we are great buddies. I got him to join the Marine Corp during WWII and you'd think with all that he had to go through he would never speak to me again, but he does. He caught hell. He is Joel's daddy.

My brothers and sisters in order are: Sora (who married Hux Coulter) and 11 months later Sallie. Sallie is 78, so Sora would have been 79 in March had she lived. Then Hugh, who is the one that got killed on the Forrestal. He was a captain, a navy captain. He was the oldest boy. He went to the University of Florida in 1929. He was born in 1915. Then Atkins, who was an honor graduate in Agriculture from Florida and Southeast Conference pole vaulting champion. He graduated in Spring 1935. He broke the AAU record vault. My other brothers were Mike and Victor.

My granddaddy was not a very successful farmer. He was Mr. Wallace Embry. You've heard of people having a green thumb, well Granddaddy was just the opposite. I don't know why they went to Dade City, I forget. The first four children were born there. That was up through 1911 or 1912 and then Daddy went to Quincy in 1912 and he liked what he saw and the fellows up there were willing to help him get a toehold.

The Embrys came down from Kentucky in 1896. There were seven boys: Uncle Hugh, Boone (my daddy), John, Milus, Ashton Fox, Barton Stone and William Edwin Embry. Uncle Ed, the youngest of all these seven boys, used to take a crew of black boys up to Connecticut to show them how to gather tobacco. He took them back in 1910, 1912 or 1913. He was a Marine in WWI.

Grandfather Embry went down to South America from 1923 to 1940 -- most of that time he was a manager with General Motors. He was 6 feet 4 inches. Had those seven boys and there was one daughter, Aunt Polly. She was about mid-way. She just died last Spring and would have been 100 if she had lived four more months. She had to go to bed about the last year her body was just so frail it wouldn't hold her up. She lived just 3 blocks from Sallie. Sallie knew everybody in Dade City. She was crazy about Aunt Polly. Everybody liked Aunt Polly. She was driving around in that Cadillac until she was about 86. Her only son, Charles Touchton, made her quit.

Six
Joe Cantey
**Cantey Home, Havana
June 5, 1988**

My granddaddy Cantey brought his slaves down to grow tobacco way back before the Civil War. He first started in Old Salem but he couldn't grow tobacco there. There was too much pine and he had to go down in the hardwood forest to burn the wood logs to make the potash to grow the tobacco. That's why he wound up in Gray Hammock down in Midway. We stayed there until I was eight years old, then we moved to Amsterdam, GA. I grew 60 crops of tobacco. My daddy grew 70 crops. After they freed the slaves, my granddaddy couldn't make a living in Midway, so he was Clerk of the Court for Gadsden County about the turn of the century right on up until he lost his eyesight. He didn't never have any opposition.

My father was Frank Cantey and my granddaddy was William Thomas Cantey. Besides my daddy, there were Robert Victor and William (Bill), his brothers. He also had a sister, Florence, who married a Higdon. My daddy moved to Georgia (Fowlstown) to grow tobacco but we had a disease – blackshank – and he couldn't grow it. In 1922, he moved to Madison to grow tobacco. My wife and I married in 1918, so we just stayed up in here. I have two brothers living in Madison now and my son is in Madison, too.

They grew cotton and stuff up in South Carolina and there was a bunch of boys bought slaves and had a wagon train all the way from Carolina down here. They owned all the land from Scotland to Little River to Ochlockonee River where they run together and they grew cotton and tobacco. His daddy-in-law came down with him. The two of them were quite big farmers back then. The daddy-in-law's name was Hudlow. They came in from Charleston, from the country, and they went on up the river and settled at a little place up there growing cotton. They grew black tobacco – this was before shade tobacco.

The Owl Commercial Company had quite a few farms -- one where the old hospital was in Quincy, and one in Midway called Santa Maria and one called Santa Clara and a good many others. They happened to have one with a lot of shade trees and the tobacco was thin and flexible where they could put it on cigars. They started off using lathes, regular building lathes, and they would put 25 lathes on top of the posts and that would give them 60% shade and the tobacco would grow thin. One pound could wrap 1,000 cigars! That's the way they started (into growing shade tobacco).

I grew my first crop before I married. I first started in the pecan business and it was too slow. I couldn't make a living in pecans so I started tobacco about 1920. I grew some for myself and then for American Sumatra Tobacco Company (which went out of business in 1955). Then I grew 20 crops for myself after the big company went out. One of the tobacco farms I had was right here where the house is and all this was in tobacco.

I built a golf course (where a tobacco barn was) for the County after we quit growing tobacco and now we're doing a half million dollar business in our golf course. We're renting $100,000 worth of golf carts alone. And I just built it because my brothers in Madison built one. I had four farms in Madison for the American Sumatra Tobacco Company and it just changed Madison with the country club golf course. I said if they can do it, I can. They give me the land and I built the golf course with the farm labor. They said it would cost a million dollars and I built that one for less than twenty thousand. We formed the company with 100 stockholders that would give $100 a piece and we built a golf course with our farm land.

When tobacco went out, everything went "ka-hooey" in Gadsden County. That was the only thing that would make money.

Well, it may have broken some of 'em and some of 'em wasn't good farmers or had hard luck. They lost it. Cecil Butler, my neighbor when I moved to Florida, he was delivering milk in a little ole cut-down Ford with 10 cents a quart milk, delivering it around town. He died two or three years ago worth in the millions.

My son had nine tobacco barns down in Madison but the storm took four of them the other day. When I was growing tobacco we had a lot of hail storms. Our farms were scattered and the hail was in a certain area. Maybe we'd lose a crop on one or two farms, but we had enough farms scattered around from Attapulgus to Midway and up about Concord, the edge of South Georgia (which was about as far as shade tobacco grew until my Dad moved to Madison).

The first farm my Dad worked was about the time I was born. A. Cohen Company came down from New York and bought 13,000 acres in South Georgia and started growing shade tobacco, cleaning up forest. They had a farm for every letter in the alphabet starting with "A" and went to "Z." They cleared up the land and burned the hardwood to get ashes and that's where it started with my dad growing it for A. Cohen Company. They went out of business and the farmers all got broke with the depression, so American Sumatra Tobacco formed a company and took all these farms around Havana and Quincy. That's the reason they got so many farms. I was a Division Superintendent. I had four farms in the Havana division and four in the Madison division, eight farms. One was named Havana Farm, Houston Farm and Lang Farm and Shelfer Farm. San Bonita was down there on 27 before you get to the River. In Madison, I had the farm of ex-Governor Hardy. They had two farms down there. One was named the Fraleigh Farm and one the Hardy Farm. I bought the Hardy Farm when they quit growing tobacco – for my son. He married Ann Blake and they're down in Madison.

I grew for myself after the company retired me and grew for Joe Budd in Quincy. I took my trained labor and packed the tobacco for Joe Budd. That's where I made more money after I retired than I made all my life. After you grow it at the farm you take it to the packing house and they sweat it (sweat the gum out of it) and it blends the colors. They put it in big bulks and run the temperature up to 110. Then you have to take it out and reverse it and cool it off. Do that for about three months. Every leaf is opened up and graded as to its quality and the length. Every leaf in that hand is the same color and the same length and it's bought for about $8 or $10 a pile then, but the farmer got about $4 a pile. It was shipped all over. Pennsylvania was a big cigar place. My brother was in the cigar business with Frank Larty. He used to grow tobacco in Madison and Quincy, too, until he died. He had a distributing point in York, PA where they rolled those cigars by hand. Of course, they wound up doing it all with machines, like Joe Budd in Quincy. Got 'em out of business.

My dad started off with Owl Commercial Company. They grew some tobacco for years, but about the turn of the century is when they started growing shade tobacco.

I grew up in it. We lived in a big old two-story house in Midway. My Dad moved up to Amsterdam to grow tobacco for the Owl Company in 1904. So they started growing shade tobacco about then.

My granddaddy lost his wife and she's buried in Midway. The cemetery there is the oldest cemetery in Florida. It was a cemetery before there was a Florida or USA. It's on the Spanish Trail and the Spanish wintered at this cemetery and buried hundreds over there. They had an epidemic and a lot of them died that winter. Now the cemetery on one side is for the American people and the Spanish and the Negroes are on the other side. They didn't have anything but a wagon to take to the cemetery so they didn't go very far. I put a chainlink fence around it 10 or 15 years ago and fixed it up. The Spanish were buried with lighter'd knots and we made some little concrete blocks where the lighter'd knots were, but we didn't know names, just a bunch of knobs sticking up where the Spanish are buried. The old settlers told me it was a cemetery before there was a USA or Florida. After the explorers left St. Augustine and got to the Ochlockonee River, they held up there for the winter.

I worked in tobacco from the time I was six years old. When I was 10 years old I worked in the packing house. I would have to walk about two miles and an old whistle would blow at 4:00 in the morning and that meant get up and at sun-up you went to work. We didn't have electricity so you had to work by daylight. You worked from sun up till sun down for 25 cents.

We moved to Fowlstown and the old Apalachicola Northern come from Apalachicola and through our plantation going to Climax to bring the seafood. We would cut up wood, fat wood, for that old locomotive to stop and get the wood. That steam engine rode from Apalachicola to Climax. Every night it would come by and blow the whistle and we would have to have two or three racks of wood. That's the only way they got the seafood out of Apalachicola.

We used to fire our barns with wood. You had to cut the wood. We cut sweetgum wood and let it dry, and we'd burn sweetgum. Then we wound up with coal, and then with charquettes. We'd burn thousands of tons of those little brickettes. Then we wound up burning with gas. About two and a half million BTUs of heat in those big barns.

None of my barns ever burned, but a lot of them did. We'd be firing in the barn because it was damp – to dry out the tobacco. That heat would bring the lightning in there and burn it up. So I finally went to grounding mine. I put a copper wire and buried it and I saved some by grounding.

Our children worked in the tobacco and my grandchildren worked in it. We have a lot of grandchildren. One of our daughters had four girls and a boy and they all worked in it. They would string it and we'd hang it up in the barn on sticks and spread it out.

I just like to farm. Out here in this place I've got every kind of fruit and vegetable growing. I've even got Thompson grapes growing that you grow in California. I've got them about half-grown now. I've got ten different types of grapes I'm growing.

To grow tobacco, you first picked a place with a clay base. Had to have a good clay base. It would get disease on the root if the land was too light. After we got rid of the pine trees, then we'd have potash. We used to get it from Chile, pure potash. We'd have to take a shingle and scatter it out. It would burn your hands before we had commercial fertilizer. Then we'd take cotton seeds and bury them and put this potash on to eat it up. And that's the way we'd grow tobacco before we had the commercial fertilizer.

There was something in this area (for shade tobacco), it never did spread except in Connecticut (East Hartford). Up and down the Connecticut River they could grow tobacco and they're still growing some, but it brings about $15 to $20 a pound for 25 and 50 cent cigars.

The last year I grew tobacco was about 20 years ago. I grew up until 1975. After I retired from the company, then I took one of their farms and grew tobacco for myself. It was the Shelfer Farm.

{Mrs. Cantey adds: We went there to stay one year until we built here. But we stayed there 10 years and then we built here. He was having such a good time making his own money, going where he wanted.}

I knew a lot of mistakes that I had made and I didn't make them when I was spending my money. I let them pay for my mistakes.

It was a very scientific time was the main thing. From the time you sowed your seed, one ounce of the seed would cost $650. But one ounce of tobacco seed would plant about 25 acres. We would take a teaspoon full and mix it with meal or something and sow it because the seeds were so fine you couldn't see them. Those were hybrid seeds that cost that much.

If we saved the open pollinated seed it didn't cost, but we had a better grade by having the hybrid seed. They were developed to make more pounds and quality. It started off with Sumatra seed – that was the old sun tobacco. It made the filler for the wrapper. We just grew the outside wrapper for cigars. Just a little strip of the leaf was all it took (1,000 cigars could be wrapped with a single pound of tobacco.) They used to roll it by hand. Mr. Budd in Quincy had machines, but a lady would have to take that half a leaf of tobacco and strip the stem out of it and she would put it on a perforating machine that would cut it just exactly to fit. Then she'd have to spread it on over a perforation with a vacuum to hold until the cigar wrapped. But we learned to grind up this tobacco and homogenize it. That's what put us out of business, that and labor, too. For each 30-acre farm we had to have 100 tenant houses. I had 125 of them on this farm here in Havana.

We didn't have transportation in the early days. You had to walk to work and you had mules and wagons and you had to have the labor right there because you had too much invested. You couldn't get out and hire labor, because it took so many per acre to do it. We'd have to recruit them from Georgia and Alabama.

We started training the labor at about six years old, pulling grass or hunting worms – the little ones. Somebody with a good switch – and they'd keep eight or 10 of a bunch and just bring them on up and at 10 or 12 years old they could do anything a grown person could do. The children seemed happier and less into trouble than they are now. Their families didn't have to buy much food, just a little meat. We didn't pay them much, but there were things like doctor's care and wood and space for gardens that we furnished. If they did get put in jail, we went their bail.

My daddy was 94 years old when he died. When we grew tobacco for filler to go inside the cigar, I used to haul it from Fowlstown to Quincy. That old big packing house they just tore down back of where Fletcher-Cantey used to be. It'd be wagons line up a mile with five or six boxes of tobacco. We'd leave right after supper and it'd take us until daylight to get there and the mules were bogging up right at the Court House knee-deep in mud all the way around.

My granddaddy was Clerk of the Court. They didn't have any air-conditioning. They didn't have no typewriters. He done everything with a pen and ink. In the summertime, it had a hallway through it, and he and the secretaries would get out in the hall to get some breeze to be able to work. But Quincy was just a mud puddle in the Fall of the year – the time we'd be hauling tobacco and it raining. We'd have to put down boards to walk across the street.

The hardest part of growing tobacco was fighting weather conditions. You had the ups and downs, you had dry weather, and we didn't have irrigation then. The first irrigation I saw was where they would bore holes through a long poplar log. They would have an old steam pump and pump it out of a creek up on top of a hill and make a big reservoir and put the shade down below in low ground and then in big troughs and you'd pull pegs out. Your water would be running through the troughs in the tobacco shade.

That's the way I learned to swim was in one of those reservoirs. Right there at the airport in Quincy, right across there they had a big reservoir. At the top of the hill and they grew tobacco all down next to the creek.

We would try to plant in 4-foot rows and about 12 inches apart. But every stalk had to be tied up with a string nine feet up to a wire and wrapped as it grew. You had to wrap it between each leaf. The first shade was built on Little River on 90. Dad built a shade over there with lathes and that was the first one built. Between Quincy and Little River. It was around the turn of the century – I don't know just what year.

Mr. D.A. Shaw was the manager of American Sumatra Tobacco Company, after it was formed. Cubans came over here, they were growing it in Cuba and a lot of them come over here and rolled cigars and worked in tobacco. I remember the Shaws, and the McFarlins. John McFarlin had a big old two story house as you go up the hill to the left. That was Jack McFarlin's where Dixon Lester used to live. As you go up the hill from Havana that big old house is still there.

The American Sumatra Tobacco Company sent a man, Gasloff, from New York out here as manager. Later on he moved to Jamison and went to growing for himself and left the company. Then they brought a man named Einstein. He built a big house in Amsterdam in the middle of that farm with every letter in the alphabet. My dad was a superintendent. They had the biggest farm in the south and one in the north. Of course, folks had to ride a horse then. This old man Einstein had the finest horses and a big surrey – every Friday a servant would hitch up that surrey and those pretty horses and take him to the Bon Aire Hotel in

Bainbridge. It took about three hours to drive there. We thought it was the biggest thing in the world to get in that surrey.

We had seven boys and three girls in our family. Two of the boys are living in Madison. The rest are dead. Clyde and my dad grew tobacco, and Captain Frank. (Just three of them grew it.) My dad grew tobacco in different places.

My wife's name was McLaughlin (Nellie McLaughlin). We were neighbors – went to school together.

Our daughter Mary Alice is married to Guyte Chester. They live here in Havana. She is our youngest daughter. They have four boys. One of their sons, Jim, is fixing to launch a Star War. He was with IBM and Ford took him away from IBM to launch a Star War. He's in Houston. When he left IBM, Ford was the biggest in space business so he went with them.

Another grandson, Steve Chester, graduated from North Florida Christian, then went in the Navy for six years and he studied nuclear physics for four years. Then they put him on a submarine for two years and he'd go out in the middle of the Atlantic and submerge and stay submerged for two and a half years and not come up. He graduated from Georgia Tech in engineering.

{Mrs. Cantey: I was born and raised about 25 miles from here, south of Bainbridge and my one brother passed away two months ago. My mother was a Fain. She was raised in Decatur County and my father, too. The Fains had the Fain Drug Store on the corner for years. We used to like to go through there in a covered wagon, stop and get ice cream. We'd go to the coast in a covered wagon.

It would take two days to go to the Coast. We'd go every October. If you tired of riding, you'd walk.}

On the 20th of May every year we'd have lemonade and fish fries. From 1908 on up until 1920 in Amsterdam we'd have a celebration, Emancipation Day. We'd send to Bainbridge and get a load of ice, lemonade and have a May pole and have prizes for the best decorated wagons and mules and just have a big time. This was for the help. Singing, dancing and drinking pink lemonade, even "light bread." You know they didn't ever get light bread except for May. And all the fish you could eat. We carried that on until 1975. As long as we grew tobacco, we didn't require them to work on the 20th. That was their day and we'd stop and have a fish fry, a big day, up until 1975.

We had a carpenter crew build our barns. George Johnson was our carpenter. He'd eat dinner with her (Mrs. Cantey) every day. We lived at Hinson, a big old twelve-room house. He'd build anything she wanted in that house. The last time I saw George Johnson at a meeting, he said, "I hope I can live to sit at her table one more time." He said, "I want to eat one more meal at Mrs. Cantey's house"!

In the middle of the day, he'd eat with us. Then we had plenty of servants. She had one in the kitchen and one in the house and one in the yard and they would do everything. She directed it. We had plenty of cows, milk, butter and vegetables.

{Mrs. Cantey: I never knew how many I was going to have for dinner – six or eight, or I never knew how many.}

She gets up on Sunday morning and fixes for 25 or 30 for dinner here for birthdays and all. Goes to church and comes back.

We've had the night riders ride around and burn up a lot of our barns. They thought we were monopolizing the tobacco business. The farmers would get mad and they'd go around and burn up our barns. Of course, they were insured by the company. They were local farmers, our neighbors. George Johnson would build the barns right back. They'd wait until they were full of tobacco and that was easy to burn. That tobacco was dry.

We got along beautifully with the labor because we didn't have labor unions. I never had any trouble. We had a superintendent on each farm. He would take the best men and the best women and direct the young ones how to work and what to do. We just passed it on down.

Anyone that wasn't in school worked in tobacco until they stopped that. Our granddaughters all worked in the barn stringing tobacco. We finally had a machine. You know we used to string it all with a needle. Put a needle through each leaf. But now they have a machine you put the leaves in there and it puts the thread through. I got my machines from Switzerland. The Swiss made it.

I grew shade tobacco from 1922 to 1975.

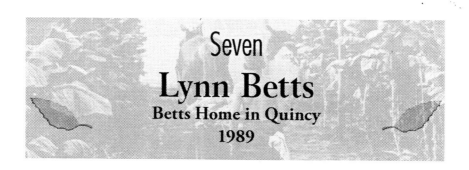

Seven
Lynn Betts
Betts Home in Quincy
1989

Originally I grew up on a farm and as a youth I worked in tobacco as naturally as most people in this area did when we were growing up. When I got out of high school in 1951, I went to work for Hav-A-Tampa, Joe Wedeles, Inc. in Quincy in the packing house. I went into the Service in 1953, got out in 1955, went back to work for Hav-A-Tampa. Then, in 1956, I married a Gadsden County girl – Helen Parramore -- who was off a tobacco farm in Gadsden Co., too. She always said she'd never marry a farmer or live on a farm!

In 1958, I grew my first crop of tobacco of my own which I started off with two acres (just across the Georgia line, near Bettstown). I was still working for Hav-A-Tampa at that time. I kept increasing. Finally, I got to 10 acres of my own. That's the largest I ever grew for myself. Then I went to work for Florida Shade Tobacco Growers, which was owned by Barry Ottinger and Arthur Fixel. I ran packing houses for that company. Then I took over a farm probably in 1963 – anyway, I started on one of their farms and ran farms for them until 1973. During that time, we grew (I believe) four crops of Candela (the Cuban type tobacco, which is a lot different from the regular shade tobacco, cured a lot different, just grown a lot different. A lot faster crop).

In 1971, 1972 and 1973, we were up to approximately 115 acres and I was still in charge of one complete farm in Calvary. Then I was also in charge of the setting, the riding and overseeing the balance of the farms. So we had farms in Gadsden County (one in Quincy and one in Havana); we had the farm in Grady County (GA) and we had a farm in Leon County (which was about the only place shade tobacco was really ever grown there, the old Bannerman Place on Meridian Road.).

In 1973 was the last crop we grew which was down to about 23 acres. That year we started harvesting on Wednesday afternoon. The superintendent that was working with us on that farm passed away the next morning. I harvested that crop living 25 miles from the farm. Had 13 barns to tend (fire) at night. So that was a pretty hard season, I guess one of the hardest seasons we had. But that was the time the tobacco business just kinda went down. Most everybody was getting out. That's when our company dissolved partnerships and went out.

We worked a lot of labor. We worked a lot of school kids, black and white. We had good working relations with them. Up until about 1970 it was really enjoyable to work because labor always worked good and got along good and then it got to where we couldn't work too many of the young kids. I think that hurt us, not only hurt us as growers, but it hurt the families, it hurt the kids by depriving them of learning how to work.

You know we saw a lot of changes in our tobacco growing in the time we grew it. At first, most all the work was hand work. A lot of it was done with mules. As years went by we went more mechanical, with tractors, transplanters, a lot of double-row cultivating with tractors -- we even had a tying machine. This was a mechanical machine that the people would ride on. Did away with our benches for tying. We went from hand stringing (all the tobacco having to be sewn leaf by leaf) until they came out with an electric stringer that teen-agers could whip off 400 to 600 sticks a day where usually it would take a well-experienced, older person to get 400, 450 to 500 sticks a day when they were doing it by hand. We went from what we called row irrigation (of turning the water down the middles) to when we put in portable type, and from that to overhead irrigation – a permanent type irrigation. There were just a lot of changes in the 20 or so years I was in the tobacco growing. People took a lot of interest in it. It's just once farming is in you, you can get out of the farming, but you can't get the farming out of you.

And we went from when you used to dust it by hand with a tin can or sack, then to hand blow-guns, then to mule-drawn blow-guns, then to airplanes, backpacks – just all kinds of different blow-guns and things for insecticide for insects.

People that were never around it just can't imagine things that went on and the changes in it. It'd be the same thing in that if some of these people were to come back now that weren't around since 1900 and see some of these airplanes and cars and things we've got now.

When you got through harvesting tobacco and got it in the barn, got it cured out, then it was taken down, tied up in what we called "hands," individual hands, then taken to the packing house, put in bulks. Usually about 4,000 pounds were stacked in one pile. Had to be placed in there just right. In the middle of that bulk would be a thermometer placed in a pack so you could check temperature on it each day. If that temperature started getting too high, you automatically take it, shake that tobacco out, re-bulk on another place, on another bulk. Or if the temperature wouldn't start going up, sometimes you'd have to shake it out, re-do it to get it heating up.

This process (called sweating) was what finished curing the tobacco to the stage that it would keep. In other words, it had to get to a certain consistency – moisture and all. Sometimes, it would take about seven to 10 days to automatically turn it, check it out and turn it. And, usually, I would say about eight to nine weeks (maybe 10 to 12 weeks) to dry it out enough. Just according to how much moisture was in the tobacco when it was delivered to the packing house.

After it was the right moisture content, dried out just right, then you baled it. Put it in 150-to-160 pound bales. And in what we called a baling box, we put a mat on the bottom, a piece of wax paper on that (a piece of wax-coated brown paper). Had sides on the box that were removable. You placed that tobacco in there in a certain way that all the heads were turned out. That is, all the stems were turned out. Then that went under a press. It was pressed down to about 12 to 14 inches. Then you removed the sides from that box and sewed it up, sewed that bale up. That's where you got what you called the "bale." If that tobacco was kept on cold storage it would probably keep seven, eight, maybe 10 years. But you had to treat it against insects.

In the latter years of packing houses they quit putting it in bulk and went to what they called forced sweating. They had steam – live steam in sweat rooms. They'd leave it in the box that it was delivered in or either pack it out in smaller boxes and sweat it in the boxes instead of bulks. It took much less labor to do it, a lot less handling and you could get a lot more in your area. But, as far as I was concerned the boxes and forced sweat never worked as good as the old-fashioned bulk.

Then when you got through with that, in what you called a sorting room, we always say "sorting." We didn't say "assorting." That's when you had the women that graded into different grades as to which cigar it would go on. We made about 14 to 16 different grades. You went by color, by size, by different amounts of holes in the leaf, by texture of the leaf. Then it was shipped to the factories to be put on the outside of the cigar, for the wrapper. All this had to be done by hand. You had to be very particular not to get holes in it, because it was used for the outside wrapper.

One thing I can always remember that Mr. Joe Wedeles taught me. He told us we had to get in there and work just like the labor did, because if we didn't know how to do it and couldn't do it ourselves, that we could never tell anybody else how to do it. And that always stuck with me. I think it's a good policy to go by. Don't ever ask anybody to do anything that you can't do a little bit of yourself.

A "slat shade" (the original design of a tobacco shade).
Photo provided by Fain Embry

Later (familiar) style of shade that set our landscape apart. Ola Mae "Sug" Jackson and Lillie Lee Smith and John Walter Pride put a little humor into their "sewing cheesecloth" work. Forrest Davis, Jr. Farm, Sawdust

Eight
"Barn Day 1990"
May 12, 1990

(On the day the "I Hear Hester Singing" Barn was dedicated after it had been restored, many friends and neighbors came to relive the shade tobacco days with us and celebrate that we were not losing our heritage completely. George Johnson, then Gadsden County Farm Bureau Agent, brought "The Ole House" Band and they gave all of us a vintage country music treat. He had real ties with the barn, because he grew up working in it and the shades – and between numbers he and fellow band member James Harold Thompson, our former Florida House of Representatives Speaker who'd grown up working on his grandfather's farm in Gretna, told their memories.)

Part I
George (Cousin Sonny) Johnson

In the tobacco business, there was a job for everybody that wanted one. From the little children that were about five years old, there was picking up leaves in the barns and the rest could go to totin' and primin' – and when I was coming along, just about one of the best jobs you could have was driving the barge. That was kinda the Cadillac of the jobs! And all the other children looked up to you if you drove the barge.

But in order to keep that job, it meant you had to be there about 30 minutes before everybody else got there, to catch the mule and get her hooked up, and be out in the field. And if you slept a little late one morning, you might lose your job. And so, I had to work about 30 minutes a day longer, for that dollar a day Johnny was paying me!

But it was a good time and I learned how to drive – when I was about 12 years old. Growing up working on this farm, one of the best things I remember was eating dinner at Cousin Olean's house. She made them good ole homemade biscuits. I ate with her everyday, so working with Johnny and Hal had its benefits. And another one of those, I remember, was we didn't miss a single picture show that came on Saturday night. Johnny always paid our way. That's just some of the memories.

Part II
James Harold Thompson

I guess most of you wouldn't be here if you hadn't had some relationship with shade tobacco. I told somebody before the music started that one of the main reasons I went to law school and got stuck in an office today was because of one of these doggone tobacco barns. Because I got convinced when I was about 12 or 13 that I sure didn't want to spend the rest of my life scrambling up in one. But it sure is an era that's gone by and so many of us learned so much in one.

My work was for my granddaddy Alex Presnell over in Hardaway, and a few of you knew him. He was a tall, slender fellow. I remember that he always wore a white, long-sleeved shirt. I never could understand that, why he did that right in the middle of the summer and this kind of work, but he always was a little bit dressed. And I remember going up in a tobacco barn the first time. You know it was a kind of a curse to be a little bit taller than the rest of the boys, because the boss man, whether he was your uncle or your granddaddy or the man that had hired you figured out real quick that it didn't take but three tall boys to hang tobacco in one of these barns. Otherwise, it took four if everybody was a little shorter. So those of us that were a little taller we had to go up in the barn a little earlier. I remember the first time I went up in a tobacco barn and I hung the tobacco – and all of you that know about that know you had to space it very evenly so that air could circulate up there and it could dry and not, you know, start a rot. Because if it started a rot in one part of the barn the whole doggone thing would rot on you if you didn't be careful. And I remember going up there on a hot day, and I finally told my granddaddy I wanted to go up there and be the hanger. You know you kinda worked your way up to that, because when you punched up you caught all the dirt and everything that came off of everybody's shoes and also the tobacco and the water and the poison. So I went way up to the top of the barn, and, boy, I topped out that section and I knew I spaced every stick just perfectly even and it was hanging just right. And I came back down and Granddaddy was sitting on the sill there and had that white, long-sleeved shirt on and I sat down by him just as proud. And I said, "Well, how you think I did"?

He looked up there, and he said, "It's pretty good, but that's what I'm paying you for, son."

So as I began my adult life working at the Legislature and all that I've been privileged to do, people would come forward and say, "Boy, what a great job you've done"! I'd say, "Well, that's what y'all elected me to do was go over there and do that job."

You remember that people from all walks of life and what they taught you. There was an old black gentleman named Will Robinson. He came from Alabama and packed barges for my uncle and my granddaddy probably the first five years I toted. And by the way, Jim Anderson, your grandson there is five years old. That's when I started to work. Brother Alexander and I doubled up for one primer. One of us couldn't do it by ourselves. But I remember very vividly that we were talking about something and what you want in life and how you get it, and all that, and Uncle Will paused a minute and he said, "Somebody give you something, they haven't done you a bit of good." And I remember that and kinda transferred that over to what to do about opportunity for people. You know, if people have an opportunity for education and can work and make good, society gets along pretty good. But a handout society is not a very good one. And that's another important lesson I learned.

So there are a lot of good lessons that followed us all through life. We learned to work with each other and we learned how to work in teams. We learned not to be scared of it. We learned to work under adverse circumstances. I remember my sister Jo Ann – some of you remember her, she went to Atlanta to Nurses' School and had such a time going way off up there. I remember taking her up there in a 1949 Chevrolet, all five of us. Papa Joe stayed home. We took enough chicken to do us a day and a half up there. Because back then, you didn't stop at restaurants. You'd buy breakfast, because that was the cheapest. But Jo Ann was well-suited for the hard work she had to endure when she went to Nurses' School, because she had worked stringing tobacco in a tobacco barn. There are a lot of you here who have done that, or whose mothers have done that. And grandmothers have done that. And it's a thing to be proud of. But Jo Ann had a sort of an allergy to the poison. A lot of people would have that through the years. Most of 'em would go to the house. Jo Ann would go outside the barn and get over it, and come back in and start stringing tobacco. And so I learned a lesson there. That you can't just give up when things get a little bit difficult for you.

All those things shaped and molded my philosophy, and me as a person – and the people that I've touched, with your help, in Florida and throughout the Country. I've had such wonderful opportunities, and so much of it started right here in a tobacco barn with a shade right out there. And I'm proud to be a part of it, and proud it's a part of my heritage and past.

Part III
Rev. Jim Anderson
Pastor, Woodland-Gretna Presbyterian Churches
Prayer of Dedication

Prefaced by these remarks: "Scripture tells us that we are to 'look back and return to the rock from which we are hewn' and this afternoon is the beginning of a look back at the foundation of this community. Let us pray.

Dear God, our Heavenly Father:

We are surrounded with so much that reminds us of the blood, sweat and tears of our grandparents and parents. In the midst of this beautiful area, we are reminded that the land has brought forth plenty. You have greatly blessed this land. We are reminded of the tenacity, of the sacrifice, of the hard work of those who were wiped out economically, and just came right back and were blessed again. We thank you for the privilege that is ours in this community. In your Name, we pray. Amen."

Part IV
Robert C. (Bob) Lay, Sr.

(George introduced Bob as "Kay's head engineer and carpenter." In turn, Bob explained that he had planned to lead the group in singing "I'd Like to Teach the World to Sing" – Coca-Cola's song about harmony, which was a prevailing memory of mine about the barn and the way we all worked together. But since we couldn't find the words, he was substituting another song celebrating that "tomorrow is Mother's Day." In a tobacco barn, mothers – key workers -- were definitely important.)

> M is for the many things she taught me
> O means only that she's growing old
> T is for the tears she shed to save me
> H is for her heart of purest gold
> E is for her eyes with lovelight shining
> R means right … and right she'll always be
> …
> Put them all together and they spell Mother
> A word that means the world to me.

Part V
John Henry McNealy
(One of the Barn's Restorers)

I'm gonna do a folk solo I remember from a long time ago. "If It Wasn't for the Lord" – and if it wasn't for the Lord, we wouldn't be celebrating this day.

> If it wasn't for the Lord
> Oh the Lord
> Tell me what would I do
> If it wasn't for the Lord
> Tell me what would I do
> Cause he's everything to me
> He's my water when I'm thirsty
> He's my shelter any time
> Cause he's everything, everything to me
> Oh if it wasn't for the Lord, Lord, Lord
> What would I do
> If it wasn't for the Lord
> Tell me what would I do
> Cause he's everything, everything to me.
> When this life is ended
> You know I must surely die
> Jesus he'll be my gangway
> Yeah, he'll take me to that home on high
> 'Cause he's everything, yeah everything to me.

Nine
M. D. Peavy
Peavy Home, Havana
July 12, 1991

My first crop was two acres back in 1950. We grew two and the next year we grew three and the next, three. My daddy and I were farming together and that was all we were growing. In fact, I went to Daddy and told him, "Daddy I'm going to have to let you have the farm. I got to get out where I can make more money 'cause I had a wife and three children I have to take care of." He said, "Well, M.D. if I got out would you take the farm"? In other words he'd quit. You know old folks don't want to grow but two or three acres. They don't want to buy irrigation, they don't want to build any barns. So when I took over I just went right on and bought irrigation, and I think I went to fifteen acres the first year. I worked on up until in 1974 I had 102 acres. That was a heap of shade tobacco. I had it here on my farm, plus I was renting a Cuban's farm up here and I rented T. W. Touchton's farm. I had that three farms. It was a heap of work.

When I was growing tobacco I could tell my whole crew what we wanted to do and a young deaf-mute girl would be the first to go get her hoe or rake and get started. Jabbo has been with me since he was just a kid. He is the only one that I've still got that I really work. Alcohol has just about ruined him.

I grew a half acre of tobacco this year under an old shade I had. I fertilized it with the regular old shade tobacco special just like we've always used. Leslie James made it for me. I got the seed from a friend of mine in Connecticut and I fixed my own little flat bed and raised the plants myself. I had cheesecloth over my seed bed only just right over the top of it. We had two or three real cold nights and I had some big tarpaulins and completely covered it up. Covered the whole thing. The flat bed wasn't as big as this room. I didn't have a problem with blue mold or anything like that. I didn't poison that seed bed but two or three times.

Jabbo and I were the two people who sewed the cheesecloth. I did all the sewing and he did the holding. I didn't do it back when I had the 102 acres. When I sewed the cloth I didn't have the first place to come unsewed. When I had different people sewing it, it would just come unsewed. We are all the time having to go back and redo some of it. None of mine came unsewed.

That was a good experience for my grandson. It was the first time he had ever really seen any tobacco. He was born about the time tobacco went out about 15 years ago. I may grow some this year if I can get hold of some different type seed.

Four generations of my family have grown tobacco. My granddaddy, my father, me and my son helped grow it. My son-in-law works with the Floridin Company. His name is Eugene Pickles.

I always heard that you could hear tobacco growing, but I never have heard it. You can be out in the field and the breeze will be blowing and you'll hear it click a little bit. I don't know that it was growing or just the leaves clicking a little bit. It's hard to say. But I'll tell you that it does grow fast.

Didn't have any problem with hail and didn't have any insurance, very few worms. At my peak I had four different crews going. I imagine each crew had thirty people in the crew. I had anywhere from 100 to 120 hands.

That little bit of tobacco I grew was almost as much trouble to me as when I grew a heap of tobacco. You couldn't go anywhere, you had to stay right here where you could watch it.

It has been fifteen years since I grew tobacco for a living. Everybody in my family worked in tobacco then. They worked in all capacities.

We used to have a mule that would go from the field to the barn and back to the field. We never drove it at all. We would get it out of the barn and it would go right on back to the field. That's been a good many years ago, though.

The first tobacco I ever fired was with wood, then we went to coal, then we went to gas.

There was one year I quit school. Mama and Daddy didn't say anything. They just went and got a mule for me and had me plow the fields. I plowed all that year! Come September, come time for the school bus to run that morning, Mama and Daddy hadn't said, " M.D. I want you to get up now and go back to school." When the school bus came. I was sitting there waiting for that school bus to come. I know Mama and Daddy laughed about that thing. They didn't let me see them, but I know they did.

My grandfather grew tobacco. Before him, I don't know of any of my folks who did. My father was Magnus D. the same as I am. My middle name is Delacy. There was Woodberry-Delacy Tobacco Company. Tom Delacy was my daddy's first cousin.

One year Mr. Cuthbert came into my barn. We had a radio playing. Mr. Cuthbert thought that this was the worse thing that we could do while stringing tobacco. But all of my hands would get in tune because they worked so well with the radio playing.

I could fill a barn with tobacco in a day. That was good -- you could fill a barn back up and go ahead and get your heat under it and it worked so good. I have seen a time when I wouldn't fill up but about three or four lights a day and that made it bad for fires. If you could start the whole thing at one time it was nice. I had portable gas heaters that I could take from one barn to another.

My grandfather's name was John Peavy. My folks came here from Dooley County, GA., around Cordele and Vienna. They came here about 1850.

Stringing machines were first used in Florida right here on my farm. Tom Delacy was the first to receive them. He went to Connecticut and saw them being used. He started right after this visit to Connecticut. Other people all over the county and in Georgia, after Tom Delacy got in stringing machines, started getting them, too. But he was the first one that had some in this part of the country. This was about the early fifties or sixties. (I bought the Delacy farm.)

My farm is the first farm to have planted tobacco in double rows. There used to be four-foot-wide rows. I built the racks myself.

In addition to tobacco, we had cows, a little corn and a little of pole beans, a little of all of it. I fattened out cows just for the compost.

I was thinking about growing tobacco about 10 years ago and Hentz Fletcher told me, he said, "Mr. Peavy, if you grow some tobacco I want you to let me bring my boy over and let him lug one day." He just wanted his boy to lug some tobacco and find out what he used to have to do.

We hung our tobacco quite wide apart because I had plenty of barn room and that made it cure out better, ventilation could go up through it. If I was really filling up a barn I'd have a stick between each stick.

One year I had all my hands one day to strike on me. It got me right in the worst predicament and they all struck. I went down and told Cecil Butler what had happened. I said Cecil what we need now is to put me some more help in there right quick. The next morning he had a big bus come driving in over there, unloaded it and they went to work. They found out that I could get help so that day at dinner they were all out there ready to go back to work. I told them, "Now if y'all want to go back to work I'll let this crew go on back, but if y'all are not going to work, Mr. Butler said he would furnish me help the rest of the year." They were all ready to go back to work and never did have no more trouble with them.

I had one of the biggest fires there was in the county. One year I had about six or seven barns burn at one time. Every one of them was full of tobacco. I had bought a bunch of barns over here close to Concord that was all in a row and one of them caught on fire. They were all so close they just burned. They were all covered with shingles. Burned every one of them.

Most of my barns were up here on the Delacy farm when I bought it. My oldest barn would be 50 years old or older. It was built back in the thirties.

Our working hours were from "can see to can't see." At one time I had three big school buses that I hauled my labor. Some would come from way down below Havana, some would come from between here and Quincy. We would go twenty-five miles to pick up help.

Everybody went home for lunch. We'd close the barn and wasn't anybody supposed to go into that barn until we come back. That would be one of my rules. I don't care what, you don't go back in the barn cause if you let them go back in the barn they'll take some of the sticks and put them back on the pile. Nobody went back in that barn until 1:00 and I was always back at the barn. The ones from way off would bring their lunch. Usually if I didn't pick up help but from maybe down Havana way I'd run them back home. The bus driver, as soon as he went around and put everybody off he went right back and started picking 'em up again. He'd put the first one off and start picking back up. We had people (rolling stores) come by during the day that had sandwiches and all kinds of things.

I remember one year it was real hot and all my hands had made up their minds that they wanted Kool-Aid, instead of water, in the cooler. I went and got 15 or 20 pounds of sugar, got my ice, my water and I put my Kool-Aid in there. Along about dinner time they were ready for me to throw that Kool-Aid out and get some water.

The last year I grew tobacco was 1976. I grew for Hav-A-Tampa, which was Joe Wedeles. Denny Hutchinson was running the packing house and Sam McMillan was there. Our last few years we delivered tobacco to Havana to Mr. Gus Bert. They phased out this place in Havana and we started carrying it to Quincy to Wedeles and Sam McMillan was there then.

{Mrs. Peavy on running the barn: I talked and I talked trying to supervise that bunch and hadn't a soul heard me yet.}

When the workers talked around my daddy it was "Mr. Peavy." They didn't call him by his name. When I come up I was just a little kid I made them call me "Mr. M.D." Ever since I was just a little kid I told all of them that called me M.D., it's "Mr. M.D."

My hands would work in the packing house, the ones that wanted to would. I had all kinds of families that lived here on the farm. Then had some that lived in what they called the Glade, people that lived back in there on their own places. I don't know where that name comes from.

Around here we had some of the best land as there was in the county there for growing tobacco.

I've traveled all over the United States, and there are other parts of the country that can grow tobacco just as good as Gadsden County. They just didn't have a market for it. If you don't have a market for it, if you don't have a warehouse, or people that will buy it, why grow it. I've seen plenty of land that I know I could grow good shade tobacco, but they didn't have any market for it. I'll tell you what, there's money that could be made off of shade tobacco right now if you could get several different farmers to grow it. They're getting anywhere from $15 to $20 a pound for tobacco in Connecticut. They can't grow as good a tobacco as we can grow. Tobacco don't get any size up there. I think we can grow just as good a quality as they can grow up there.

I used to think my tobacco when it was being harvested in the field and going to the barn, was getting tore up worse than anybody's tobacco in Gadsden County. But when I delivered tobacco to Mr. Gus Bert, which was Hav-A-Tampa, he told me a million times he said that I delivered one of the cleanest crops of the less tore up tobacco of anybody that brings tobacco in down there. I reckon because I thought my tobacco was getting tore up and would just be on them all the time about it. I just couldn't stand to see a leaf of tobacco get tore up. He always told me I had the less tore up tobacco of any farmer that brought tobacco in there.

I can remember when I was a kid, we grew sun tobacco we'd get in the bottom and we'd walk it in. Just get in there and walk all over it to just see how much we could put up. We grew sun tobacco before we grew shade tobacco. In fact, the first crop of shade tobacco we grew was back in 1950. But, I had been working in tobacco ever since I was big enough to walk.

My granddaddy grew sun tobacco, the same type of tobacco that we grow under shade only out in the sun. It was for cigars. Same type of tobacco barns and all, just didn't have the shade. It made the tobacco be the least little bit thicker. The leaves wouldn't be as thin and delicate.

My granddaddy grew tobacco and tended to it just like we do shade tobacco. He even grew the type tobacco that they used to spear on the stick. That was chewing tobacco, but that was grown way back before my time.

I remember when I was a little kid we use to thread sticks ahead of time. Instead of using a knife they'd go get a top out of a sardine can and they'd nail it up side of the wall. Where you cut the sardine thing off it would be sharp and when we would thread the stick we'd pull it across and that's what we would cut the string with. Cut it with a sardine lid. The string would be in a little ball. If you didn't have but an acre, acre and a half of tobacco it wouldn't take that much.

I can remember a person right up the road here -- he wouldn't count his sticks, he would just give 'em sticks, but what he would do he would cut the string off, and every time he'd give them a bundle of string he'd give them a punch. Well, it can't work like that because every time they'd go to the bathroom they'd have a pocket full of string to take with them. He'd go out there and kick around the bushes and just find all kinds of string where they threw it out. You'd find the sticks where they threw them out the window.

{Mrs. Peavy: Some of the people that worked in our barn used to use the string to crochet.}

I can remember when I was a kid my granddaddy would have a fit if you talked about bringing a watermelon in the barn to cut. He said it would rot tobacco. As far as I was concerned if somebody wanted to bring a watermelon in the barn and cut it and everybody eat it, it didn't hurt anything. But according to my granddaddy that watermelon would make tobacco rot.

My grandmother didn't work, she was strictly a housewife. A school teacher. My mother would work you slap to death. My mother worked.

I did my own irrigating and I did my own barnfiring. I couldn't trust it to anybody else. I don't even remember what the average temperature was, but I think it was about 95 to 100 but I declare I don't remember. I expect 150 would hurt it if you were doing that temperature when it was green, but after it gets cured out then the temperature wouldn't hurt it.

Ten
Ernst and Barbara Bietenholz
Bietenholz Home in Quincy
1992

(Ernst and his wife, Barbara, both Swiss natives, came to Quincy to live in the 1950s at the behest of the American Sumatra Tobacco Company. Theirs is a unique perspective on shade tobacco, as they were able to see the "big picture" and yet at the same time, they and their family threw their hearts into helping and being a part of this area that would soon be out of the tobacco business.)

Ernst begins the conversation: Deli Maatschappij was a Dutch corporation from the Netherlands and it had tobacco operations on the island of Sumatra, which was at that time a colony of the Netherlands. In 1955, a merger between American Sumatra Tobacco Corporation (originally named American Sumatra Tobacco Company) and Imperial Agricultural Corporation with headquarters in Hartford, CT was a division of Deli Maatschappij.

When the Japanese occupied Indonesia during World War II, many Dutch colonists became Japanese prisoners of war. The Japanese used these prisoners to build a railroad system (as shown in the movie, "The Bridge on the River Kwai" –1957). Many prisoners died.

The Dutch were able to ship their last Sumatra-grown tobacco out of the country to New York, were it was sitting on Pier 81 for over a year. During the War, no tobacco was shipped out of Sumatra/Indonesia to the West.

To enlarge their productivity in the U.S. after the War, Imperial Agricultural Corp. acquired American Sumatra Tobacco Corp. AST, which was formed in 1910 with holdings in Connecticut, Massachusetts, Florida and Georgia, is a company which became an important source of cigar wrapper leaf in the U.S.A.

Deli Maatschappij was a publicly-held corporation and tobacco was only one of its many products. The corporation may have been the second or third biggest coffee importer in the United States. A large amount of lumber was imported and the corporation was also big into the commodities market.

Under the new ownership, AST soon realized that tobacco might not be grown much longer in the Southern Division. Qualitatively. Florida tobacco was not equal to the one grown in Connecticut. It was strong, leaving a bitter taste. The company decided to find an alternate crop to grow in Florida. AST experimented with crops such as peach orchards, nursery plantations, vegetables, cattle, hogs, poultry and increased interest in timber production.

The Connecticut tobacco was somewhat similar to Sumatra tobacco, which was being grown again after World War II when Sukarno became president of Indonesia (Note: Sumatra is one of the largest islands which make up Indonesia.) However, there was no chance for the Dutch to return to Indonesia. The colonies were lost. Indonesia was now an independent country with Sukarno as it leader.

The Florida tobacco probably had the biggest boom during WWII because the government bought up cigars to hand out to the army, the military. Of course, during WWII there was no export; but after the War quite a bit of Florida tobacco was exported, especially to England wishing for a cheaper cigar. But when homogenized tobacco was invented, there was no market for this tobacco anymore.

Before coming to America, we had a dairy farm, fruit orchard, and grew potatoes, corn and wheat. Barbara and I had degrees in horticulture and agriculture from the agricultural college, Strickhof, in Zurich, which were beneficial in our professional life. However, I had no experience in growing tobacco in Switzerland, although sun tobacco was grown there.

I was employed April 1, 1955 by American Sumatra Tobacco Corporation – Southern Division. My initial responsibility was being in charge of the seed program, whereby I developed the strain of tobacco named "Moonlight" in Amsterdam, GA. (Note: Many old tobacco farmers will be able to explain how this tobacco variety got its name of "Moonlight.")

During this same period, Dr. Clayton researched at AST's research center of Mission Road in Tallahassee (which later was sold to

FSU). Dr. Clayton had previously retired as a plant breeder and scientist for the government. After his retirement from AST, he did research for May Tobacco on one of their farms – but that is the Mays' story.

As a new employee in the tobacco industry, it was explained to me that one had to be born into tobacco in order to know how to grow, cure and sort it. Therefore, this was a big challenge for me to learn. The best way was hands-on, and I learned to hang, cure, bulk and sort it myself after it was cured. The stringing of tobacco was done with the Swiss-produced machine rather than by hand.

I was active in the curing, warehousing and sorting of tobacco grown in Florida and Georgia. We also sorted Connecticut tobacco in Amsterdam, GA. In the '50s and up until 1969, the main office was located on West Jefferson Street, the entire block where Hardee's is now standing.

The first seed plot was at Bruce Farm located on the west side of Quincy, which later was owned by Manning Taylor, Farm Bureau, Suber & Johnson which later became The Fletcher Company. I dealt with Manning Taylor in the sale of 11 acres of Bruce Farm on the north side of the railroad track.

Barbara was hired in 1956 to supervise the growth of peaches and to teach employees how to prune and cultivate the trees. Sometimes she worked with a crew of 100 people.

It was around 1958 when I was placed in charge of all warehouse operations at AST, the Southern Division which consisted of

Quincy, Hinson, Havana, Madison, FL & Amsterdam, GA areas.

In 1961, I was advanced to General Manager of the Southern Division and made a Vice President of AST. Responsibilities also included being a Director of the AST stamp machine production, located in Miami; the name was Hilsum Sales Corporation.

At times, we sorted the tobacco in one of our many warehouses in Amsterdam, GA until 1962. We employed as many as 1,000 people to sort and pack the tobacco. The Florida tobacco was sorted first, then came the Connecticut tobacco to be sorted. We also had a warehouse and four farms in Madison, FL.

AST stopped growing tobacco on their own in 1961, but the company had partnerships with two individuals: Adrian Garland in Havana and Maurice Owens in Quincy. In these partnerships, we grew nearly 100 acres of tobacco.

When the Surgeon General came out against cigarette smoking, people went wild. They said right away, "Now they going to smoke a cigar"! We needed more tobacco and I negotiated contracts with Consolidated and a 3-year contract with at that time Kohn Brothers, which later became part of General Cigar.

In Connecticut tobacco was grown in the Connecticut River Valley and the Farmington River Valley. We also had farms and a large warehouse in Massachusetts.

Shade tobacco is grown in Mexico and the Dominican Republic, British Honduras now known as Belize. In 1959, I was sent several times by AST to Cuba to harvest tobacco seeds there. It was a very interesting journey. The last time I was in Cuba, I got out two days before Fidel Castro marched into Havana. That was a nervous time. Connecticut was short on seeds and happy to receive them from Cuba. The Duys Family had tobacco operations in Cuba – but that is their story.

In its search for a profitable crop, AST discovered that the timber production and nursery operation were the more successful replacements for its tobacco production. In 1959, the first two to three acres of nursery stock was planted on Krausland Plantation (also known as the Willoughby Shackelford Gregory home). The Connecticut Division had already begun its successful nursery operation in 1954.

Now Florida had to discover ways for its nursery to become successful. Since the climate was different in Florida, the nursery grew plants in 1-, 2- and 3-gallon pots on top of black plastic to help control week growth and diseases. Plants were set under shades if too much sun could damage them.

Charles N. Harris of Quincy was in charge of the nursery operations, Florida Division. After his death in 1977, John P. Sparmann became Production Manager.

In 1967, AST was split up into three different areas. Most farm and timber land was sold to Coastal Lumber Company. The Quincy Corporation, consisting of mainly building lots, was sold to a group of investors, and Imperial Nurseries, which retained the name of AST Corporation, was sold to General Cigar.

In 1970, I was appointed President of Imperial Nurseries, Connecticut and Florida Divisions. I had the opportunity to establish the first wholesale yards in Connecticut and Pennsylvania. During my 15 years as President, Imperial Nurseries were one of General Cigar-Culbro's most profitable divisions.

On January 1, 1985, I retired. My wife Barbara has worked along side of me and has been my partner throughout my life.

Barbara and I enjoyed our trips back to our home country – Switzerland, but we never had the desire to return for good. We made our life here. And, how could we leave our dear children and grandchildren? This is where our home is today.

Barbara (continues the conversation): Our children's names are Brigitt, who raised her children in South Carolina; Ulrich "Rick," who lives and works in Quincy; and Andreas "Andy," who lives and works in Blountstown. When our children were growing up, they all had to learn to work in tobacco, and later they worked in the nursery business. This gave them the opportunity to understand how some people have to work under hard physical conditions all their lives. We needed them to understand how fortunate they were to be able to choose a good education.

Ernst demanded always good work from his salaried as well as hourly employees, but he was also concerned about their well-being. It began in the warehouse when each employee received a green apron to protect clothing while sorting tobacco.

Later, Ernst had electricity installed in the employees' primitive dwellings. Windows and screens replaced the shutters, which had been a primitive way to control day and night – or keep the mosquitoes out of the house. Water faucets were installed by each house, which enabled the families to have running water in their kitchens by attaching an inexpensive water hose with cut-off valve.

Electricity was probably the biggest money saving for these families. Instead of having to spend a great deal of money on buying ice, they now had light, refrigerators, washing machines and more. What a blessing for people who worked eight to 10 hours daily!

As the tobacco acreage was reduced, those people could still live in their tenant houses – rent free. Some families later bought their own homes under the low income house laws. Others remained in their homes until they passed away. However, Ernst did not permit new people to move into the homes, because he knew they were substandard for today's requirements.

Ernst was also very proud that when he retired from Imperial Nurseries in 1985, all of the full-time employees and laborers were covered by health insurance, a pension plan and a small life insurance through their employer.

After being successful with the nursery operations, Ernst with his team was very happy to help other tobacco farmers, who stopped growing their crops in 1967, get started with their nursery operations. They were in Havana – May and Shelfer Nursery; in Sawdust – Suber Nursery and in Greensboro – Fletcher Nursery.

Ernst closes with the Havana Story: When we came to Quincy in 1955, Havana was completely surrounded by AST land. There was no room for this town to grow in size. I was privileged to sell several farms to help Havana extend its borders.

Perhaps the most important of these sales was land for the development of the Havana Golf Course. It was so designed to create a nice golf course. The Company retained the land around the course to sell lots for residential development at a later date.

The Havana golfers were thankful for my cooperation that they later offered me a lifelong, free membership, which made me quite happy. However, I had to decline this generous offer. After all, I just did my job in the interest of my employer.

In his later years, Ernst would often say, "I could not have been successful without a good team. That is what life is all about."

Eleven
Jim Campbell and Archie Hubbard
Visit to the Barn
July 13, 1992

Archie Hubbard: I grew up working in tobacco. My father worked in the AST Company. They started off paying me a quarter a day and it was real good when they went to sixty cents. I went to Connecticut in the late '30s before the War started. I couldn't find a job down here and Lamar Munroe gave me a job in Connecticut working up there. So I went up and worked for three years and enjoyed it.

They grew more tobacco per farm in Connecticut than in this area. Farms of 25 or 30 acres were about average here. Up there 100 to 225 acres is about an average farm. They grew a lot of tobacco on the farms.

Up there they didn't even tie it up, just wrap it to start with and it would blow down every Saturday night.

I bought some plows and carried them up there and they didn't want to plow. They'd rather take a hoe and pull dirt up around each plant. They had some kind of a cultivator and just went right down the middle of a row.

They had mule-drawn plows but not as we used them here. We dirted our tobacco with a plow, put dirt on it, loosened up the dirt and everything. But up there all they did was just run down the middle of the row. But it grew pretty good. It was a lot of work, a lot of work to do it their way. Of course, later on, they got to doing a little bit better, but they never did cultivate it up there, I didn't think, like we did down here.

Their labor included a lot of foreigners, Polish. They didn't carry labor through the winter like we did. They just hired when they needed it. The day they needed a man to work, well that's the day they hired him. They had boarding houses to put them in. They had some kind of sauce they heated all day long.

After I came back down here I went to work for Mr. Dick Shaw after the War. I ran the Love Farm for Mr. Dick Shaw. We grew about 25 or 26 acres. It was located right there by the Gadsden Country Club. I was with Mr. Love until he died about 1961.

Jim Campbell: Mr. Love was Mr. Dick Shaw's nephew. When he was a young man, my father worked for Mr. Dick Shaw. That's where Mr. James Love learned to grow tobacco was working the summer time with my father on Mr. Dick Shaw's farm -- Osceola. He was just a young man then but he would come out there and work and learn the tobacco business under my father, more or less. My father was A.H. Campbell. He farmed for Mr. Dick Shaw for a number of years, then he farmed for Mr. James Love. Then in

1934 he moved down to Hardaway. Actually it was several farm units. Some of them had sharecroppers on them. It was nearly five thousand acres and it's all gone now. There's not a building, not a barn, nothing left.

There was a big packing house in Hardaway that burned during the War. It had a big peanut oil mill built back in WWI and a big syrup mill where they made hundreds of barrels of syrup. There used to be a big operation out there. Hardaway owned it. Old man Hardaway that bought it, my understanding was that he helped build A and N Railroad and bought this land. The railroad ran right through it. And then his son is the one my father worked for. There was another Hardaway that was about my age and he was the last of them to own the farm. Back then the community of Hardaway had most everything. It even had street lights.

Mr. Hubbard: During the War they grew about 30 acres and I grew about 10 or 15. A lot of it was sharecropped out and they might grow a little bit.

Mr. Campbell: I don't see how they grew tobacco during the War with so many men gone, but they did. There was a feeling it would really go bust at War's end. I know several people told me, Mr. Horace Curry and some other folks. I was intending to buy a farm myself, and they said, "Oh no! The War is over. Now prices are going to drop back down." But they never did. They just kept going up and up. So I didn't buy one. I decided not to. But I was a lot better off.

I worked my father's tobacco and Archie and I grew some together for a couple of years after the war. We grew ours almost over to 90 in front of Mr. Amos Davis' house. See that farm ran from over there almost half way to Greensboro. It was a big place. And they had another 1,000 acres down in Liberty County. They'd go in and cut trees for fence post -- cedar trees.

Mr. Hubbard: Hardaway had some nice houses. I wouldn't say they were very expensive but nice houses.

Mr. Campbell: You had hail and wind that would blow your shades down.

Mr. Hubbard: We always got by some kind of way. Mr. Amos Davis had a hail storm one day and it came down and beat it up pretty good everybody came from places and helped him cut it off so it would sprout again, make the suckers. It made a nice crop of tobacco.

Mr. Campbell: He had a crop when he and I were growing some. We were out standing in the shade when it started hailing and we run and jumped in the truck and it near'bout filled the back of that truck up. So much hail fell down and all the cheese cloth sagged down between the wires. We got in there and cut it so the ice would fall through rather than take the shade down. And it stripped those leaves right off the stalks. It wasn't very high only about 8 inches high, but it stripped everything but the little stem and bud, and that came back and made as pretty a crop of tobacco as you ever saw. I wouldn't advise doing that but as long as that stem is alive, that bud is alive it will come back.

Mr. Campbell, showing pictures: And I came down here to the old depot to the "Absolutely Nothing Railroad" as we all called the A & N -- Apalachicola Northern Railroad and that's the old wooden packing house and this is the farm commissary and tenant houses and that was our house right there. So this is looking west from the depot. This is out in front of the farm commissary and there was a tool room there and they were just loading material on that going back to work.

Every year at the end of the season they'd usually throw a big fish fry or barbecue or something and that's some of the farm hands. We segregated even pictures then, that's all the blacks that worked on the farm and here is all the whites that worked on the farm. That's Perry Cantley -- he was the lot man. A lot man does everything. He worked seven days a week on call 24 hours a day. He looked after all the mules and cows, fed the cows. He was quite a character.

Some of the others in the picture were Eubanks, there's a family of Eubanks there and those are Hills. Some of the blacks are Jack McDonald and Louise, his daughter. She was our cook. She cooked for us. Some are still around.

Mr. Hubbard: We had two cooks. We had one that every time she filled the last dishes she'd say, "There ain't no mo'."

Mr. Campbell: This is a family of Jackson children. There was a whole family of Jacksons. They didn't live on the place but they worked during tobacco season. Those are bags of peas on their heads. They'd been somewhere and got bags of peas.

My mother kept books for the farm and kind of helped in the store. That was the only place around they could trade because they couldn't go to town. A few could go but most just traded at that store.

My mother's maiden name was Suber, but not from around here. She came up from around Atlanta. Her first name was Edith.

Here they're building a shade. They're pulling the wires with just a rope and block and tackle. Later on they got these winches and pulled them.

Here they're putting hay up in the mule barn. We made hay all summer long it seemed like.

There was a machine that marked where the tobacco should be planted. Then the worker would know to drop a plant in each one of those little indentations. The worker has a peg in his hand that he makes the hole a little bigger, puts the plant in and pushes the dirt back a little bit and then workers with buckets of water come along and pour a little water on each plant to wash the dirt around the roots, about a dipper full of water.

The wires for the shade were about 4 feet apart.

This shows workers bud poisoning. Each one of them had a little bag around their waist with arsenic of lead. Nowadays the EPA has stopped that kind of stuff. They'd mix arsenic of lead with cornmeal and then open the bud with two fingers of one hand and take a little poison put in there with the other hand. Go to eat lunch they'd just wipe their hands and eat lunch.

Here, they're weaving slats with weaving wire – they'd put them about four inches apart. I can't verify it but that could very well be one of the last slat shades built in Gadsden County. After this they started using cloth. Years ago they used just slats then they'd put cloth under the slats. After while they had a ribbed cloth and they just did away with the slats.

This is sewing cheesecloth: when putting up cloth it takes one to hold it and another to sew. They had two benches every run. They'd get on one bench and somebody would bring the other bench and put it in front of them so they didn't ever have to get down.

We raised a lot of syrup cane and put it in big 55 gallon barrels.

Mr. Campbell worked for Higdon Grocery Company until he retired.

Mr. James Love's farm was called the Malone Farm. (Picture he's showing has: C.P. Suber, Sue Hubbard, Mildred Suber, A.B. Hubbard and Ed Suber Neeley.)

A roadway and a terrace. They'd go prime everything off and take those stalks down and give them access so wagons could come through and they wouldn't have to pull it so far. The terrace was where they had to build it up where it wouldn't wash. If land slopes too much you'd have to have terraces, follow the contour of the land.

When I was in college (Univ. Of Fla.) I'd come home in the summertime and I'd run the barn. I didn't hang but I'd push it up. Sometimes you'd have to get up there and show 'em how. You'd put a young boy down low -- they'd hang on to one side and hand up. It could take about three men above him to get the tobacco sticks all the way to the top.

Mr. Drew Haire lived in Hardaway and all his children were girls and I've seen them hanging tobacco. Now they look sophisticated and ladylike, but I can truthfully say I've seen them hanging tobacco. You had to get it in anyway you could.

Hardaway was several different farm units. When he bought all that, there were several different farms like the Money place and Rosemeade and what we called "Number Two." Each one of those farm units had a house and barns on it. Some two barns, some three or four. Time you count them all up I guess there were 15 or 18 of them at least scattered over ten miles. Some almost down to Greensboro almost to where I-10 crosses there and then some as far over as 90 in front of Mr. Amos Davis. The Money place had two or three barns. A family had lived there one time whose name was Money, I believe is how it got its name. Just like Little River. Little River is not because of the small river. It's because some Littles lived out there. So a lot of these places were named after somebody who once had lived there. Rosemeade was by Mrs. Atwater. Mrs. Atwater lived on Atwater Road. It belongs to the Governor now.

Mr. Campbell: My sister Mary Frances (Mr. Hubbard's wife) was principal out at Mt. Pleasant for a number of years. She taught there and then got to be principal out there. Miss Rachel (Mr. Hubbard's sister) was a secretary in the office. During the War, Mary Frances ran the barn.

In the early twenties when they first started growing flue-cured tobacco around here my daddy worked for Mr. Dick Shaw and I was about five or six years old. They planted about sixty or seventy-five acres and they built about a dozen of these little tobacco barns, the little log barns, square with flues. I was about five or six years old and I can remember driving a barge hauling into the barns from the fields. They had built two great big tobacco packing houses down by the old JFNA Depot down at the bottom of South Adams and they auctioned the tobacco off. On the 4th of July they had a great big dinner down there for everybody. All farmers brought in corn and potatoes and barbecue. It never did pan out too well. They sent these what you call tobacco demonstrators down from the Carolinas and Virginia to help us grow it ... show us how to grow it down here. One of them was name Mr. Arnold. He lived with us out on Osceola (Mr. Dick Shaw's farm down on Little River) and he stayed us with all that summer to show the farmers how to grow flue-cured tobacco. Then another year or two went by and my dad went down to South Florida and stayed a couple of years and then came back and started growing tobacco with Mr. James Love. What happened with flue-curing tobacco I don't really know, but it played out.

Twelve
Rev. Louis Mims
Backporch at Sawdust
October 1, 1992

I was born on a Sunday, May 10, 1908. My daddy's name was Alan Mims and my granddaddy was Frank. I would have been 10 years old in May and Mama died in January. She was the mother of nine children and all of them was babies but one; she had one miscarriage.

I only went to the seventh grade. My first wife died in 1969. I'd been single for over 20 years, then I got married again, but I'd have to go to heaven to get another one like the first one I had.

Mr. Pittman built the Antioch Baptist Church in Wetumpka. Black and white used to all go to church in one church. They used to have a time. Wetumpka had one store and two houses and one of the houses had the post office in it and the other run the little store. They had to haul the mail once a week. She had a little go-cart thing with two wheels on it and the horse had to pull the mail from here to town. My grandmother used to be a mid-wife for black and white in Wetumpka. Her name was Phyllis Bradwell.

She was Phyllis Cannon by birth but she married Robert Bradwell. I started preaching at Ebenezer Church. I pastored for 44 years.

Mr. Joe Pittman, he was a professor and he walked to town. When he got a car he'd let anybody drive that could drive, but when he drove it he'd come out to see how the road was. If it was muddy, he wouldn't bring the car out. If it was ok he'd go back and get the car.

I was born right over on Lake Talquin. My daddy was Grandpa's oldest son. And my mother was a Tennell. My grandmother was from Roanoke, VA. She was half-Indian. They came with the Mims crowd (the white Mims). Old Man Will Stoutamire was the one that freed our family, and then they farmed. They farmed corn and potatoes and peas and beans. Wasn't much else but okra and and tomatoes and growing hogs.

When they first came, they farmed turpentine – at that time it came from the tree – you caught the gum in a bucket and you carried it to the barrel and to the still.

I never did know why the white Mims came. See this county all around here. You got two schools named Mims now, one of them over there in Spring Creek. And I saw in the paper they was born in Orangeburg, SC. My daughter's boy, Eddie, plays football at FAM and she went to Carolina to see him play a game. My daughter is Arrie Battle and she works in the Welfare Office, now HRS. That's my baby.

There were four children in all, but one of 'em isn't living. My oldest daughter got killed in a car accident. I have two girls and one boy by my first wife. That accident was when I had my first heart attack. She was talking to me that morning and that evening she was dead. When I drove up to her car (he had a spot where I could park – all the rest of it was blocked) and I … walk up and he was toting her. And I just had a sick heart attack.

They put a pacemaker in there. The first time they cut me, they stopped the arteries. I came out of the hospital and I went to preaching that Monday. And I've preached in three churches (Fountainhead, East Violetta and Stewart Temple) – 44 years. And didn't get $100 a month.

When I went to school, they didn't have but six weeks. You'd go out in the woods, pick up lighter'd knots and tote water from the spring (gets tickled).

No, but it was down there where I was born at – called Wetumpka. I could sit here now and tell you all the books of the Bible. (More laughing – he recites).

Kay: You did pretty good. They taught you like they taught Mama. She can remember everything she learned.

I ran for 11 years to keep from preaching. I didn't want to preach. I got that leg sawn out from under me. And I said, "Dear Lord, if you let me live …" He said, "If you grieving about your leg, it could have been your whole body." Next he said: "You running from me. Now cut out your running." (Laughs.)

Kay: But you didn't lose your leg?

That's a wooden leg there.

Kay: All the way up?

It comes to right there.

Kay: How did it happen?

I was working on the railroad. And I had that railroad to heart. I didn't want to hear nothing else. And I told the boys in November. "Boys, I'm leaving the RR the first day of December. Something bad's gone happen to me." Friday morning, 1st day of December, 1944. That motor car jumped the track and caught me between the wheels. Cut me right up to the stomach. Caught that leg and just ground it up, ground it off. And it just drug me as far as that carport yonder. See the push cart didn't jump, the motor car jumped. I fell between the wheels, and it dove and drug me. I said, "Boys, I'm ruined for life." The blood was shooting out.

Bob Lay: Sure, pumping out. The heart pumping …

So I said, "Come back and see. I'm hurt. I'm ruint for life. They put me on the motor car and brought me back to town and laid me on the ground. A black man lying there bleeding. It was nine in the morning (a white ambulance went right on by) and I didn't see a doctor until …

Kay: It was cold, too, wasn't it?

Yeah, it was so cold. I tell you something. I laid there. It was already ground off. And when they got me to the doctor (Dr. Davis), he just sewed cotton in it to put back over that bone. I wish you could have seen it. I just laid there and suffered through it. At 9:00 when they took me and it was 6:00 when they come to me. And they had to paralyze me through my back at 6:00. I was wide awake. In two days, I could walk on a stump. In eight more, I was walking on a carved leg.

Kay: You were determined.

Did you know I put down the blocks to build your brother's house over there? I hauled concrete for 30 years for Oakland Concrete. I drove the City trash truck for seven years. Had a job of taking down trees with a crew of men for the City. And I left that and went to Oakland Concrete. And after I went there the City tried to get Oakland Concrete to fire me, wanted me back out there 'cause I could do the work. Mr. Johnny (Bostick) told me: "Long as he do my work I'm satisfied." And everyday they would call me to do the difficult things. And I say to him: "Mr. Johnny, why you all causing me to do all these things"?

He said, "Look here, we not trying to give you a hard time. We knew you'd do the work for us. So if I had a whole crew like you, one-legged or two-legged, I'd be satisfied."
And I'd still be there`... that little boy that's running it now, he was just a little ole thing. I got to call him Mr. Alan. (Laughs.) Well, I tell you what he told me, "He said, Louis, I sure hate to see you go. You've been our backbone."

You know, remember, I stayed there 30 years, plus then went back out there and stayed five more years. But I didn't do nothing except stay on the yard. "I don't want you driving no trucks," he said. "Just work here in the yard." I stayed there five more years. And if I didn't have heart trouble, I'd be with 'em right now. I tell you the truth. I want y'all to love us right on, 'cause this skin's deep.

And when we get to heaven, that's gonna be one heaven. Think about it. He said, "One Lord, one faith, one baptism." People fight holiness – I don't care what church you belong to. Holiness is right. If you fall, you know what that word holiness means. The Devil can shout. The Devil can pray. The Devil can preach, but he just can't lead the life. He'll just kick out somewhere.

Kay: I like that. Maybe that'll be the saying that saves our world.

We have to do it that way, 'cause, Baby, the time is winding up. He said before the end of time, peace would be taken from the land. We would search for peace and couldn't find it. Nobody satisfied now.

Bob Lay: That's a good sermon!

About tobacco, I did work in tobacco. Down at a place called the "Captain Taylor Place," down below the Grove. He had a big farm down there and us people down at Bradwell would go across through the swamp and work tobacco over there with Captain Taylor.
It was joining "Magnolia Grove." All side the road down there was magnolia trees. There were farm houses on back behind it. And going down to Magnolia Grove, there's a big church on the left called Mt. Olive Methodist Church. When you passed Mt. Olive Church, you come to Mr. Tom Winn's place there where Mrs. Carr's got that place now.

Mr. Winn was growing tobacco on that side and Magnolia Grove was growing it on that side and Captain Taylor was growing back down the road there. That was the crop then – tobacco.

I toted tobacco and had to tote a blow-gun to blow tobacco. Captain Taylor was running alongside us. "Whoopee, whoopee"! His boys was blowing just like we were. "Whoopee, just catch your breath now"! See, he had a son. He'd say to the others, "All right, I'm gonna give you a little water now. Now, just a little bit on the roof of the mouth." Because he said, if you drank too much water back then you'd cramp when you be hot. He had a son there – Hugh Taylor. And one named Jack and one named Frank. Another one, but I forgot his name.

Kay: So you blew tobacco with Mr. Hugh Taylor – the one that was the Judge?.

His father was Frank Taylor – Old Man Taylor. My grandmother was a midwife with all that crew. She did all the midwifing back then. My mama's mama.

Kay: What grandparent was it that came from Orangeburg, SC?

Franklin Benjamin Mims. His daddy and them come from Orangeburg. My great-granddaddy died before I was born. But see, my grandaddy Frank spanked me a many a day (Laughs.) He never would work cotton. The chilluns had to get out and work in tobacco. And Grandma Fannie would be plowing them little wild oxen. He'd have an oxen with a loop 'round the ox's head and he'd lead 'em and Grandma would come out and plow them two plow lines. She'd run the cart and he'd pick the crop like that. He'd get through with the crop and he'd put that cow to death. Next year, he'd have another one that was trained to pull that plow. And the first horse he bought, my daddy bought him for a hand of nails. He was used and my daddy bought him from a man named Mims. And I remember the old horse was named Pigeon!

Kay: Did your grandfather tell you anything about the early days?

No, he just talked about different things. But he was unconcerned. I'd say he was just unconcerned.

Kay: Well, did they hate the Mims?

Uhn uh. I wouldn't a come here to see your Mama now. (Both of us laughing.)

Kay: Well, she doesn't know very much about the Mims!

Note: Rev. Mims' grandson Eddie Battle (the FAMU fotball player he mentioned) went on to complete his education at FAMU, earning his BS and MS. His mother Arrie informs that he now lives in Orlando, FL.

Thirteen
Elise (Scrap) Jackson Williams
Backporch at Sawdust
October, 1992

I was born in Whigham, Georgia in 1930. I've worked on several tobacco farms including the Forrest Davis'.

Up in Whigham, my daddy worked on a turpentine still. I believe the first time we moved down here to Gadsden County I was five years old and we moved over there to Mt. Pleasant on Lee Parramore's place. He was growing tobacco. We stayed down there several years until about 1939, when we moved back to Whigham. We lived there until 1941 and then we moved down on Mr. Joe Suber's place in Greensboro. We stayed there six months then we moved on Rock Comfort up the hill. Along then, it was called the Old Merger Place. I was 11 years old when we moved there. And I was living there on Rock Comfort until my husband Willie D. and I moved into a home your daddy built for us over here and we worked for your brother Johnny (Forrest, Jr.)

But even while I was a young girl about 15 (1945), staying on Rock Comfort, every chance we could get we came down here on the Davis farm. All of us girls (your sisters Saradee and Betty and you were a little fat baby) – all of us would work in the barn. Your brothers Johnny and Hal worked in the field and the barn. We walked from Rock Comfort to down here. Along then girls just wore dresses. We would pin our dresses and go to the top of the barn and take down tobacco, and, before it was hung up there, we would string the tobacco. We would have so much fun.

One year, your father had a tobacco crop over in Greensboro, and he had a little Jeep truck. Saradee, your oldest sister, didn't have a license. But if they left the Jeep and we were "caught up" stringing that tobacco, she would take us all for a ride! We would go over to Greensboro. There were some other white girls that worked in the barn – Iris Johnson, Hazel Burns and her little sister June. We would have quite a time! One day, she ran in the ditches. But she got us out and we went home and back to the barn (where Saradee's mama thought we were!).

At that time, my oldest sister Stella Mae and all of us were able to work both farms. There were a lot of people up on Rock Comfort and that meant we would run out of work. So in our spare time we could work down here. The Merge had a lot of farms. They had one at Rock Comfort, they had the Bruce Farm (near present Talquin Electric Headquarters), they had Sandy Lee (across from the present State Farmer's Market , also on Hwy. 90.) And then, on the old Bainbridge Road, they had El Consuelo and the Shaw Farm – and just lots of farms all over. As time moved on then the Merge sold out to the "Dutchman." Before that, they had #8, #9, #10 and #11 Packing House here in Quincy. But the "Dutchman" moved all the packing houses to Amsterdam, GA. That's when we moved down here on y'all's farm.

I worked it from all angles. We would poison. First I remember, we would poison it with our fingers. Then later on they would get a cup or a can, tomato cans and things and nail it to a stick and you'd walk around and shake it – you'd try to keep from putting too much. And the boss man, he was a colored man, Mr. Gabe Martin, he always would tell us … he said, "Well y'all tired of bending y'all's back – which y'all ain't got no back. Y'all ain't got nothing but just a little gristle"!

He said, "One of these here days, the airplane coming and gonna spray the poison on the tobacco. Y'all won't have to poison."

We said, "How in the world the airplane gone poison the tobacco"?!

We were young and we thought that airplane can't put that poison in the bud! (Scrap laughs.)

So then he said, "Yeah but one day that's what you gonna have. And we gonna have tobacco loopers and tobacco stringers." Back then we strung it all by hand, done everything by hand. But time moved on. When machines first came down here, they looped that tobacco on the sticks and that didn't work so well. Don't you know it would fall when it gets dry. It'd fall on the ground.

Kay: You're talking about the electric stringing machines?

It was a looper first. It just put the string around the tobacco. And then later as time moved on, they learned how to make those machines with the needle in them.

Kay: Well, now did you ever do the other kind of looping (and wrapping) out in the field?

Yeah, I did all of that. You put a ball of thread on the end of the bench and you would pull it. A man would be on top and a woman on the bottom and she'd loop it (down low, to the little plant) and hand it up there to him . (He'd be standing on the tying bench, and he'd tie it to the "row-wire.")

Kay: Now, did I remember this correctly. Did you say Mama helped do that one time?

One day ... Mrs. Davis, you remember that day when you and me and Mr. Johnny was all alone when that shade was right there and we didn't have nobody to wrap but us – you remember that? (Mama laughs.) You remember that day you came out there and helped till eleven o'clock and then you had to come fix dinner?

Mama: Yeah, I remember that. And somebody'd put a bench – and another bench. And you'd walk from one bench to the other.

Kay: Mama, you didn't do that part. *That* was sewing cheesecloth. Scrap, did you ever sew cheesecloth?

Yes, Lawd! I sewed cheesecloth. Uhmmm hmmm. It'd take about a week to sew it. And it'd be according to how many you would have. Sometimes you would have nine benches.

Kay: Did they put up the top first?

Uhm hmm. But then later I think they went to putting up the walls and then the top.

Mama: One time bad weather was coming up and me and you ran over there ---

Sure did! And let the shade down. It was lightning and you came by. I was sitting on the porch of that house – you know where that house is. I was sitting on the porch and she said, "Well, Scrap, what you doing"? And I said, "Nothing."

(We all laugh, because what else would she be doing with a thunderstorm coming!)

And she said, "Will you go with me over there and see to the shades? Johnny's over in Tallahassee and he called back and told me his shades were up."

And me and her went on over there, and it was a good little piece to go, and we went over there (and pulled the side cloth down) so the wind wouldn't blow it. It was a little puffed up from the flood, lifted up from the water, wasn't it?

Mama: Yeah.

Kay: Why were the sides of the shade up?

They'd lift it up to go in and prime it. And it was lifted up all the way across the end, so they could go in to work.

Kay: So y'all were going over there to check to make sure it was down?

Uhm hmm. See, Mr. Johnny, he wasn't here. He was over there in Tallahassee. And he called back and wanted his Mama …

Kay: His right-hand man! (Scrap laughs.) You reckon he would've ever been able to have grown a crop if it hadn't been for her being here.

Mama: I remember me and Mr. Roy – Johnny'd leave me kindly in charge of the barn and Mr. Roy Strickland would come along and he'd tell me what to do. So I'd try to see that it got done, 'cause Johnny wouldn't be here.

Scrap: Mmh hmm!

Kay: So y'all lived in the house that's going across the creek?

Mmh hmm. When we first moved down here, we lived across the creek, way over yonder in that house. Then after Miss Hester's son Wendell moved to Miami (about 1962), we moved on this side.

Kay: Were you and Willie D. married by then?

Mmh hmm. We moved there after the Dutchman (company that bought AST Co.) sold that place to Mr. Dewey Johnson. Then my husband was working with Mr. Johnny. They wanted him to work with them, but he wanted to work with Johnny, and so he had to move. And your daddy – he had told us he was gonna build us a house and so he built this house where we live now.

Kay: And at that time how many children did you have?

Well, when I stayed over here on y'all's place, I had several. I've had two since I lived up there.

Kay: Did they help in tobacco?

Yes, five of them worked in it: My girls Lillie Belle, Willie Belle and Mary Jo. And my boys Allen and Willie D., Jr. My girl Dorothy, too, but she mostly stayed home and kept the babies and things. But my baby girl Loretha, she hadn't ever seen tobacco. She was born in 1973.

Kay: Scrap, I wondered how you could work all day in the daytime, then go home and fix up supper for 'em all. And then get ready for the next day, all the clothes!

Mmh hmm. One thing I had good help – 'cause Willie D. has helped me with 'em. I'd start washing on Monday and that'd be through Wednesday. And I'd let the children iron and sweep the yards and everything. And be back to work. I remember one time we were working (chuckles) and Johnny had that barn right down there that blowed down. One night it came up a bad rain, a storm. Do you remember how Johnny'd have the 'bacco bulked?

Mama: Yeah.

You know, when it would be "in case" and we'd take it down and it'd be in the bulk. On that night, I mean you talking about some bad weather! Oh, some bad weather had come up and I mean that barn – water was in that barn that big and I mean all the tobacco was bulked down there on the ground.

Mama: And we had to hang it back up.

Scrap: Mr. Johnny came down there – he had flashlights and things. He came down there and woke us up. He said, "There's water running in the barn and wetting all my tobacco."

We jumped up out of the bed – me and all my children, Willie D. and then Kate (Hester's daughter) was living down here and they came down and helped. Got all that tobacco up off that ground and hung it back up on them tiers.

Mama: And fired it.

Scrap: Mmh hmm.

Mama: You remember when … I remember toting slats to build a slat shade over at Greensboro. I toted slats in my arms to cover with slats.

Scrap: I remember that. But you know what. The first year I started working. That's what it was – they were weaving them slats in there, over the top of them shades.

Kay: Did they put some cloth under the slats? Or was it just slats?

Scraps: They'd have just the little slats. (To Mama): Would they have cloth with them old slats?

Mama: I just can't remember. I remember toting the things and I had a miscarriage. I ought not to have been out toting those things. (Scrap remembered working at Granddaddy Davis' shade at Greensboro – the farm Mama is talking about. Papa and he had started their first crop there in 1928 and some must have been grown there until about 1943, when Granddaddy died.)

Scrap: About 1942 or '43, your daddy had this place up here what they called the "Red Quarters." Right up here in front of the Bible Store. All of that back over there he had. And a man named Mr. Flournoy, he worked, you know as the boss over it.

Kay: Mr. Flournoy? I remember him.

Scrap: Mmh hmm. And we worked up there in that shade. We would "drop" – the men would peg it. We put the plants in a basket, see it'd be full, and we would drop them one by one, about a foot apart. Then the men would get down there and peg it. They had a stick and they would push it down in the ground. There'd be three of us in a row, 'cause one of us would be dropping, one pegging it and one watering it.

Mama: They didn't have irrigation then. They had to tote the bucket.

Scrap: And then when they first irrigated, there weren't any sprinklers over the top. They would tote them pipes and lay 'em down those rows. And they'd run the water down them rows. But later, as time moved on they had the sprinklers and put 'em overhead. You wouldn't have to worry about toting them pipes from row to row.

Mama: I remember taking off my shoes and wading up and down that row. (Scrap laughs.)

Kay: I'd roll up my blue jean legs and run barefooted, too – oh, it felt so good!

Scrap: Pushing down them loops – that's what I hated. That's when you looped that 'bacco. See, it was supposed to go right around the bottom, the bottom leaf. You would put it in a loop, and the ladies be on the ground (and the men tying it up to the wire).

Mama: On the transplanting machine, you know, it would tickle me when Willie D. and different ones of 'em were sitting on the back of it, feeding the plants through it and I'd just stand out there and laugh!

Kay: It was cute – and so much simpler than hand-planting. It could do two rows at a time, with four people riding behind and all they had to do was stick a plant through a wheel. The machine made the furrow and covered it and everything.

Scrap laughing: I and Willie D. – we loved to work in that tobacco!

Kay: Well, you never did tell me how you managed to feed 'em all. On the days you worked … did you bring all y'all's lunch?

Scrap: No, we'd go home. Mr. Davis would carry us home. Most of the time, because we didn't have freezers and things like we have now, we'd cook up something or 'other. Open canned goods and I'd feed 'em. And then at night when I'd go home I'd have more time. You see I'd be doing something else while Willie D. – he was always good to help me.

In the summertime, we worked in the fields and in the winter we'd go to the packing house. We would carry our lunch then, but in the summer we would just run in and fix up something or other – fry us some fish or some chicken, somethin' or 'nother like that.

Mama: Well, you know Willie D. has really been good to me. One time I fell out there by the road and I couldn't get up, and he came along and he led me to the house and got me to the bed. Twice he's found me, that I couldn't get to the house.

Kay: He's a mighty nice fellow. How'd you meet him?

Scrap: We were working in the tobacco field. He moved … we were already living on Rock Comfort and so he moved up there when I was about 17 years old. Mr. Harry Bassett had a farm there, and he had houses. Uhm hm. So (Willie D.) moved there to Mr. Bassett's on Rock Comfort. And me and him courted two years, before I married him. I married him in 1949.

Kay: And you've got nine children?

Scrap: Mhm hm.

Kay: Scrap's like you and me, Mama. She believes in having 'em and loving 'em and making the most of 'em. Not like the new generation – if they don't want 'em, they don't have to have 'em.

Scrap: That's right. 'Long in then, people kept babies. But now …

Mama: I always believed if the Good Lord gave 'em to me, I could find a way to take care of 'em. And I'd do the best I could with 'em (laughing).

Scrap Mhm hm. He'd make a way for 'em 'cause He had made the way before ever they came into the world. Now, my Mama – she was the mother of 19 head. She didn't raise but 12.

Mama: Well, that was pretty good, out of 19.

Scrap: Mhm hm. And the oldest one she had to die, in raising them, was nine months old. Then there would be scarcely little babies two and three weeks old.

Kay: What, out of all your experiences in tobacco, was the best and what was the worst? The best first!

Scrap: Well (gets tickled) ….

Kay: If there was one!

Scrap: Well, I liked to string. Of course, I liked it all, though. Except looping. I just didn't like that. Pushing out them loops. It was a tedious thing. Ooh, that was backbreaking. I believe sometimes that's what ails my back now – the way I'd have to push down them loops. You see, you had nothing to rest on. You had to use both hands. You wouldn't have to push down but once cause you see when you finally looped it, you could go behind 'em and push down them loops.

Kay: The wrapping, though, was not so bad

Scrap: No, the wrapping was easy. Every other day, you would wrap that tobacco 'cause it'd be growed up and if a wind would come it would blow it over. That's why we wrapped it more than we did anything. And 'course, once you started out you sometimes had to re-set it. Maybe sometimes twice, you know, things had died. Sometimes a lot of it would die if you set it behind a rain. You know we didn't have no irrigation when we first started. You know it would be so dry it would die. Now I tell you another thing I hated. Was that tobacco, after it got tall, dripping over your head when it rained. Lord, you'd have to go out there and all that water pouring down on you. I have left out that field many times.

Kay: It'd be good to get to the barn though when they'd have the heaters going – wouldn't it feel good?!

Scrap: Yes, Lord!

Kay: Scrap, do you remember the times the barn caught on fire? Once, the shade did.

Scrap: Mmh hm. We were stringing and looked down there and the shade (laughing) … the shade was on fire. That was right out there. We were stringing in that barn right there. The shade was back down there where them peaches are. Ann was bossing then. Some of 'em run ahead and cut that burning part off. Mhm hm.

Kay: Did you ever work down at the Rudd Place? Johnny used to rent down there. Well, that shade caught on fire once, too. I think it got burned pretty bad.

Scrap: Yeah, I remember that I come down there and helped string some of that burnt 'bacco. I remember that. But that's just been so long. That's been a long time ago.

Mama: Well, one time Johnny was in Future Farmers. These two men stayed all day, ate dinner with me. We'd have to change, put on different clothes. Future Farmer clothes and dress-up clothes for Johnny and Hal. So I had to keep the clothes going. These men stayed and stayed several days. Johnny couldn't get his work done. So finally, we thought they'd left. So he got out there with his tractor at 11:00 at night. They came back and went down there and took his picture. That's the picture that went in the national magazine. He was so embarrassed he didn't know what to do. (Laughs).

And the shade was across the road, the road over there (65). It had a hole in it, 'cause it was October. He sure was embarrassed. It was in all the papers, too, you know.

Kay: He was such a perfectionist. If it showed a hole in his shade, it really would be a calamity to him.

Scrap: Mhm hm.

Fourteen
Vivian Allen
Visit to the Barn (with friend Betty Yuhas)
November 9, 1992

(Talking about an era of the Quincy tobacco that preceded our shade tobacco era. Mrs. Allen's grandparents, J.H. and Addie Bushnell, lived on the La Camellia Plantation for about 14 years. They came from Pennsylvania at a time – the early 1880s -- when the Owl Cigar Company was reviving the crop of tobacco in our area, after the War Between the States.)

My grandparents and their three children were enjoying life here until 1893. It was all cut short by the Financial Panic of '93. It was really a major depression. High tariffs just really destroyed our trade at that time. Then also, in the local history book (written by Miles Womack), when I looked that up about four years ago, it spoke of the discovery of Fuller's earth on the Owl Cigar property and that is what they are still mining, just where my mother was born. On that property.

Showing a watch of her grandfather's:

The inscription reads: "To J.H. Bushnell compliments of Owl Cigar Company." That was given to him apparently when … you know they always used to give someone a gold watch when they left. He left because of all this business that came on in 1893. Now they may actually have left in 1894.

His initials were J.H.B. – James Hyde Bushnell. He was born in Pennsylvania. Both of my grandparents were born there. My mother's older sister is the one that told me all the stories. My grandmother's name was Addie Diana Dart Bushnell. It was their youngest child who was my mother. The other two children were born in Pennsylvania. Mother was born here on New Year's Day and they didn't have a name for her and someone came in and said the yellow jessamine is blooming early this year. So she was named for the flower. She was "Jessamine Adele Bushnell." She always had an interesting name to me. Since I have come here to live in Tallahassee, I have planted a yellow jessamine on a fence and it runs riot, but is pretty.

I actually am a native of Oregon and I am living here now because my youngest son is here and has my only grandchildren. After my husband died four years ago I came here to be near my grandchildren. So this is actually closing a circle, much to our surprise, because the family was entirely Northern, from Pennsylvania, with some in New York. My grandfather, my mother's father, came here in approximately 1881, I would say as an employee of the Owl Cigar Company, to manage their plantation out north of Quincy, very close to the Georgia border. It was the plantation known as "La Camellia."

Today, as I said, it is owned by the Floridin Company and is being mined for Fuller's earth. My mother was a "little trailer" in the family. She was twelve years behind her sister, and I grew up with her sister (because of a break in the family). The sister's name was Isabelle Bushnell Smith.. "Aunt Tee," as I called her, was seventeen when they left their plantation in Quincy. I heard all through my childhood in Portland, OR, clear across the continent – I heard all these tales of Gadsden, Quincy and plantation life.

Now I can't remember but part of it. The house burned while they were here. They had the typical old plantation set-up with the kitchen outside in a separate building with the shacks for, as my aunt always spoke of them, the "darkies." She never said the "N" word. They were the darkies and she was very, very fond of them. They had many servants around the house and she had a very warm, close feeling with Uncle this and Aunt that. I've forgotten their names. I understand the plantation had several hundred employees. It was quite an operation at that time. George Storm, whose exact office with Owl Cigar I do not know, was one of the top executives. He was apparently responsible for overseeing this business down here. He came, I would judge, maybe every year, two or three times every year. And when he did he stayed with the family because his name was very, very familiar to me. My aunt was 17 when they left and by that time she had been a bridesmaid for at least three families in this area. I'm sure one of them was the Nicholsons. I seem to remember that name. Munroe, I think, was another one. She was still in touch when I was in my teens with a family by the name of Love here, and they came and visited us in Portland, OR. I remember them very well.

I have a very vivid memory of the Loves because I must have been 12 to 14, somewhere in there when Mr. Love and his wife, and his sister Miss Hattie Love came. And my aunt and her husband went down to the railroad station to meet them. When they got out of the car, I went out of the house to help bring things in. Of course I was young and overeager and not very experienced. Miss Hattie was a fairly tall woman and as she got out she had a little box in her hand and I reached for that box to help her. It had a handle on it. I would say it was maybe 10 inches square, more or less, and black. She yelped. That was her battery for her hearing aid and it was connected by a wire and I almost yanked the hearing aid out. I had never seen a hearing aid in my life. She had to carry that box with her everywhere she went. One of the primitive hearing aids. That's why I remember Miss Hattie. I don't believe they stayed in the house. I believe they stayed in a hotel, but they were there for dinner. I remember my aunt – we did not have permanent help, but we had a good-sized house and had a cleaning woman – but my aunt did hire a black cook to come in and prepare the dinner and serve it. That was done in honor of the Loves from Quincy.

I'm speaking now of my aunt and her brother, my uncle, not her husband. They did use a horse to go to school in Quincy. I remember her speaking of the two of them going on horseback to some country school near the plantation. That would have been in the early 1880s. The two of them rode on one horse to go to school at least for a time. She ended by being sent to Virginia to finishing school at Staunton, VA. I don't remember the name of the school there, either. Mother, of course, was only four or five when they left, so she did not attend school around here at all.

She was born on the plantation. I do not know if there was a doctor in attendance, but when Social Security came in the 30s she wrote for proof of her birth and there was no public record of her at all. Only the fact that my aunt was so much older and could give an affidavit, even proved my mother was born, much less where she was born. I am sure that was more or less typical of rural areas at that time.

Some of the things that I remember my aunt mentioning, not about the tobacco specifically, but she mentioned picnicking and boating on the Ochlockonee. That was not a strange name to me at all when I came here.

There was apparently quite a lot of social activity then even though getting around in this red clay must have been a problem at times. Aunt Tee had very happy memories of her years here. She would have been maybe four or five when she came, so she was here 11 or 12 years, through her real developing time. She never worked a day in her life. She did tell me about the tobacco barn, but I couldn't really picture how the tobacco was hung up in it. Now I can. And about the smell. She also referred to Tallahassee. It was quite an event to go over there, the big city, from here.

When my grandparents left, they went from here to Missouri and eventually to Oregon. My parents met in Oregon and that is why I was born there. (As I said earlier, why they left was a dual combination: the Financial Panic of 1893 caused by the tariffs – my aunt always mentioned "the tariffs" -- plus the fact the Owl Cigar Company discovered Fuller's earth on the grounds of the plantation.) That particular property is still valuable as a source of Fuller's earth which is used, as I understand, in the petroleum industry, and also supplies a lucrative kitty litter industry!

My grandparents lived in Susquehanna County, PA., I think, shortly before they came here. They were married there Sept. 16, 1874. Grandfather J.H. Bushnell's paternal grandfather had come from Lebanon, CT. as a pioneer of that northeastern county of Pennsylvania. He would have had some expertise in tobacco, because he came from the Connecticut River Valley.

I don't know if there is any connection with Bushnell Co., FL. That probably could be checked out because the family was a long-time American family. His first American ancestor was a signer in Connecticut of the Guilford Covenant, which was comparable to the Mayflower Compact back in the early 1600s. So the family has been in this country a long time and maybe that's a collateral line there. I really don't know.

It must have been an experience for a family from the Northeast within a generation of the Civil War to come into the Deep South when my grandfather had had a brother in Libby Prison in Richmond, and my grandmother had had two brothers in Andersonville and lost one of them there. I have been there and I saw his marker. But this was a generation of that very divisive War. That must have been quite an experience, I would think. And yet they had happy memories of the time. Apparently, there was no antagonism.

As I said, their house burned. My aunt probably told me all she knew. She was a child. The only thing that she saved was a wax doll and she told me of standing outside holding her wax doll and watching the house burn. I am assuming they rebuilt the house because they continued living there. That was my aunt. It would have been before my mother was born, I imagine.

In their type of tobacco (which was before shade tobacco), they used a lot of black laborers. They were all black. She was very definite about that. She never referred to any white laborers. There might have been a very few. She referred to the colored people a great deal. She never referred to any real problems. There might have been individual problems, individual people. She did refer to what she called lax morals, but that's something I wouldn't want to repeat, not want to spread. As I said they had several people working in the house and in the kitchen. Doing the cleaning, the laundry, taking care of the children, the cooking and not just one or two. There were several. So it was probably a good-sized house, I imagine. I picture it as being much like the Nicholson Farm. The house is probably no longer there. It may have been bulldozed for the mining. I really don't know.

Before they put a gate across that road, I did drive on to the property a time or two and I never saw a structure. If there was a house there they must have knocked it down.

Now, the name "La Camellia" was because the drive going up to the house was lined with camellias on both sides. That I do remember hearing.

My grandparents were burned out twice in their married life and the only thing that survived to come to anyone, and I had it at one time and now I could kick myself for having let it go, was a small set (part of a set) of either four or six blue-and-white Spode dessert plates and cups and saucers.

I have three sons – two in California and the youngest one here. His name is Tod Kent Allen. He is a consultant and works with the Dept. of Environmental Regulation. He has his own business. His wife and her family came up here from the Canal Zone. He will be here permanently. This son has the only descendants in the family – two daughters. To think, we have closed a circle that began with my "La Camellia" grandparents!

My Aunt Tee lived to be 82. She died in Oregon in October 1959. My mother died at age 67 in California, in 1957. Their brother, Uncle Howard, the one between them, never married. He lived out his life in Los Angeles. He had a marvelous baritone voice – top operatic quality. As a result of things falling apart here in the 1880s, he was not able to train, so he never used it. I heard him when he was about 70. I thought, "Oh, my word. What a tragedy that voice was not heard." Since he never married, there is no Bushnell line.

I called my aunt "Tee." That was my baby attempt at "Auntie." She liked it and we kept it as "Tee." I am named for her – Vivian Isabelle. (She was Isabelle Adelaide.) She never had any children, though she did marry. She married someone from Indianapolis. She had a lovely personality – was a very bubbly, outgoing person. Small, just 5 feet tall. She had beaus around here and I used to know the names, but I don't remember them.

After her husband died in 1948 she made a train trip here to see who might be left and she didn't find anybody. We'd had two World Wars in the meantime and there were lots of changes. It was interesting, but she couldn't even locate the plantation.

She lived with us the last few years. She was the "grandmother" in the house. She had a summer cottage at the beach in Oregon and that's where she was when she died.

The main office for the Owl Cigar company was in New York. Mr. Storm is the only name I remember. He was the one who came here. He was my grandfather's boss (superior). My grandfather was in charge of the plantation, but there is that red brick building on

Madison Street that says Owl Commercial Company. That was probably warehousing, marketing. That was Owl Commercial Co. rather than Owl Cigar Co. My aunt always spoke of Owl Cigar and that's what's on the watch. So there had to be another operation. I imagine George Storm was in charge of that, but he stayed only with the family when he was here.

Fifteen
Maidee Barnett
Visit at "The Arbors"
December 28, 1993

I was Maidee Meeks. I was born in Lowndes County near Dublin, Georgia in 1905. It was in the Valdosta area they called central Georgia. Later, I came to Florida and now I count Florida as home.

My Bachelor of Arts degree was from Wesleyan College, in 1927. And then summer schools were at Duke and Tallahassee (Florida State College for Women). I received a Master of Arts degree from Peabody University in 1934.

I met my husband, Edgar Barnett, Sr., in 1930. He went to college at Auburn and majored in agriculture and surveying. He was from Dothan, Alabama. I lived across the street with my aunt (Mrs. Tom Nixon – related to Gene and Mary Neal Nixon), and he boarded across the street with the Keys. The Keys were from Quincy and the street is named for them. Edgar, Sr. was involved in tobacco at that time. He was manager of the Quincy Creek Tobacco Company. The name was changed from Douglas, Carmichael and Malone, when the Alabama outfit (from the Dothan area) purchased the property. Malone and Barnett were related. They actually grew the tobacco.

We were married in Georgia in 1936. Edgar, Jr. was born two years later. He was eight years old when his father died at age 46. We lived at Douglas City.

We tried to grow a special kind of tobacco without bugs. We also began experimenting with a little wheat and oats. In addition, we grew corn to feed hogs and cows for sale. We had over two hundred workers on the farm.

The farm was sold to Henry Weinberg in 1946 after my husband died. I started back teaching in 1950. I taught English Literature, 9th and 10th grades, in Quincy.

Note: In the early 1930s, Maidee Meeks first taught history at Gadsden High in Quincy, according to a former pupil, "Miss Julia" (Munroe) Woodward.

Pearl Pride stringing tobacco on Swiss-made stringing machine, mentioned by M.D. Peavy. (Davis Farm, Sawdust)

Rev. Louis Mims and Olean Davis swap tales ("backporch at Sawdust")

Sixteen
Building a Shade
(for Display Crop of Shade Tobacco)
Forrest (Johnny) Davis, Jr. and Nathaniel McNealy
Spring, 1997

Kay: How many posts you reckon you've ever put up in your life, Johnny?

Johnny: I've dug a many of them holes and put a many one of 'em up. Whoa, wait a minute. Let me move that.

Nathaniel: Okay.

(Sounds of post-hole digging – as the two men put up the first shade post.)

Johnny: I always tried to build a neat shade where most of 'em just stuck em in. Didn't measure or anything.

Nathaniel chuckles: That's for darn sure!

More sounds of dirt plopping.

Kay: Does Nathaniel know what the "dead man" is?

Johnny: Yeah.

Kay: Nathaniel, do you?

Nathaniel: It's the lug. (Referring to the short log that's used to anchor each guywire to the outside posts of a shade.)

Kay: And that's how you measure how high it's supposed to be? (Referring to a stick with a red mark. It's used to make each post the same height.)

Johnny: Most of 'em just stick 'em down there like that.

Kay: And leave it to chance?

They don't care what it looked like. (More chuckles from Nathaniel.)

Kay: About how high is it? Eight feet?

Johnny to Nathaniel: See if it's bumped down enough.

Johnny: It's about eight feet and three or four inches. You got to have some room to tie the wire.

Kay: And how deep is the hole? About three feet?

Nathaniel: Yep, three feet. About three feet.

Kay: Nathaniel, the tobacco we're planting here was grown in a hothouse.

Nathaniel (laughing): That'll be fine.

Kay: No, really. That's how they grew that. It's in plugs.

Nathaniel: How you gonna cure it out?

Kay: We don't care about curing it out. We just want to grow it! Or at least, we'll wait till we get there, won't we, Johnny?

Nathaniel: There you go! (Skill saw noises drown Johnny's next instructions.)

Kay: What kind of fertilizer do you put on it?

Johnny: Well, if we'd done like we belong to, we'd have put some stable fertilizer out here and then put "tobacco special" …

Nathaniel: Cottonseed meal, right?

Johnny: That's an organic …

Nathaniel: Right.

Kay: And then you come on with the nitrogen and potash, is that right?

Johnny: Well, if it hadn't got enough fertilizer under it.

Kay: Is there something about this dirt, that it can grow here and maybe not other places? I've heard that it's maybe because there's not any lime in it.

Johnny: No. You have to put lime to get the PH up. It can grow up there in Georgia. It can grow anywhere.

Kay: But they couldn't ever grow it in Tallahassee!

Nathaniel laughs.

Johnny: Maybe they didn't try it.

Kay: They sure did. Benjamin Chaires tried it.

Johnny: Bannerman over there raised it. He raised some of the best tobacco. Over there before you get to the Meridian Road.

Kay: Mr. Shanks used to tell us this was the only place in the world it would naturally do well. He said it had to do with the humidity, something about the humidity.

Johnny: No, they grow better tobacco in Connecticut, because of the cooler nights. We would have grown good tobacco here this year because we've had cool at night – it doesn't grow so fast, has more strength to it.

Kay: Nathaniel, am I in your way? I think I'm hindering you from your work!

Nathaniel: No. That's too deep, ain't it? (Digging sounds.)

Kay: Johnny, what was the biggest shade you ever grew?

Johnny: 20 acres. The one over at the Brinkley Place had 20 acres. This one by the barn had 10 acres. And the one across the road was five acres.

Nathaniel: You had to have an allotment on it, didn't you, Mr. Johnny?

Johnny: No, we didn't have any allotment.

Serious digging sounds ensue.

Kay: So you wanted hard-packed soil?

Answer lost in digging.

Kay: When they had the wooden shades, I guess it took whole ditches and long logs to anchor those down?

Johnny: You had a wire every four feet. You had to anchor that wire, because there was so much weight. (Instructions to Nathaniel.)

Kay: The posts in the middle of the shade didn't have any lugs? Just the outside ones and the corner posts?

Johnny: All them that you tied the wire …

Kay: The guywires. Otherwise, there would be too much stress, wouldn't there? Nathaniel, you said you plowed a mule in one of these shades …? And those mules got off with you one time, didn't they?

Nathaniel: Yes, goodness. Okay, Mr. Johnny!

Johnny: Now, we got to dig the lugs.

Kay: And that's the hard part!

Johnny: They hadn't got to be down so deep, 'cause there isn't gonna be….

Nathaniel: That much pressure on 'em. Where you want 'em out there?

Johnny: Let's see if we can sort of gauge them … bring it out some.

Kay: You put 'em out eight feet from the shade post?

Johnny: Yeah.

Nathaniel: Okay, Mr. Johnny. I need a round-point shovel now.

Johnny: Huh? Take the hole-diggers and do it.

Nathaniel: All right. That'll get the little old bitty thing in? I believe I could do that better with a shovel, Mr. Johnny.

Johnny laughs. Well, you can do it with one. I'll go get a round-pointed shovel.

Kay: Mr. Adams, that you worked in tobacco for … he was just a regular farmer, like Johnny?

Nathaniel: Just a regular farmer, like Mr. Johnny. Yeah.

Kay: Johnny, did you know Mr. Joe Adams?

Johnny: Yeah.

Kay: I just wondered. That's who taught Nathaniel tobacco.

Nathaniel: I need to go down deeper, don't I, Mr. Johnny? (At this point, with the ground so hard, it's looking like a hopeless job to me.)

Kay: Oh my, we all need to get us a shovel. I'll get one, too. (Surprisingly, though, Nathaniel soon has the 4' trenches dug all the way around the perimeter of the shade – he dug seven, Johnny and I one each. Next step is anchoring each lug to each outside post with the end of the guywire.)

Kay: Wrap the wire around twice and then curl it on and … cut it about how long?

Johnny: Well, it's got to be enough to go up yonder. (Indicates that the heavy wire from the lug will then be stretched up to fit snugly around the top of the shade post.)

Kay: You eyeball it?

Johnny: Yes. (Nathaniel chuckles. Sounds of bird singing.)

Kay: I'm gonna one of these days learn how to video-tape, 'cause I bet it'd be a lot easier than trying to take pictures and tape-record people! But right now, it's too high-tech for me.

(All the while I'm yakking, Nathaniel and Johnny are zipping through their task of securing the guywires to the ground.)

Kay: That little gadget that you're twisting with … do you call it a "twister"?

Johnny: Yeah.

Kay: Is that something you got at the store, or did you have to make it?

Johnny: No. This is a mowing machine part. I just find anything that's got a hole in it – that's flat.

Kay to Nathaniel: You ought to see the hoe he made out of a sawblade!

Nathaniel laughs.

Kay: Johnny can make something out of anything!

Johnny: The one I hoed them onions with – I got them so close – I took a mowing machine blade (Nathaniel: Uh huh) and made me a hoe out of it. See it's at an angle like that and got them sticking things on the side of it … Boy it'll cut it. See, a sawblade's made out of better material than … (birds are singing in the background).

Kay: ... just a regular hoe from Lowe's, or somewhere. (A real bird serenade here.)

Kay: Wirecutters, to cut it off. Y'all be careful with the tobacco! I better watch out after my crop! I replanted one today, Johnny.

Johnny: You did?

Kay: Was that bad? Nathaniel, I pulled the bud out of it. I was trying to straighten it up. See, that one's got the bud in it.

Johnny: Well, see once it starts to doing like that you can't move it very much. It gets brittle.

Kay: Okay, well I won't touch anymore. I learned. But I replanted. I hope that's okay. That one.

(No reply.)

Kay: I guess this is the first time you ever put up the wires after the crop was planted. You never had that problem before! Stepping on the tobacco.

Johnny: Papa did it.

Kay, laughing: Papa's done it? I imagine Papa did it anyway he could make it work.

Johnny: He wasn't even through with it when we were gathering tobacco. There was grass in it. It was growed up in grass. I don't believe in doing that. Just like these lugs. I'd be ready when I went to doing ... (Nathaniel tickled: You're darn right!)

Kay: But Papa (laughing) … I'm not gonna let 'em talk about my Papa! (Nathaniel: I heard that!) If I have to fight!

Johnny: Laughing, too. But he sure wasn't no farmer. I can tell you that right now. He was busy sawmilling and he didn't have time to do that. And that first year and I didn't know nothing about tobacco and he was down yonder in the logwoods and he left me up here with this tobacco to gather, and I didn't know how to fire it or nothing.

Nathaniel: Man, you was in trouble then, wasn't you?

Johnny: Firing it with wood …

Kay: How old were you, Johnny?

Johnny: I was about 12 or 14 … or 13 years old.

Nathaniel: Mmhmm. Man!

Kay: Papa'd send 'em down to Liberty County with the log truck to get the firewood. They didn't even have a license!

Johnny: And no brakes on the truck. And it was during the War …

Nathaniel chuckling: You couldn't make it without 'em on there now! You couldn't make it!

Kay: So he left you with … was it this barn?

Johnny: Yeah.

Kay: That was the only barn you had then.

Johnny: Well, he growed that crop up yonder and did good on that crop (referring to a farm at Rock Comfort). See, he had it contracted and that was – some of 'em said that was the prettiest tobacco they'd ever brought in that packing house. That was some good tobacco dirt. He moved a boiler there with a steam engine and pumped that water out there and irrigated it, and I mean that was some fine tobacco. But Lindsay Smith was growing it for him, and he really knew how.

Kay: That's when he was building this barn.

Johnny: Well, he built this one the next year. Because (Eugene) Griffin built that barn. I mean that was a well-built barn.

Nathaniel: Which one was it?

Johnny: Well, I mean it's done been torn down now. (Bird serenade.)

Kay: What did they call that place? Who were the people that first lived there?

Johnny: Wrosdick.

Kay: The road you turn to go to Gretna.

Johnny: All that place, that place where Stanley Burns lives ... all that.

Nathaniel: How long was Mr. Davis in sawmilling, Mr. Johnny?

Johnny: He was in sawmilling all his life. (Nathaniel: Good gracious alife!) That's what they come over here from Walton County …

Kay: You gonna have enough wire?

Nathaniel: There's a big roll out there.

Kay: Well, how did <u>your</u> first crop come out, Johnny?

Johnny: It wasn't too good.

Seventeen
Hal Davis
Backporch at Sawdust
May, 1997

First of all, I remember in Greensboro when we had the crop of tobacco there and Papa had me priming in the sand-leaves. It was a job stooping down to get those sand-leaves! But anyway later on when they were growing it over here, before they had overhead irrigation, my typical day was getting up at 4:00 or 5:00 in the morning, going in the truck to Dellwood in Jackson Co., and bringing back 20-25 people to work in the tobacco crop. And we had to be back here by sun-up.

And so, then, they gave me an easy job during the day. All I had to do was take the tractor and pull the tobacco from the shade to the barn. Then at sundown, I would take the hands back to Dellwood, come home – we'd irrigate the tobacco at night by running water down the rows. So Brother Johnny would stand there and guide the water by ditch down the row. It'd go down about ¾ of the way. I'd lie down and go to sleep and put my feet up and when it'd hit my feet, it'd wake me up so I could tell Johnny to cut the water off, where he could put it down another row.

So it went. I'd go home, maybe sleep in my bed a little, have one of Mama's big breakfasts, get the truck, go back to Dellwood and get the laborers.

That was a typical rough day in the tobacco field, as I remember.

Well, I can't tell you all my experiences, but I fired the barns at night, too. And there was a certain time that we had coal and then we had to go to some kind of short logs from some kind of mill in Hosford. We'd fire by wood. That was before the gas burners. I was off at school when we had the gas burners. I was before the stringing machines. We strung it by needle when I was growing up. But the stringing machines and the overhead irrigation and all that came after I was gone off to college.

Hal's mama: The women, like Hester and Mrs. Hamilton, used to bring their babies and lay 'em on the benches while they strung. Don't you remember?

Yeah, yeah. Not on the benches. They'd have 'em out on the floor (ground) in the tobacco barn, and they'd string.

Kay: Well, did you ever hang it? Did you string it?

Oh yeah, I hung it. I never strung it! You'd have to get up in the barn and have somebody hand it on up. Remember when Saradee saved the barn?

Kay: Saradee and Betty.

Betty, too?

Yeah! And Mama and I carried the buckets of water. And they (Saradee and Betty) carried 'em on up to the men at the top.

I didn't remember ...

Kay: Well, just the women were here. It was Sunday afternoon. You and Johnny were over at the Johnsons'.*

Hal: I remember when the Barn was built. I think it was about the longest in the county. Supposed to have been. (By 1942 standards.)

Kay: Remember Mr. Joe Black asked Papa: "Why do you want to build a big barn like that? When it burns, it's gonna be a big fire"!

Hal laughs.

Mama: And your Granddaddy Davis said, "Forrest never will grow enough tobacco to fill that barn"!

Kay: Didn't you have to help clear the ground for it every afternoon after school?

I don't remember that. But if it had to be done, we did it. (Another big Hal laugh.)

Mama: I remember somebody walking behind me, and throwing a worm on me!

Hal: The worst experience I had was when we were over there at Greensboro (and I don't know if it was Papa's crop or Granddaddy Davis') – and I was priming those sand-leaves! Remember where the old Davis house was (on the corner of Coleman and Jackson Streets)? You turned right on Jackson Street (if you came from Quincy) and kept going straight. Right behind Rufie Tolar's house, there was a 40-acre field and a house over on the right-hand side that the Faircloths lived in. Papa gave us a penny apiece for the hornworms that we pulled off. That shade had slats on it as well as cheesecloth.

Mama: I remember totin' slats to it.

Kay: Mama helped build the first one. Did you ever poison the tobacco?

Hal: Oh yeah. Mama'd make us these little pouches and you'd put that (cottonseed) meal and poison mixture in the bud of the tobacco when it was growing up.

Kay: Mama made me a pouch and I poisoned, too.

Hal: Yeah, we started young! (All of us laughing.)

Discussing a picture:

Kay: That was your T-model, that you had off in college?

Hal: Yeah, that I had off in college. Well, I had it more than a year – had it here. I hadn't ever changed the oil, so I decided I'd go change the oil and when I went to take the plug off the bottom, it wouldn't come out. So I had to take the screwdriver and there was a band or something at that time that was around the cylinders had worn out. That T-model would run today. It was running 70 miles an hour, coming back from where I bought it. But Papa was gonna do me a big favor. So since it needed to be something redone, he took it to Tallahassee and they bored that thing so tight after they overhauled it, it broke my arm when it backfired in cranking it. So then I never did drive it in Gainesville. It sat there until somebody – one summer when I was gone – gave it away. Before I had it "repaired," that thing was a loose Goose!

Kay: Well, one time you were carrying the help home in it. And you had Coot locked up in the back part (just kidding around with him). He was hollering: "Mr. Hal, Mr. Hal -- let me out, Mr. Hal"! Y'all were just fooling around. But that was funny to me.

Hal: Well, that couldn't have been. There was nothing to lock him up in. It might have been later on, when I had the '48 Chevrolet coupe. I got that right after college. And I may have been home during the summer.

Kay: Well, how old were you when you were priming the tobacco?

Hal: Eight or ten. My first job was working in sun tobacco for Fletcher Edwards. And it made me mad because he paid Johnny 25 cents a day and he paid me 10 cents! I knew I worked just as hard as Johnny! (All of us laughing.)

Now that was 1938. No, probably in '36. So the priming was after that. Before we started in tobacco, Papa would have these fields planted in two rows of corn and a row of peanuts. And then he'd pay us 10 cents a row to hoe the peanuts. And he circled the rows.

They had these contours, and some of these rows you'd think you'd never get through with it. You'd hurry to get to the short rows 'cause the fields would be rectangular so you had to have short rows. And we'd really make the money on those short rows. But when you'd hit them long rows, it'd even out. And Johnny and I were about six and eight years old. It was when we had the place up there on Rock Comfort, just this side of Little Rock Comfort Creek. The field was back there where we had the fish pond. We'd go over there at daylight and Mama would fix us a lunch and we'd quit at sundown. And we'd come by that cemetery, coming home. (Big laugh.) The Edwards Cemetery – and it would scare us.

Kay: Going by your ancestors!

Mama: And nothing ever did catch you! I remember being in this house and somebody saying it was "hainted." I never did see any ghosts in here, and I've lived in it a long time. If there are ghosts, they're friendly ghosts. They've never done anything bad to us.

Discussing the view of the old oak and stockade out back:

Mama: I call that the Queen Ann Oak. (Her great-grandma Queen Ann Edwards planted it "to shade her kitchen." In those days, kitchens were built off from the house.)

Kay: Hal, did you tell me you built the stockade?! Something about it being your FFA project?

Hal: It may have been. We used a lot of things for FFA. Me and I forget who Papa had (it wasn't Tom Durden), but it was somebody from Greensboro – Pitts!

Kay: Buddy Pitts' daddy?

Hal: Yeah, I believe so. Buddy Pitts' daddy and I built that mule barn.

Kay: Well, I always attribute it to you.

Hal: Big laugh. I did that on purpose.

Kay: You're not laughing 'cause you're not taking credit for it?

Hal: You said you wanted to hear my laugh …

Kay: Yes, I would …

*(Saradee has since told that Papa was one of the men chopping the burning timbers out at the top. The other man was Claude Ward, from Liberty County, who had seen the lightning strike the roof. We heard him blowing his horn, and all ran out to see. He jumped out, grabbed an axe from his car trunk – and he and Papa proceeded to the top. Between us all, we saved it – and it's still standing: "The I Hear Hester Singing" Barn!)

Eighteen
Herschel Edwards
Pewter Farm, Sawdust
July 13, 1997

I'm a native of Sawdust and I was born August 26, 1903. I'll be 94 years old on my next birthday.

My daddy was Henry Lee Edwards, the son of Henry and Queen Ann Edwards and they lived up there where your mama (Olean Davis) lives now. That's the old Edwards homestead. Lee was born there. As a boy he worked for his brother Dan. Dan's house is still standing. Then when he left there he bought this land down here. He grew cotton and paid for this land with the cotton proceeds -- the land below the Sawdust crossroads, going south toward Hosford about 2 miles.

Many things have happened in my lifetime. Everybody that lived up and down this highway has either died or moved on. This highway was a dirt road and to go from here to Quincy in a buggy took about an hour. If it was loaded with whatever material you wanted to put in it, it took three hours. Long journey. Generally,

I rode with my daddy. There wasn't anybody but he and I, so I rode on the seat.

Quite often, Daddy would have a basket of eggs or sweet potatoes, or he would kill a pork, to take to town. Back in those days there wasn't any refrigeration. So what you did was kill a pork and carry it to the market. They'd cut it up that day and sell it. Sometimes we'd do that. We'd take this to town to trade.

We would bring back sugar, rice, flour, coffee and that type stuff. Sometimes we would eat with my daddy's sister, Aunt Ida Owens. She ran a boarding house and we'd go eat dinner with her, and she generally had good meals prepared for her boarders. She was on that corner that's across from Bell and Bates now. It was called Owens Boarding House.

My daddy grew tobacco. He grew sun tobacco back in those days, didn't have shade tobacco. It was used for filler in cigars. He only got about 15 or 20 cents a pound for it. I think Mr. Alex Shaw built the first tobacco shade. He got in to business with a man named Peter. They came out here and talked to my daddy and he grew two or three acres of shade tobacco under the slat top covering. In other words they rolled the slats out of the timber and cut them into strips kind of like a tobacco stick and you rolled that stick on top of the wire that you stretched across your land and tied it in and that was your shade. Later they discontinued that and began to make cloth.

There may have been other folks growing shade tobacco at that time, but I wasn't aware of it because I was a small child.

I started working in tobacco when I was about 8 or 10 years old. My first job was poisoning tobacco. You generally had a tin can of some type that you put a handle on and then you would mix up a mixture of "Paris green," cornmeal and probably some sand in it. Then you would put that stuff in the cup and walk down the row and shake the cup over the bud of every stalk of tobacco. You had holes in the bottom of the cup sort of like a salt or pepper shaker.

My oldest sister was named Ola. Back in those days they were chipping turpentine on the long leaf pines in the woods. A man came here from Blackshear, GA., and he was what they call a wood driver. He checked on the boys that were chipping trees. Ola met him and they got married. They lived a year or two roughly up there where granddaughter Beth has that mobile home now. Then he decided that farming wasn't for him so they went down to Wakulla County and he ran a turpentine still down there for several years. My sister Ola, when she was thirty something years old, had pneumonia and died. My daddy decided to quit farming and go to Gainesville, FL and make a living some other way. So he got him a grocery store and was doing very well with it. Then he got unhappy and came back up here after about two or three years down there. In the meantime, while he was down there, my other sister, Lalla, was a young girl and this man, Mr. Petty, came. He was an insurance man. My mother was taking in boarders and took him in as a boarder and as a result he and my sister Lalla married and they had four or five children. They had Pauline, who died recently, and Virginia, who lives in Tifton, GA. Eugene was living in Atlanta. He died in the last few years. Virginia is the only one in that crowd that is still living.

I had a brother, Newell, who was 10 years older than me, who lived up there in that house for several years and he died 20 years ago. I was the baby. I was an accident.

Everybody worked in tobacco. My mama -- she would work in it until about 9 or 10 in the morning then she would go to the house to cook dinner. She cooked with wood and half the time there wouldn't be any wood cut. Somebody would have to come out of the barn to cut wood for her to cook dinner with. You drew water out of the well with a bucket. It was rough living back in those days.

I was five or six years old when my daddy left farming. When he came back from Gainesville, he stayed here until he died. His wife (my mama) was Della Suber who was George and Elmer and Joe Suber's sister.

I went to the Sawdust school. I walked from here to the school house. I didn't have any way to ride. There were some other kids walking, too. The Howells that used to live up here. Dolly Edwards used to live in that house where Thomas Fletcher has now. They lived there and some of those children went with us.

Daddy wound up growing eight-10 acres of shade, the last crop of shade tobacco they grew. He didn't get paid well enough for it so he quit growing shade tobacco and went back to growing sun tobacco. About that time I had graduated from high school. I went to Jacksonville to Massey Business College. At that time my sister Lalla and her husband were living in Palatka. The manager at the Southern Utilities Company, which was a power company supplying power to all that area, asked my sister if I would be interested in taking a job with him. Of course, I had just finished

Massey Business College and I readily accepted. So I stayed there a couple of years. Then Electric Bond Share Company in New York bought out Southern Utilities. When they did they sent me to Miami to their general accounting office. I stayed down there six years and married Miss Ethel (Fambrough) in that six years. Brought her up here to the woods. She came out of North Georgia, had never been in the woods before and accepted the lifestyle without any complaint.

The reason I came back from Miami -- the depression came on in 1932. The office I was working in, I think there was about 139 people and when they let me go I think they had 35 left. That's the way they were cutting down. But it was the biggest blessing that ever come down the pike when they did that to me. Of course, at the time I didn't think so. In the meantime, my brother Newell, had found out that this little store up here in Sawdust was for sale. So of course, he didn't have any money and I didn't have much so he asked me if I would put up half the money and we'd go in half owners. Fortunately, I had a few hundred dollars so I sent him some money. Then after they let me go in '32, I came back up here and the depression was in full rule at that time. He and I fished about once a week for a couple of years and I spent what little money I had trying to operate this farm and lost it all, of course. Then he decided that maybe we should open a grocery store in Quincy, which we did. Had two in Quincy at one time. One was the Jitney Jungle and the other was the Blue Ribbon Store. I was keeping all the records, sending all the reports to the Internal Revenue Service and all that stuff you have to do.

In the meantime, I had decided I had to do something else. At that time, they had begun the New Deal. Roosevelt had put in different agencies – WPA, et cetera. Mr. E. C. Jackson, who was

Stoney Edwards' brother-in-law, was in charge of the Quincy office. So he came out here one morning and wanted to know if I would be interested in coming to work in the office. I said, "Well, I don't know. What does it pay"? He said, "$15.00 a week." I told him I didn't think I could go that route right then. So when he left Miss Ethel flew all over me like a hawk. She said, "You've been sitting around here two or three years doing nothing. What you think you're going to do. You better take it."

So I went over there and took it. They evidently liked what I did because they sent me to Madison, which was the district headquarters. Then they moved the district headquarters back to Tallahassee and then they decided they were going to send me to Pensacola, which they did, but I was too far away from Miss Ethel and our two children. I told them I was through with them and I came back home. I'd been home about two or three weeks and they sent me a telegram (back in those days they had telegrams). They wanted to know if I would be interested in a job in this district, checking on all these projects they had going. They gave me that job and I kept it until the War broke out with England and France and all that group over there ... the last World War. So they disbanded the project.

When they did, Mr. George Munroe came to see me wanting to know if I would be interested in working for the Munroe family. I told him I thought I might be. He said come by my office Monday. I went by there and we agreed. Pat Munroe had just died, so the first thing he did was put me on that estate, working on it. I worked there a while. George, at that time, was operating five tobacco farms and I was in charge of the office, seeing about all the payrolls, and all that stuff, did all the bills. He was growing a hybrid seed corn. It was a specialty that increased the corn yield tremendously in this county. We sold a lot of that seed corn and we had to keep up with all that and try to collect. Then he died. When he died, Bradley and Bobby took over and they started what is now the George Munroe Tractor Company. Then they both died and Dwight Clark and Little George Munroe had the knowhow so they brought the tractor company from the estate that was formed. Dwight Clark is still operating that tractor company. George got on a tractor one day and let it kill him.

We had a partnership. First it was just with my father-in-law. Marcus (my son) went in the military and went to Europe for several months. When he got back home, he wanted to stay here and farm so we set up a partnership between my father-in-law, myself and Marcus and we grew anywhere from 20 to 40 acres of tobacco. We did really well, we were fortunate.

At first, Henry Weinberg was packing our tobacco and selling it. There was a little friction there, and we went with the Bayuk Cigar Company. Mickey Selzer was Bayuk's representative. We built our own packing house. There were several farmers in it: Maxwell Strom, Kenneth Maxwell and Max Fletcher from Greensboro was in there. We did real well with that.

When I first went to work for George Munroe, the office was down there where the old post office was. About a block north was the packing house. Then they sold that packing house. There was another packing house across the street from where R. E. Blitch and Sons was and I worked in that building for several years. When George got to selling hybrid seed corn and bahia grass seed and all that type of stuff they decided they'd build a building out there across from Talquin Electric. When they built that building

I moved out there. Then I ran that thing for four or five years and did all this other work on the side.

Then when George died Bobby and Bradley took it over. They were not active in the business, they'd just come by every once in awhile.

When we were farming we had Wilbur Suber as superintendent of Pewter Farm. That was in the '50s. We had 50-75 farm hands. We had a bus that we ran to Quincy to bring help every morning and we had a truck we ran to Blountstown. It came loaded every morning. There was a pile of them. Every once in awhile now when I go into Winn-Dixie, one of them will come up and speak to me. It's hard to remember them all, though.

We had four or five tenant houses. Mose Madry was one of my mainstays. He drove the truck and transported hands part of the time. I think he's dead. Willie Chestnut lives over here on this highway. They were two of the leaders. Another was Pierce Rolax that drove the bus bringing the school children. He used to live up there on the left.

We had seven barns. The old one, my daddy built. Marcus and I built all the rest of them. We cut most of the timber on this place. George Johnson built one of the barns that we had.

We had all the problems. We had aphids, blue mold, blackshank and all that stuff. We just fought it the best we could. Finally, they developed a few varieties of tobacco that were more or less resistant to a lot of these things.

Our daughter Marian worked in it a little, not too much. We had mostly black workers. We had six mules when we first began. They'd die out and tractors were coming in so we began to buy tractors. Of course, they weren't efficient like they are now. Had all kind of problems with them, but we worked it out.

When the hands came in at night they would feed and water the animals and then they would come back the next morning and hitch them up to go to work. We didn't have a regular lot man. We'd just tell somebody to see about them.

One shade was out here back of this barn that my daddy built, and we had one down there between there and the pond. King Ferguson, a black man, who lived back in the plantation, built that first barn.

Shade tobacco was the best thing that's ever been in Gadsden County for the farmer. Of course, some of them didn't make any money. Some of them didn't deserve to make any money. See they had a deal whereby the tobacco company furnished a portion of the cost of producing the tobacco. A lot of boys, when they'd get that payment -- instead of paying for the fertilizer and the other stuff that they had to have to grow tobacco -- would buy new pickups and take off fishing and all that type of stuff. And some drank a lot of liquor and were living high instead of putting that money in the tobacco crop. That got a lot of them in trouble. Too, there were some tobacco companies that weren't exactly honest. I think everybody knows that.

The 20th of May was what they used to celebrate back then because that was a freedom deal for blacks.

Your Grandpa Will Chester used to drive a buggy to Quincy (from down below Telogia) and sometimes on his trip he'd spend the night with us to break his trip. The Shuler that was the game warden in Liberty County (your mama's kinfolks, too), used to ride by here checking on things.

Nineteen
Pat Carman and Barbara Bietenholz & Brigitt Bietenholz Clark
Visit to the Barn
Summer 1997

(Discussing possibility that a relative of Pat's may have helped build the "I Hear Hester Singing" Barn for my dad):

Pat: My uncle, Colin Hanna, built barns. He lived in Hanna Town, between Mt. Pleasant and Bainbridge, and he died in May of 1942.

Kay: We wish we knew for sure. Mama just always said, "The man we had building the barn came to eat lunch with us everyday. He had only gotten the pillars laid and he died." She thought his name was Mr. Griffin. And there *was* a man who built barns and died about then, named Eugene Griffin.

(Acting the daily scenes so dear to anyone who's ever worked in a tobacco barn):

Pat: The stringers would get their rhythm and they might hum or they might sing. As they leaned backward they picked up the leaf and as they leaned forward, they put it on the needle. They constantly went in that rhythm *all* day!

They would string until somebody at lunchtime would yell out: "String up the stick you're on"! Which was a signal to stop for lunch. And then they said that again in the afternoon to say, "Stop"! And some of 'em barely stopped for a drink of water or anything else. And if they ran out of tobacco, you would hear 'em. Or ran out of string or sticks. They would start yelling when they had three or four sticks left – or when the tobacco was getting low. They'd holler, "Bring me some bowcka"! Or "I want some scring"! Or "sticks"! And they didn't ever say, "Bring me sticks" – just "sti-icks"! And I can hear 'em, when I stop and think about it, "Bring me some bowcka"!

Each one had their own song and their own rhythm. They more or less rocked back and forth. And some of 'em would bring something to stand on, because they were paid by the stick. At the time I was working in tobacco, they paid a penny a stick. I'm sure it probably got to be more. I made $3.00 a day when I first started. And my job was to wait on tables. Sometimes I carried it after they got it strung on the sticks down to where it was being hung up in the barn. Clearing the rack, they called it. The stringers would get mad if their rack piled up. You could only put two or three sticks up there, and they didn't want anything to slow 'em down.

I worked on the Love Farm which is north of town on Solomon Dairy Road, and the Ward Farm and Malone Farm. It's on South Adams Street, at Crossroads. I worked for Tom Maxwell. Archie Hubbard, at one time, owned the Malone Farm. Mr. Brady was on one of the farms at one time, and I think it was the Love Farm. My daddy ran the barn. He was Dave Carman, and he supervised the packing house.

(At this point, we stop to introduce Pat's great-nephew, Aubrey Allen, from Atlanta. He's getting a glimpse of the old tobacco days. It's a hot day – about 100 degrees.)

Kay: What was nice about the barn, was that the tobacco usually came in wet and it kinda cooled things down. We wore a long-sleeved shirt, some of us.

Pat: And a cap – because it would drip. In the morning when the first tobacco came in, it usually had little frogs in it, and hornworms. (A listener nearby laughs.)

Kay: We also have with us, for our tape, Barbara Bietenholz and Brigitt Bietenholz Clark.

Brigitt: I remember working on those machines (the stringing machines) – but I have no memories like Pat. I worked one or two summers, probably '61 and '62.

(Her mother, Barbara, reminds her that she worked earlier, in 1958, on the farm across from George Ford. The farm was San Julia on the Old Bainbridge Highway.)

Brigitt: I married Stan Clark; he was Edgar Clark's son.

Kay: Georgianna and Mike's brother! If you keep on, you can get all this Gadsden County connection.

(Telling Pat: But now, Barbara was born in Switzerland. No connection there. What was the name of the farm you lived on when you came to Gadsden County?)

Barbara: El Consuelo – on the Old Bainbridge Road.

Pat: Back in the teens (1910-20), my daddy worked on La Violetta, going toward Midway.

Kay: I didn't know it was "La" Violetta. In fact, I used to think they were saying "Lockarona," when it was really "La Corona." And another was "La Camellia." They were all Spanish names. What does El Consuelo mean?

Barbara: I think Consuela is a girl's name. It seems to me it should be "La Consuela." But they told me, the black people told me, it was named after a girl!

Pat: Probably one of the first to own the farm.

Barbara: We lived on the farm, but there was never tobacco, while we were there – unless it was rented out, you know, to Thomas Smith or someone.

Discussing Barbara's Swiss background:

In Switzerland, I went to horticultural school and we made shades to put over the greenhouses and over the hotbeds, you know. We made them out of wood. The girls in that school made the shades, ourselves, and then we, according to the way the weather was, we had to roll 'em up or we had to spread 'em out. They were not so heavy, not longer than this here.

When the sun was too hot under the glass, we had a lot of flowers that needed shading. And the greenhouses – we had lettuce, all kind of things in the hotbeds. And the coldbeds – we had to shade them and open the glass.

Kay: For us, shade is soothing. Why shouldn't it be to the plants?

Discussing Quincy's Sumatra tobacco ties:

Barbara: I'm not so accurate like Ernst. But Sumatra in Indonesia was taken over by the natives, the Japanese, I think – and the Dutch had to leave and they could not grow there anymore. And then they had to have a place to go, and that's why they came here. Connecticut has always had a better crop of tobacco than Florida, because of the milder season and the leaves are thinner, and the veins are less pronounced.

Kay: Lots of people have asked me: Do they leave the veins in when they roll it?

Barbara: With artificial wrappers, they don't need to have such a good quality of tobacco to produce cheap cigars. They would use broken tobacco and also the good quality of tobacco to produce homogenized tobacco, which came on rolls like paper. Homogenized tobacco is only used for the inner wrapper (I forgot what it was called). It is my understanding that the outer wrapper was always real tobacco.

Kay: Tobacco pulp!

Barbara: Before homogenizing the leaves had to be cut to fit the cigars – which wasted a lot of tobacco. Therefore, the Connecticut tobacco with dainty veins produced a better and more economical cigar.

Kay: Well, I know theirs is a smaller leaf, because when Mr. Peavy grew that crop – well, this tobacco in our little shade is Connecticut tobacco. But it grew bigger because of the sun and the climate.

Barbara: Everything grows slower and finer there in Connecticut.

Pat: And they didn't get through with the crop as early as we did here. We would be through by the 4th of July – before the hottest part of the year.

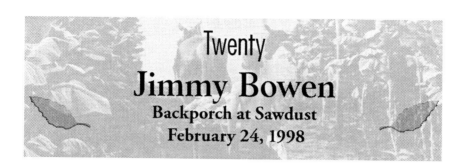

Twenty
Jimmy Bowen
Backporch at Sawdust
February 24, 1998

Fannie Campbell was seeing after Daddy's tobacco farm that was located on Providence Road. She had her children there and, of course, all of Daddy's that were old enough were there. Fannie divided the rows of tobacco up between the children. You had to poison so many rows. Fannie kept at me because I wasn't bending over like I should to put it right in the buds. I was just kind of dashing it at them. Fannie would tell me, Jimmy you're not doing it right, you'll have to do it over, and I kept telling her no, no, no. When she told me I had to do mine over again, I said no I don't listen to black people, they don't tell me what to do. So she got a switch and told me I was going to do it or she was going to switch me. I told her if you do I'm going to tell my daddy and you'll be sorry. Anyway, she got her switch and I had to do it over. In the meantime, she saw Daddy and I ended up with two whippings. I must have been nine or ten years old about then.

Back then we started working real young. It was my job to shuck the corn for the mules and get the nubbins for the milk cows and chop them up, sprinkle some cottonseed meal, and give the mules so many ears of corn, so much hay or so much fodder like we used to get off the corn stalk, feed the hogs, and get the calves up. Back then we kept the cows and calves separated until milking time.

J. W. Chason lived just across the little branch from us. Bill Chason was J.W's uncle and they used to have striped cane. There wasn't anything to do back then like there is today so when it was watermelon time a bunch of us boys would got a kick out of sneaking a watermelon out of somebody's patch and eating it. We would always do it out of some of our own people's. Well, J.W. thought that because Bill was his uncle, and Mr. Sam was his granddaddy that it was a great thing for us to go down there and get us a stalk or two of that striped cane. Mr. Chason was bad about drinking and we used to love to go down there on Saturday night because that was usually when he would be drinking. The striped cane was close to the house so we would make a little noise and get him to come out. He would chase us up and down the cane rows and we would lay quiet and let him run by us. Oh, he was going to tear up whoever was out there. Well, we would let him run by us and get way down to the other end and then we would make some noise up where we were and he would come running back. We just had a good time doing little mean things like that.

My daddy (Lamar Bowen) used to come up here and cook syrup for your daddy (Forrest Davis, Sr.). He did it for years. That's when your daddy had the grits mill and the sawmill, when your brothers Johnny and Hal were boys. Daddy used to get a kick out of seeing your mother (Olean Davis) come down to the sawmill about 8:00 or 8:30 each morning with the biggest platter of biscuits you have ever seen. Those boys would get syrup that was just cooked and

Daddy said they could eat the most biscuits of any boys he had ever seen.

I had five sisters and one brother. My brother, Murray, who lived in Chattahoochee, passed away about ten years ago. My sister, who was next to the oldest, died, but the rest of us are still living. We lived right across the branch from where one of my sisters, Essie Rudd, lives now. My uncle, Alec Bowen, ran Shepard's Mill for about eight or ten years in the fifties.

When I was young, slingshots were our guns. They had this road (Hosford Road/Hwy. 65) paved part of the way and we were all wishing they would hurry and pave the rest so we could get the gravel to shoot in our slingshots. We didn't realize that the gravel was so light and it wouldn't travel like a rock.

I remember when the government had all that land down there that St. Joe owns now (Brent Wildlife) up for sale at 50 cents an acre, and how people would say they wouldn't give 50 cents an acre for that. If they had the money to pay 50 cents an acre back then and bought it, they would be rich now.

My mama's sister, Vanna Black, was my favorite aunt. She bought me a pair of overalls when I was a little bitty thing. They had an old T-model Ford, and they would let me ride on the running board while somebody held on to me. Uncle Joe would sit in a chair and jiggle his feet, and his old cat would get up in his lap, meow and get jiggled along with Uncle Joe's feet

I was in the Service twice. I went in the first time in 1942, and I came out in September of 1947. I was overseas thirty-seven months in the European Theater. Then I was called back in 1949 during the Korean War and stayed until September 1951. I enjoyed my time in the Service except for the twenty-two months that I was in actual combat. But otherwise, I got to see a lot of things, I got to learn a lot of things that I never would have seen or would know about if I had not been in Service.

I was on the third tank at one time, just out of Berlin, with "Blood and Guts" Patton and he was on the head tank. I heard General Patton make many a speech. I never will forget, he said "Those blankety, blanks can't hit you ... follow me ... I'll lead the way." And he would darn sure lead the way. I was right near when he got killed in a wreck in Germany.

When I left here for the Service I had maybe been to Tallahassee two or three times, and the furthest I had been from Gadsden County was Lake Mystic. I had been to the beach one time. Daddy carried us all to Mexico Beach one summer after tobacco. I guess he made a good crop. Otherwise, I had never been out of Gadsden County before.

I started growing tobacco in 1948 at my old home place, and raised around twenty acres. I had about 50 or 60 people working for me at the peak of the season. I farmed for myself until 1963, and was working for King Edward when tobacco went out. It went out completely in 1975. I have done everything there was to do to tobacco. I could string tobacco, I could tie tobacco, I could move the benches, I could build the shade, I could do it all. My theory was if you couldn't do it yourself, you couldn't show anybody else how to do it. There were certain ways you had to do the looping and tying up to the row wire or you could reach up and pull it right down. Down at the bottom you could either get it too big or too little to where it would cut the plant off when it grew.

I just loved the work because I love to work people, I love to watch stuff grow and you were always proud. As one fellow said ... a tobacco farmer was always proud until November. He was proud when he got his plant bed ready, he was proud when he got his field ready, and he was proud when he got his plants transplanted, he was proud when he got it tied up, he was proud when he got started priming, he was proud when he finished, he was proud when he finished delivering it to the packing house out of the barn. Then in November they used to give you your settlement and he said that was the only time you weren't proud. A lot of times you lost money so that killed the proud part. But just as soon as you found out you could raise another crop of it you started being proud again. All of Gadsden County loved it. It was a good way of life. None of us ever thought tobacco would be completely out.

I worked for Fletcher Company for several years raising tobacco after I quit, and ended up with King Edward raising tobacco. There were good times and bad times, and in fact it was the bad that put me completely out.

I had one barn of my own that burned. It wasn't lightning. Something evidently happened in the barn because it had not been long since I had been in there and refired it. Along then you were trying to cut corners, cut your expenses. That was before we started firing with gas heat and gas heaters. We were using coal. A lot of us would go down to Hosford and get veneering blocks. We would saw them in to and lay some of them on the charcoal to help save on the charcoal. I think that is what burned my barn.

I was over in Tallahassee two or three years ago sitting in Morrison's Cafeteria, eating. I always sit where I can see everybody traveling in and out. This colored guy passed the window and then came back and beat on the window and waved at me. I didn't recognize him, but I waved back. In a few minutes he came in to our table. He said, "Get up, Mr. Jimmy. I got to hug you." After he hugged me he said, "You don't know who I am, do you"? I said, "I ought to know you but I can't quite place you." Well he was grown then and it had been some fifteen or twenty years since I had seen him. He said, "Mr. Jimmy, I used to hate you and really wanted to kill you. You used to whip me real hard with tobacco sticks. Do you know who I am"? I said, "Yes, I don't remember your first name, but your last name is Fields." He was from Gretna. He has a real good job, and owns his own home in Tallahassee. He said his Mama still tells him that he ought to thank the Lord that Mr. Jimmy came along and made a good man out of him.

That's what's wrong with our children today. They used to have discipline, and anybody that was older than them could give it to them. They wanted us to know what life was all about. Now the mama and daddy can't even give it to them.

Last year Mr. Tom Hopkins built a six acre shade. He's going to have some this year and he's talking about doing it like we did tomatoes, not doing it under a shade this time. Hentz Fletcher raised some tobacco last year without the shade. If I was going to raise tobacco now, that's the way I would do it. Because real good posts would cost you ten or twelve dollars. There's a lot of work to it, and when you get in to acres, there is a lot of work.

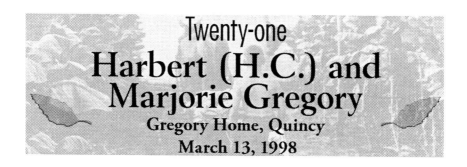

Twenty-one
Harbert (H.C.) and Marjorie Gregory
Gregory Home, Quincy
March 13, 1998

(This conversation reflects that Harbert and Marjorie are telling the story together. It begins with Harbert):

I was born July 24, 1911 in a two story house on Jefferson Street in Quincy and have lived in Quincy all my life.

My father, Scott Gregory, owned a shade tobacco farm that was called Peppergrass. Peppergrass Farm was located between Little River and Shady Rest Road. It went from Little River around the corner down to the creek in the next bottom. The farm got its name Peppergrass, because a lot of peppergrass (which is a ragweed) grew out there. We grew about 100 acres of tobacco that we sold at a market in Gadsden County. I worked on the farm until I was about 21. I went to college at the University of Florida majoring in engineering, and during the summer I would come home to help with the tobacco.

I was eight years old when I started working on the farm. My first job was as a toter. My daddy paid me a little bit of money ... token wages. We lived in town so I rode in a horse and buggy the six miles from town to the farm. A man named Jim Dunham drove the horse and buggy and he also took care of the horses at the stable on King Street. I had three older sisters, Mae T., Nelle and Gladys, but I was the only one who worked in tobacco.

{Marjorie: At that time it was mostly only boys who worked in tobacco, as my brothers did. I was not even allowed to go out to the tobacco fields when I was growing up.}

I liked working in tobacco and the big tobacco barns. The shades were pretty. Back then they had slats instead of cheesecloth. We carried lunch out to the farm everyday and everybody ate together.

Joe and Mamie O'Neal lived in Quincy and worked at the farm. Mamie also cooked for my family. The O'Neal's house was on King Street. They kept mules and horses behind their house where White's store is.

{Marjorie: Right up from their house on King Street was the Hinsons' house where all the Hinson boys grew up and right above that was Al and Sara Wilson's house. There were a lot of pretty homes all along Jefferson Street. That was the place to live then ... one of the main places in town. When Harbert's sister, Mae, moved here and bought the house between Nelle's and ours, the two story family home was sold and torn down. At about that same time the Wilson house, the Hinson house all those were taken over and taken down for commercial use.}

Tobacco was quite different from the time I was in it and in later years when it went out. It was raised in the fields and then put in big wooden barns. I didn't help make the slat shades, but I drove a barge, hung it and primed it, but I didn't pack it. The tobacco had to be in exactly the right, condition ... cased ... not too dry and not too wet. I rode many a mule, but my favorite one was named Queen.

My father was Sheriff of Quincy for 28 years. He sold the farm when he was elected Sheriff because he didn't have time to run it.

{Marjorie: One time he was taking a prisoner from Quincy to Jacksonville. Going through Lake City, a lynching mob stopped him, took the prisoner and lynched him. Harbert's father was trying to take the prisoner to safety in Jacksonville because the jail in Quincy was going to be raided.}*

My grandfather was Harbert Chapman Gregory. He grew up in Wakulla County and is buried at the New Light Cemetery just in the edge of Wakulla County. My mother's name was Kate Saunders. She was born in Jefferson County. The house in Wacissa is still standing. My father was working a cattle drive bringing cattle up from Wakulla County to Quincy when he met my mother. She was teaching school in Shiloh and lived at the Bostick house. He kept coming back courting her and they got married. When they were first married they lived in the Bostick house.

{Marjorie: Harbert's mother, or it may have been his aunt, came down the Chattahoochee River on a cotton barge and got off right between Chattahoochee and Torreya Park to visit family down there. We went down there one time and found an old colored man, real, real old who remembered when the barge came down and when she got off to visit.

I grew up in Havana out on a tobacco farm. My daddy's name was Arthur Butler and my mother's name was Sophie Garland. Both my parents came from South Georgia. My daddy grew tobacco from about the time I was born and when he died Cecil, my brother, took over and grew tobacco for as long as they grew it there. They still have the farm in Havana. When my father was born his daddy had slaves and each of his sons was assigned a little black boy. The little black boys were to teach the sons how to hunt and fish and take care of them. The black boys stayed with my daddy and his brothers all through their lives. The one that stayed with my daddy was called Albert Butler and when Mother and Daddy married and bought the farm down in Havana they brought Albert with them.

Albert started courting a lady named Millie who lived across the Ochlockonee River in Leon County. There was no bridge at the time and he had a terrible time getting across the river to court her. They eventually married and Millie Butler came to the farm as our cook when I was three years old. I remember Millie tying an old piece of sheet dipped in turpentine around my toe where I cut it or did something to it. She stayed until Harbert and I were married, had our children and our children got married. She, like a lot of the black people, was very superstitious.

Every year when they finished the tobacco season in August they had a Tobacco Festival and I was one of the contestants from Havana and that's how Harbert met me. He was in the Chamber of Commerce in Quincy. The Chamber of Commerce was sponsoring a parade and the afternoon of the parade he saw me. At the dance that night I had a date with my college roommate's cousin who had come up from Daytona Beach. But that same night Harbert told Christine Smith that he was going to marry me.

I graduated in 1938 and taught for a year in Chattahoochee. The next summer on June 28, 1939 Harbert and I were married. We have two children, Scotty, who was born in 1941 and Joe, who was born six years later.

Harbert was a surveyor and did a lot of surveying after we were married to make a little extra money on the weekends. He would go out and survey on Saturday mornings and come in and while it was fresh on his mind he would take his notes and make the drawings. We lived right across the bridge in a duplex apartment when we first got married and had a big drawing table in the back bedroom. He would sit up all night trying to get on the drawing what he had surveyed that day. He was the first to make a complete map of all the land in Gadsden County and up until recently that's the one they used at the Court House.}

Looking at some plaques on the wall:

{Marjorie: Harbert was Assistant City Manager for Quincy from 1940 to 1948, and City Manager from 1948 to 1971. He was President of the Florida City Managers in 1955-56. He was also President of The Florida League of Municipalities from 1962 to 1963. After he retired from the city of Quincy, Tallahassee was needing help because Tallahassee's City Manager, who was a good friend of Harbert's, developed cancer and asked Harbert to please come over and help him. Harbert was a consultant and got a release from the city of Quincy to go help the city of Tallahassee. He was only going to stay one year and they kept him three years.

He served in WWII as a combat engineer under General George Patton. Harbert frequently saw and talked to General Patton during the time he served under him.}

Note: The prisoner incident is recorded in Florida history books, according to Dr. Scott Gregory, Harbert and Marjorie's son. Scott adds that the Governor was quoted as saying that Sheriff Gregory, an upstanding man, had done all in his power to protect the prisoner.

Building a small shade and growing a small crop of "shade tobacco" is still work! Forrest (Johnny) Davis and Nathaniel McNealy "did good," though! Visitors Barb Bietenholz, Brigitt Clark, Pat Carman and Aubrey Allen (and many others) enjoyed the results.

Twenty-two
Betty Davis Morrison
Backporch at Sawdust
June 13, 1998

I grew up on the Davis farm in Gadsden County, FL. I was born in 1933, the fourth of four children. My brother Johnny was only four years old when I was born and he was the oldest of the four. So we were a close-knit little group, fighting and having good times along the way.

In our early years we started working in tobacco and absolutely enjoyed it. But one thing, Betty was always afraid of worms. The first time I remember being in the tobacco barn in Greensboro when I was a little girl, there was a Mr. Tolar that was the foreman of the barn crew. They put everybody they could to work in those days – older people and little children included. Sister Saradee was afraid of tobacco needles. The boys (Johnny and Hal) would chase her with a tobacco needle. And they would chase me and get me to scream and holler with a green hornworm! I remember trying to hide behind Mr.Tolar and ran circles around the sweet old man with long white hair.

Papa had started growing tobacco in I don't know what year, because I am not very historically connected. I don't remember the dates, but I do remember that we grew a lot of things before we grew tobacco. An early memory was the big old stock barn out back when Ed Chambers worked for us. We grew corn and peanuts and had mules and hogs as the mainstay, and Papa had the sawmill going meanwhile. We children used to sell slabs from the sawmill on Saturdays and got to keep the money.

I remember one time that Johnny, Hal and Saradee came home from the sawmill and said that Betty was standing on a pile of lumber cussing real loud. I probably was and I probably got a good whipping when I got home. I don't remember the whipping, but I remember getting corrected for it.

My earliest memory of tobacco on the homeplace was across the road. Saradee and I were paid a penny apiece for each grasshopper we killed. We would swat them with a bolo paddle. They caused a lot of damage to the growing tobacco.

In the planting process, one person would drop plants from the apron around their waist. The next worker would stick a hole in the ground, put the plant in it and cover the plant with the little stick leaving a hole to the side for water to be poured in. The next worker dipped a little water in each hole. There were several little teams working at one time in different rows. Sometimes the cheesecloth was already up on the shade when this was going on, around February or March, depending on the weather.

The tobacco reached a certain size and it was time to tie it up. Two workers to a long bench did this on several rows at a time. One on the ground would loop string around the young plant and hand the string up to the worker standing on the bench, who would tie it over a wire which ran overhead on each row. The two of them would move the bench further down and repeat the process. They worked quickly and efficiently being paid by the day and expected to get a lot done.

Saradee always said "Granneddy Davis." I followed her around wherever she went since I was the little sister. Granneddy Davis would shell pecans for us on the porch of the old Davis House when we went to visit, usually on Sunday afternoons. He had a windmill that pumped their water. He was retired from his businesses, which had included growing shade tobacco. A Mrs. Edenfield took care of him, Grandma Sarah D. having died earlier, about the time I was born. The old Davis House had three stories, I think, which included the attic. It was of Victorian style. You could tell all of Granneddy's children inclined that way had gone to college, as the living room was lined with bookshelves full of books. Upstairs in the attic area we may have seen some WWI helmet or the like of one of the Uncles. There was a large bathroom on the lower floor and I remember a big old footed bathtub and pink soap (probably Life Buoy).

The house could be seen as you entered Greensboro, and on down the dirt road from that was the Tolar House, and others, of course. Turning to the left at the Tolar House, you could find a small house down there where Mama and Papa rented during their early marriage days. Most folks would know it as the Ora Suber House.

Aunt Farris (the oldest of the Davis clan) used to tell me about the Teddy Roosevelt days when she and Uncle Mac used to run down the hill to Shepard's Millpond and back early in the morning.

Teddy Roosevelt was a very motivating leader who inspired the youth of that day to want to be strong and healthy. I stayed with Aunt Farris in Tallahassee some while I was attending FSU.

Back to the tobacco business. Papa bought the Smith Place up near Rock Comfort. At that time he wasn't doing as much sawmilling and was more in the house building business. He also was building dams and paving roads. The Meadows Store (back then we called it the Rushing Store) and some of the houses in Forrest Dale were built by him about that time. Mama thought up the name of Forrest Dale. I don't know if it has stuck. When Papa left one enterprise and went to another, the first one would go downhill. Mama inspired Johnny to help him keep the farm going. (He was just 13 when Papa and she let him take charge.) He grew corn and oats and raised some cows and had mules to plow and pull barges of tobacco.

Mama was so busy and was such a good disciplinarian. She'd tell you to do something and you better do it, and Papa would back her up. He taught us children to respect Mama. But Betty was a bad sasser. (I didn't know I was talking back. I just thought I was giving my point of view.) I learned pretty quick from a good many whippings what sassing was!

Mama would tell us not to go off somewhere. We loved to go see Cousin Betty Edwards and Aunt Edna Chester in particular. Mama would get busy and we would slip off somewhere. Cousin Betty used to let us hunt eggs in her barn and would sometimes bake oatmeal or rice cookies. She would give us some cookies, which was a sign she liked for us to come. Her family was grown and gone by then and she was alone and lonesome or she would have shooed us away, we thought. One time Mama came across the cattle gap which led up the lane to Cousin Betty's.

"You younguns, get on home. You're going to get it when I get there"! Whatever she said that was the general idea. Well, Saradee waited for her while she got a peach switch. But I decided I would outrun her. Well, she followed me across plowed rows, and boy did I get it! I don't remember the switching, but I sure remember what I got it for!

During World War II when I was about eight or nine years old, Hal had a "victory garden" down near the sawmill. I'm not sure if Saradee was along when I tagged down there where he was plowing with a mule. I begged him to let me ride the mule home. Finally he gave in, and helped fat little Betty up on the mule. Well, the startled mule took off, and the next thing I knew I was on the ground and the plow sliced across my thigh! We were so scared, but it didn't bleed. We didn't want Hal to get a whipping for letting me do such a dumb thing. I took my bath and put on my pajamas. But Saradee and Hal looked at it and said we better tell Mama. When Mama looked up the pajama leg, she screamed. So she called Dr. Wilhoit who met us at his office and put in about nine stitches. He said if I hadn't been fat it might have cut my big leg vein and could have had very severe consequences. The scar remains to this day.

We children liked to slide down the big old sawdust pile. Mama warned us about snakes and spontaneous combustion fires which were sometimes in them, and of possible cave-ins. At an earlier time at the sawmill, Saradee had gotten too close to a burning sawdust pile or something and her clothes caught fire. One of the hands was trying to beat it out – she didn't realize he was saving her life. She thought he was trying to kill her! Like me, she has a scar that is still there.

One time we took our sweet little sister Kay on one of our escapades. She was just a walking tot and we older four took her out for a little joy ride. We were careful and sensible except we decided to go up to the top of a fire tower! We held her hand all the way up. While we were at the top, who should go driving by below but Mama and Papa. We all waved. In a few minutes, the fire tower phone was ringing like crazy. "Bring that baby down from there," they said!

Ed Chambers, Bunion Chestnut and Jake Harris were workers from way back that I remember so well. Once, while riding in the wagon behind the mule with Ed Chambers, we got to see some dogs chasing a fox through the woods. We also rode the wagon almost to Greensboro to get some cane ground into syrup one time.

My brother Hal had a Black Angus steer named Inky, and Johnny had a white-faced Hereford (I think) steer. That steer would hear or see me coming and go berserk for some reason. One time he got after me and I climbed a fence and ran and ran trying to get back around to the house. I thought he could get over the fence to me. I kept running and climbing fences and finally got back to the front of our house. My side was killing me, but I made it!

Saradee and I had show steers, too. My last one was a Shorthorn I called Roany (because of his color). When I was showing him for sale, he kicked me goodbye and ran away. Pat Thomas caught him for me and I sold him.

I had my own checking account. We sold steers to the highest bidders and the went for $200 to $300 each and we got to keep the money. Papa and Mama tried to teach us good business and gave us all the opportunities they could.

Twenty-three
Robert and Harriett (Hattie) Parramore
Parramore Home, near Old Federal Road
November 5, 1998

I had the rolling store from 1936 until June 15, 1975. It was called White's Rolling Store. I operated out of the White's Store in town. White's Store was owned by Lee White. After he died his wife ran it and then his daughter and son-in-law, Elma and T.M. Burns. T.M. also did a lot of good barbecuing. Back then some of the roads weren't paved and you couldn't go down some of them on account of the limbs.

The rolling store was 7 ½ feet wide. That was the width the law allowed. It was about 12 or 14 feet long. They built different sizes. The sides were made out of metal, the framing was wood and the top was flat. Every once in a while they would build a different one, a bigger size. The last two they built were sure enough big. They were built over in Chiefland, but I don't know how many rolling stores were built. There were shelves on each side and in the back except for the back window. There were things hanging from the ceiling too. We had everything that you could buy in a store.

Sometimes people would get up in it. Some did, some didn't want to and some were too old. If they wanted to come in they could. It had a step that was built on to it and hung out the door. The back door was a double door so the store could be closed up.

{Mrs. Parramore: He carried meats. He had an ice chest and had to get ice every morning, but later on they had a cooler that he hook up to electricity at night. Like charging a battery.}

I carried all kinds of cold drinks. I carried some ice cream packed in dry ice, but after I got that new unit I carried more ice cream. I got my ice at Barnes Ice. A black fellow named Ed Chambers worked there. We got dry ice out of Jacksonville.

We bought from people on the run most anything they had to sell from big cans of syrup to big cans of honey. We carried chickens and eggs too. I've handled my share of them.

{Mrs. Parramore: He loaded up every morning.}

Mr. White was going to change that. He had made plans to build me a big semi-rolling store where I could load up once a week or maybe twice a week so I wouldn't have to go and come so much, I would just keep going. But getting to some places would be a problem with a big one. With the size we had we could go to most places. There were a few places we couldn't get to.

{Mrs. Parramore: People would come out and meet him. When we first married he'd stay out to 12 or one o'clock on Saturday nights. They'd meet him right on.}

I worked mostly in Liberty County. There were some kind of times back then. I worked a lot in Gadsden County, but more so in Liberty County. I went from here to Sumatra straight through and come back up what was called River Road through Lake Mystic and so on in to Bristol and then home in one day. Six days a week. I had a different run each day.

People in the communities where I couldn't go with the store would walk a mile or two to buy groceries from me and they'd sit there if I was 12:00 at night getting there. They'd be there waiting to get groceries. It wasn't nothing for people to give me money to carry to Quincy State Bank. I have carried as high as $5,000 for people. Make bank deposits, pay their light bill and everything else.

At one time there was twelve rolling stores in this area. White's had two for a long time. Different people ran the other one, they couldn't keep nobody on. Miss Betts ran the other one for several years, and Mr. Ingram. I had been working for a construction company in Jacksonville and Mr. White asked me to come to work for him. I don't know how come he came to me, but he sat there until 1:00 one night begging me to come to work for him. I finally agreed, but he had to have a truck built before we could start. He had a farm on the other side of Quincy and he told me if I wanted to work some he would let me work out there on the farm until he got the truck ready. So I went to work out on the farm.

Mr. White told me when we were getting ready to start the rolling store, if you can bring in $350 a week that will pay off. Back then things were cheap. The first day we went out we took in about $600 or $700.

I started in 1936, and it wasn't long after I started there were twelve that I know of in this county. Just after we started they began to get more and more people. Two or three people came over from Alabama and started rolling stores, but they didn't last long.

I heard of a Maloy from Jackson County with a rolling store, but I didn't know him. Red Hall, Paul Moses, Spud Jacobs and Mr. Nix. There were also two brothers and I don't remember if they had two rolling stores apiece or one apiece, but they were some rough customers. They sold moonshine and everything else.

{Mrs. Parramore: Back before Prohibition, he used to sell sugar and never knew what is was used for.}

I used to sell sugar by the ton.

My daddy and mama were Robert and Minnie Parramore. Right up the road about a quarter of a mile is where I was born and reared. There were eleven children, Ferris is one of my brothers. Mr. Andrew was my daddy's brother. He still owned about 710 acres of land across from where my daddy lived. His wife Gertrude willed it to my daddy's and one cousin's children and they sold it.

{Mrs. Parramore: One man bought 300 acres and he has a six acre fish pond and a fine home. Part of the old Cannon place was sold and divided up in 10 acre lots.}

I don't think there were any rolling stores until about 1932 or 1933, during the Depression.

{Mrs. Parramore: When I was small, we went to town with a mule and wagon.}

Red Hall had the first rolling store that I every saw. His wife was Bonnie Hall and her sister was Daphne Layerd.

I didn't have a sign on the side of the rolling store at first, but most people called me Mr. White, and still do. I see some people at a store or around and they say, "How are you, Mr. White"? An old colored woman that used to trade with me called here Saturday night and she said, "Hey, Mr. White."

{Mrs. Parramore: She asked me if I was Robert Parramore's wife and I said yes. She said, "Well, I used to trade with him on the rolling store and I was just wanting to know how he was getting along." I said, "Well, would you like to talk to him"? She said, "Yes m'am, if he is able to come to the phone." So he went in there and talked to her. They all loved him.}

I had a different run for each day. I had Wednesdays off, but by the time I got it loaded and shaped up it took a half day.

{Mrs. Parramore: He had to keep books, because he did credit business, too. After he got to where he shook so bad he couldn't write I kept his books for him.}

Anybody who has ever done credit business gets burned sooner or later, but they could count it off a certain amount on income tax.

{Mrs. Parramore: I had one man come to the house one day after Robert was off the rolling store and he said to me, "I'm so and so and I owe Mr. Parramore some money from the rolling store and I want to pay it." And he paid it. He said he was trying to get right with the Lord and he owed that bill and wanted to pay it. Two or three people sent payment in the mail. Robert kept the money on the rolling store in a cigar box. He did all his figuring in his head and he could add just as fast and good as anybody.}

One of my customers told me one day that he had been checking behind me ever since he started trading with me and I ain't never found a mistake that you made. He asked me how I did it and I told him, I don't know I was just good in math in school.

{Mrs. Parramore: Robert graduated from high school and back then not too many graduated from high school. He could add real well and he used it every day.}

I went to school in Quincy and graduated in 1930. Even though there were eleven children in our family and it was during the Depression my daddy was a good manager. He did farming and logging work, he kept them busy all the time. He dealt in real estate for a while, selling land.

{Mrs. Parramore: Mr. Parramore and Uncle Ralph bought a bunch of land for fifty cents an acre way back then, and when they sold it I think they got about $45 an acre for it.
{Mrs. Parramore adds: I was an Edwards, my grandmother was a Hawkins. My mother was Mittie Fletcher and Papa was Meade Edwards. His daddy was Dan Edwards and his mother was Florence Hawkins Edwards. She was an only child and her father died with malaria or something in the Civil War. She came from Liberty County. I don't know if she was related to any of these Hawkins or not.}

Something Gold

Somebody else that had a rolling store was Mayo Flournoy. The body of his rolling store is still in the front yard where he died and left it. His wife never had it moved. The body of a rolling store sat on a wide bodied truck, not a pickup truck.

My grandson Jimmy rode with me about three or four years during the summer when he wasn't in school. He called it his job and he was good help too. Then Mike worked with me one summer before he started to college. We were married in 1949. We have nine grandchildren, two step-grandchildren and five great-grandchildren, one just born yesterday in Colorado Springs, Colorado. Three boys and two girls.

We bogged down one time in the Apalachicola National Forest near Telogia going toward Sumatra. Back then there wasn't anything round there but forest roads and they weren't kept up too well. One morning we went to a fellow's house in the woods about seven or eight miles back that we had been going to all the time. But it had been raining a lot and when I drove in, the truck settled down so that the back door where you walk in was level with the ground. We worked all day trying to get that thing out of there. Finally we got some big poles and jacked it up on them and got it out on a little higher land. I didn't spend that night there, but I have spent nights bogged down or something happened to the truck and there was nowhere to call anybody. We carried sacks of horse feed so I'd just roll out some and sleep on them until somebody would come along the next morning. They'd go to a telephone and call the boss and tell him I was broke down or bogged down. I never got held up, but there were times when I was sure scared 'cause I would have all the money I'd take in during the day plus checks that people gave me to put in the bank for them. I sure wouldn't do it now 'cause it has sure changed since then.

{Mrs. Parramore: A long time ago people used to give him squirrel meat, turkey meat and things like that.}

There were some boys down there below Bristol -- brothers, and they stayed in the swamp all the time. About all they did for a living was hunt and fish. I've brought fish out of there by the wash tub full. I didn't bring them home. I'd sell them. It was against the law and I got so near to getting caught selling some. The game warden knew I was selling and one evening when I was waiting on his wife, he said, "Robert, I got to talk to you a little." I said, "Okay, what you want, Mr. Bloomie"? He was Bloomie Shuler. I liked him. He was a fine old man. He said, "I know you been buying fish." I said, "Yessir, I ain't going to lie." He said, "I know you got some in there now. I'm telling you you've been reported so don't get no more." I sold them and did what he said. When I went back the next week the man had a tub full of the prettiest bream. I didn't take them and got out of the fish selling.

{Mrs. Parramore: I went to Sawdust School, the only one in the eighth grade. Two of our teachers were Carmalotta Fletcher and Miss Pearl Fern that married George Edwards. I think she boarded with them when she came here to teach and that's how they met. Another teacher was Miss Audrey McKenzie. She married a Sanders. I think she was from Crawfordville or somewhere down there. I went to Greensboro to high school. Mildred went to Palmer School in DeFuniak Springs. The Presbyterian Church sent Mildred the last few years of her high school over there and then they sent her to Atlanta to nurses' training. There was nine in my family, I was fourth from the oldest.}

The rolling store also sold kerosene. We had two 55 gallon drums, one on each side held on with metal straps. Back then people used kerosene for lamps, stoves and everything else.

{Mrs. Parramore: When the chickens saw the rolling store coming they'd get on the nest and try as hard as they could to lay an egg and if they couldn't they'd get down and cross their feet cause they knew they were gone to the rolling store. This was told me by a man!}

When you go in to Chattahoochee from Greensboro where the road forks and one goes to Liberty County and one goes to Chattahoochee I'd carry the regular egg cases that you put eggs in but I had filled up the case and went on and bought some more from two or three or four people, I don't know how many dozen, and I went to turn the corner down there and they everyone rolled out on the floor. I never will forget that. I have never seen so many broken eggs in my life. I was just leaving a lady's house and she was good enough to give me some things to clean with.

{Mrs. Parramore: He carried fresh vegetables and canned goods, dry goods, shoes and a lot of things he didn't carry they would order through him and he would go to town and buy them. He didn't carry too many toys.}

I went to a lot of tobacco barns. One was Hubert Clark's. I never will forget one time, it was tobacco time and when they saw a rolling store they just quit work and come to the rolling store. They waved me down so I stopped and he came out and got all over me and told me he didn't want me to come here anymore and stop on my place and get my workers stopped. I'm going to have something done about this. I said, no sir you're not going to have anything done about it because we pay taxes to run this truck and I ain't on your property. I'm on the state highway and there ain't nothing you can do about it. That made him mad 'cause he knew there was nothing he could do about it. And I had a run-in with Adrian Fletcher. He told me he wanted me to quit stopping at his place -- he was paying them to work not to meet the rolling store. Well, later on one afternoon the road going from his place into Sycamore through the cemetery they were gathering tobacco and they saw us coming and they just walked out in the road in front of us. They knew he told us not to stop, but we stopped. He came up there to get on me, but I told him the same thing. I said we did not stop here, they got in the road and you didn't want us to run over them did you, he said no. About that time one of the workers spoke up and said yes sir, he didn't stop, we stopped him. That ended that.

My route took me mostly to tenant houses, but I would stop for anybody that waved me down. We carried plows and everything for horses, ax handles to you-name-it. Farmers were as glad to see us as the workers. In the spring we sold seed. All kinds of people traded with me. I had people with plenty of money that would trade with me rather than go to town. Martha and Boony Stoutamire used to trade with me.

Two or three ladies were always baking us a pie for the rolling store. None of them made it home though. One of the ladies was Mary Loney. She lived across from Alfred Shuler.

{Mrs. Parramore: I drove the school bus for Quincy ten years from 1967 to 1977. I stopped in 1977. At first I drove the Lake Talquin run and I kept the bus here at night. I started out at 7:00 in the morning and I hauled elementary and high school on that run. Because it was such a long run they couldn't afford to send two buses down there. That was before integration. I got off of that run, I said I was going to quit, but one of the men that was on another run above town quit and they asked me to run that one. So that one I ran two different runs. A high school run and an elementary run. The high school run was from Quincy to St. Johns School and the elementary run was from Quincy to Joe Allen road and back. We had defensive driving courses every year and they would tell us about all these things, wrecks and all those things. I would think to myself, "What in the world am I doing on this school bus?" But I got through it.}

A certificate on the wall reads: Harriett E. Parramore … In recognition of ten years outstanding service as a bus driver … Gadsden County School Board 1977.

Mrs. Parramore remembers this about firing a tobacco barn:

The Barn-Firing Party

It was when cigarette tobacco was cured by wood heat. That night several of us sat up all night and kept the wood heat going. This was Uncle Deck Fletcher and Uncle Tom Fletcher's children. They did it often, but this was my one and only time. So we made a party out of it. One boy went to sleep on the ground. His mouth was open and another boy put a toad-frog in it. Needless to say, he awoke!

Twenty-four
Fount May
Backporch at Sawdust
May 18, 1999

My brother Don and I inherited May Tobacco Company from my father and uncle and in the process he ran the farms and grew the tobacco and I ran the packing house and did the packing and it made a good arrangement for the two of us.

When you pack tobacco it comes in from the farm in a cured state it has to be "in case," what we call "cased" is tobacco that has been taken down in early morning hours when moisture is in the air and it makes the tobacco soft and pliable like a cloth, like material. They box it up and bring it to the packing house and as it is received it's weighed in. Originally it was put in bulks. A bulk of tobacco is a platform. The tobacco is laid down hand by hand in layers, usually making layers or reams up to twenty reams high, no more than that and would hold around 5,000 pounds of tobacco. In that bulk was a tube you could put a thermometer in to have the readings of the internal heat of the bulk. Because in this bulking process it was used to generate its own heat, it was a continuing of the curing that had been started in the barn. This though was with heat and moisture or the release of the moisture. The bulk was turned at least three times and during that time it was a complete reversal. What went in on the bottom ended up, on the turn, on the top and what was on the inside ended up on the outside. That gave you a uniformity and your fermented heating and drying process. This process made the colors run even better and made the leaf more uniform.

At the end of approximately four weeks time the tobacco had gone through the heating process and was then boxed up. After it went through the bulking process it was taken up and boxed and held in boxes until time for it to go to the sorting room. To get it ready for the sorting room it was then unboxed and each hand was hung individually in a casing room where under high humidity and fan it was given back the degree of moisture it needed to handle it. Then it was taken down into the sorting room and each leaf was gone through individually by women, approximately 50 women. They went through each leaf of tobacco pulling out off color and torn tobacco and other degrees of tobacco that were undesirable thus giving you a uniformed hand of cigar wrapping tobacco. It was then repacked in bale pound lots -- a bale of tobacco being approximately 100 pounds.

Then from that point it went in to what we called the heating room and there under high heat and high fans it went through the gradual drying out process making it ready for sale. At that time it was then sampled and each bale labeled. It might be interesting to mention at this time, when tobacco came in, it came in by priming and shade in names. And it stayed that way. It was identified by the shade crop and the pickin' from the stalk which was the priming and it was sold that way. A priming usually consisted of going through the entire crop getting approximately two leaves at a time. You started out with sand leaves and then first middles on up, depending on the crop, to about fifth middles or sixth middles and then the tops and that would complete an entire crop.

In later years we gave up bulking tobacco and started using the hot room entirely. That is, when it came in from the farm it would be put in boxes and then put in the hot room and it would artificially go through the same fermentation and heat process it had in the bulk only by boxing it and putting it in the hot room this required less handling, less labor, and a more uniform system of curing in the packing house.

That was the only main change that was made during my lifetime within the packing house. After it was baled and ready for sale it could stay stored for years as long as you kept tobacco bugs out of it. There was no limitation on when it had to leave the packing house, but if you were lucky it was sold and moved out by next spring before the new crop came in. And that's about the story of the packing house.

May Tobacco Company, as I knew it, was founded by my father, Fount H. May, Sr. and Fred L. May right after World War I around 1920 and at that time they secured a building just off the square in Quincy at 103 E. Washington Street which prior to their packing venture was a wagon and buggy agency downstairs and Dr. Davis' office was upstairs. They converted this store building into a packing house and added the sorting room across the back. It was used as a packing house until closed with the phasing out of tobacco in 1970.

I was born on what we call May Farm, that's the home place, therefore was exposed to the growing of tobacco all of my life.

My first job was 10 cents a day being gate boy, they were just babysitting for me at that time. But then I went on to work in the barn, I never worked in the fields, but I worked in the barn and became stick man and then in the end I was barn boss. About that time I went into the service and got married and came back and then went in to the packing end of it.

May Tobacco Company through the years acquired two other farms, May Farm being the home place and we bought a farm nearby called the Ball Farm, and we had a farm in Havana called the Shelfer Farm. The May and Ball farms grew about 40 acres each a year on those farms and approximately 20 acres on the Shelfer Farm which gave us an annual packing of around 100 acres. It was not feasible to run a packing house with less than 100 acres of tobacco. It would be cost prohibitive if you got less than that.

May Farm was located on Woodward Road. I don't know about the road numbers, but I think it's 270, but I could be corrected on that. Ball Farm was off State Road 12 (the Havana Hwy.) about 2 miles northeast of Quincy. Shelfer Farm was located right at Havana, part of it actually in the city limits of Havana at a crossroads called Old Salem.

We have two tobacco barns left on May Nursery which we use as storage. I might mention at this point that after tobacco went out rather than liquidate and sell out we utilized the land we had, and equipment, and went into the nursery business making the Shelfer Farm which was the most adaptable into a container grown nursery for landscape plants for the northern market. On May Farm there are about four barns still left, and Ball Farm we have since sold.

The products we grow at the nursery for the northern market are primarily azaleas and junipers, and as we call them, other broadleaf evergreens. If it's hardy enough to grow in New England we grow it, if not we don't grow it. It has been a very good venture for both of us, my brother and I, he has since passed and I'm retired. His two sons and my two sons now own and operate it successfully.

The business end of tobacco growing was usually financed by a manufacturer whether it be a large one or a small one. We happened to always have a small manufacturer in Pennsylvania that wanted our tobacco and he was our primary source of financing. However, people like King Edward and Swisher Company we also dealt with them, and with all of that we had one broker, a man from Baltimore that handled all of our selling for us and sold off grades and the by-products of the tobacco for us.

To my knowledge, one year was never like another. Some were good. My uncle used to describe it like sharecropping, sometimes you were even, but never ahead. But it did make a living for four families and to my knowledge only one year was a complete wipe-out. My father did not grow a crop of tobacco in 1933. But by him not doing that I got to go with him on trip up to Niagara Falls. At my age that didn't bother me.

The beginning of the May family here in Gadsden County came with my great-grandfather Joel Farris May who came in the 1820s and he was a tailor until the time he bought what is May Farm, the home place in 1855. He had been living in Quincy. His home is where the present house of Mort Bates is now and Frank May built right next door. My grandfather inherited the farm and it has been in the family since 1855 and tobacco of one description or another has been grown out there during this period.

Prior to the shade grown tobacco I'm sure the tobacco my grandfather grew was of a different type and I have heard that in the curing of it they cured it sort of like burley tobacco is cured now in Kentucky. They cut the stalk down, then spear it and hang it upside down in barns that are not as elaborate as the shade grown tobacco barns. I really am not familiar enough with that to give a good account of that crop, but they did grow tobacco prior to shade grown tobacco.

The house of May Farm is the original house that my grandfather built to raise his family. It's still standing and in good repair and good use. I was born out there in 1919 and lived the first six years of my life out there.

Our packing house on Washington Street is now used as a restaurant and it has rental property, offices and one apartment upstairs. The upstairs has been made into living quarters.

May Tobacco Company packing house, as I said, was a wagon and buggy agency and between it and the corner where the Leaf Theater now stands was a livery stable and in between our packing house and the livery stable was a pen where they kept the horses.

In 1944 I married Carolyn Brinson from Monticello. Her parents were Dr. Jack and Martha Brinson. In this marriage we had three children, Fount, Jr. and Martha and John Bradford. Fount, Jr. married Beth Suber, Mr. E. L. Suber's granddaughter. Martha married Bill Sapp, A.D. and Ruth Sapps's son, and Bradford married Crystle Johnson, one of those many Johnsons and Edwards and Fletchers from Gadsden County. All live in Quincy. Out of those marriages I have a total of eight grandchildren.

Twenty-five
J. L. (James Louie) Barineau
Kitchen at Sawdust
March 23, 2006

Eugene Griffin was my cousin and he lived with us on my granddaddy and father's farm. He was a carpenter and he was a bachelor. Carpentering was his profession and building shade tobacco barns and repairing them was his specialty.

Mr. Griffin had a technique of building barns that was so good. I'd say it was the way he braced them. He put braces east and west and then north and south with long timber. They would stand quite a bit of wind. He was definitely known as one of the better barn builders in the county.

I grew up on that farm in south Decatur County. I was born in 1918 and lived there until 1941. On this farm we produced cigarette tobacco which is very different from shade tobacco. Cigarette tobacco was introduced to South Georgia in 1925. My dad grew one of the first crops that was grown and he continued to produce it as a money crop as long as he farmed.

Ross and Ida Barineau were my father and mother. My dad was a farmer and my mother was a school teacher and she taught school in Faceville, Georgia for four years and then moved to Attapulgus for the next 25 years until she retired. I graduated from Attapulgus High School in 1935 along with my wife Nita. We were classmates from the sixth grade through high school.

During 1929 was whenever we had the stock market crash. During the thirties, which was known as the great depression, and unless you lived through it why there is no way to explain just how bad it was. Living on a farm we always had plenty to eat, but money was a different story. If you could find any work that would produce some cash money you certainly took it. So after I finished high school I did not go to college. I stayed on the farm to help my father. And in the meantime Mr. Gene Griffin was in the process of building tobacco barns in Gadsden County and the following winter, after most of our work on the farm was done, I helped him build tobacco barns and we built quite a few in Decatur and in Gadsden County. We built some barns for Dick Shaw. He could have very well been the fellow who built the first slat shade. I can remember building five for one company, Emory Collins Tobacco Company, which was located north of the Quincy Airport. In 1938 we were repairing a barn for Mr. Forrest Davis. We had about a week's work and since I was with Mr. Gene Griffin and he was invited to lunch everyday, I was invited also. And it was Sunday dinner every day and it's something I've never forgotten.

In 1939, I was fortunate enough to get a job with the Attapulgus Clay Company which is the Fuller's earth mine. But then in 1940 war clouds were hanging over Europe. Germany had already invaded Poland so they initiated the draft. If I remember correct everybody 18 to 28 had to register for the draft. You were given a number and then the President of the United States drew out the numbers from a fish bowl which would determine how soon you would go. I had a low draft number so I decided not to wait. On January 15, 1941, I enlisted in the U.S. Army Air Force and was stationed at McDill, Florida. From there I was sent to radio school in Scott Field, Illinois. I completed that course in September 1941. December 7, 1941 was Pearl Harbor. Of course immediately after that everything changed. The United States at that time was in no position to fight a war, but I reckon just by providence everybody pulled together. They began to made war supplies and everything. They did get the planes and ships built fast enough to eventually win the war, but it was quite trying times.

In January 1942, I was sent to gunnery school in Las Vegas, Nevada to get my training for air service. When I came to Barksdale Field in Louisiana, that's where the outfit was when I returned. Stayed there a short time and then got orders to report to Ft. Myers, Florida. And there I was assigned to a B-24 group which was known as Halpro or Halverson Project. I was a radio operator and top turret gunner on B-24s. This Halverson Project, we were selected from the 98th bomb group that was stationed at Ft. Myers. Prior to that Jimmy Doolittle with B-25s had initiated a raid on Japan from the carriers close to Japan. We were a task force and we were headed to China. We were going to bomb Tokyo from a base in China, but on the way we stopped in Khartoum, Sudan and at that time German General Rommel was making a move through the desert trying to get control of the Suez Canal so he could get control of the Middle East oil. Our orders were changed and we were assigned with the British to do bombing missions all along the North African ports, all those ports. That's what we did for several months. Finally at El Alemain the British got Rommel turned around. The world made a drastic change then. They started driving him out of Africa and as he moved back why we moved up in the desert and continued to fly and bomb the ports where they were bringing in the supplies. And eventually we were able to move him out of Africa, then we started bombing southern Italy. When we arrived in Africa we thought we would be there for the duration of the war, but as providence I reckon they finally told us when we had completed 300 combat hours we could come home.

I completed my 300 combat hours when we were stationed at a place called Suluch, which was about 30 miles south of Benghazi. My last mission was to Naples in Italy. When I returned home, I left Cairo, Egypt on Easter Sunday morning in 1943. That morning when we took off it was solid overcast. We got above the clouds and then the sun came up over the clouds. Now you talk about a pretty Easter sunrise, that was it. We landed at Khartoum to change planes. When I walked into the mess hall or dining room I looked over there and there was a nurse from my home town. It was just unbelievable. She had enlisted in the service, an Army nurse. She was on her way over and since we were going to be there awhile why I had a long talk with her. It was just something to see her, meet her on the way over. She is still living today. She lives in Augusta, Georgia. She was originally from Dothan. Her aunt lived about two miles from us and she spent a lot of time visiting there and I got to know her.

Anybody that said they wasn't scared was just telling a fib to be honest with you. You always kinda felt like when you went out there was a very good chance that you wouldn't come back and of course some of my buddies didn't come back.

The nearest community that I lived in was close to Bettstown. A lot of people know where Bettstown is. There were three brothers came down from South Carolina and established Bettstown. It was quite a flourishing place. We lived about a mile from Bettstown.

After high school Nita went on to college. She became a teacher and during her teaching days we were courting pretty heavy. When I went in the service in 1941 course I got home on furlough and got to see her once in awhile. Now in 1942 whenever I knew it wouldn't be too long before I would be going over she consented to marry me. She was taking an awful gamble, but she consented. On April 11, 1942 we were married in Ft. Myers. Mother came down with her and on a Saturday afternoon we went to the Methodist parsonage and it was a production line waiting to be married. There were two couples ahead of us that the preacher married and then we were the third couple.

In fact we left the states on May 20, 1942 and our outfit dropped the first bombs by American bombers on the continent of Europe during WWII. Upon returning to the United States after my service I was assigned to Salt Lake City for reassignment and I asked them to send me as far back east as I could go and they assigned me to Dyersburg, Tennessee which was the final phase training for B-27 pilots and crews. I spent the rest of the war there. We were fortunate enough Nita came up and we lived off base for the rest of the time which was very good. Our daughter Anita was born in January while I was overseas, and Nita was living with her parents.

{Mrs. Barineau: My daddy was William Riley Thomas and he was a foreman for AST Company. They lived at Watauga, which was about 2 miles east of Attapulgus. All those farms had a letter and our farm was "V" with the AST Company. Mr. Joe Cantey lived about 2 miles down the road, Mr. Ed Smith lived in between and his farm was "S" and Mr. Joe was "C," but I'm not positive.}

The war with Japan ended in September 1945 I believe, thereabouts. I was discharged on September 15, 1945. I returned home and with all of us service men coming home jobs were kinda scarce. Of course, they had the GI bill which anyone who wanted to could take advantage of and go to college. That was one of the greatest things that ever happened to service men or to this country because there were so many that went on and got their degree and helped make the United States what it was after the war. But since I was married, I felt like I needed to go to work. I was offered a job with the A. L. Wilson Company in Quincy. I worked for them for one year. My uncle, Marvin Barineau, and his partner were in the lumber business. It was going pretty good and he took me under his wing and I went to work for them. I worked for them for eight years in the lumber company. Marvin had purchased a pretty good size farm right near home where we were living and they had grown shade tobacco in a small way for some time but he wanted to get into shade tobacco in a big way because it was going pretty good at that time. Having the sawmills and all it wasn't any trouble for them to get the lumber so started building tobacco barns. A Mr. Johnny Davis who lived at Gibson was the carpenter and built those barns and I was the one that was to take over and operate the farm. So in 1955 I came to the farm and we started building shades and getting ready to produce tobacco. This was a farm that Marvin owned. He and his partner Mack McCall had a large farm. We made it into a corporation. It was known as Barineau and McCall Farms on the Attapulgus Highway about a mile from the Georgia line in the white house where we are living now on Barineau Road.

After we got the shades built, and we built quite a few, you had to rotate the shades -- you couldn't plant in them two years in a row. One year we would have 28 acres and the next year we would have 33 acres just depending on which shades were up. The first year we grew for King Edward Tobacco Company and packed it with the co-op. Adrian Fletcher, Thomas Smith and Maurice Owens had formed a co-op and we packed with them that year. But the next year a company by the name of CULBRO came down from Connecticut and they wanted to get a foothold in Florida. They asked if we would like to produce tobacco for them. We consented and it was one of the best things that ever happened to us. For the rest of the time that I grew tobacco which I grew my last crop in 1973, we produced tobacco for Cullman Tobacco Company which was CULBRO and later became General Cigar. Our tobacco, most of it which was the number one grade, went on what was the White Owl cigar. And most of the other tobacco grown in Gadsden County either went on the King Edward cigar or the Hav-A-Tampa cigar. That was a ten-cent cigar which was a little higher priced cigar than your King Edward cigar and the other.

In about 1961 or so they put an embargo on Cuban tobacco. Cuba had developed a method of fire curing wrapping tobacco which nobody here had ever tried. The Candela was fire cured. So they asked us if we would consent to Candela some. We did and started modifying two of the large barns which were 42 x 160 and modifying them so we could fire cure it. Cullman had connections with the Cubans who had fled Cuba to Miami and they brought these Cubans up to help us so it would be cured as it was supposed to. They did the curing. We put it in the barn and they cured it for us. The Cuban that was in charge of our curing was Silvio Perez. And even after we went out of the tobacco business Silvio and I exchanged Christmas cards up until his death which was about two years ago.

I could communicate with him but the ones he brought up that actually stayed with the barns and did the firing could not speak English. He was the go-between. They all went back to South Florida. Before Castro deported them, Silvio had been the superintendent on a large Cuban farm. They probably cure tobacco both ways in Cuba now.

The good part about the Candela method was that within about 45 hours after it was put in the barn it was completely cured and it was cured completely green. Then you had to put it through what was called a mulling process and it would come out an olive drab color and that went on expensive cigars. Now why they wanted it that I couldn't tell you because I'm sure it probably affected the taste some, it had to. That's the way they wanted it and the good part about it you would come out with a lot higher percentage of number one wrapper than if you cured it the other way. The first two primings we cured natural and from then on the center part of the plant we Candela it. Now King Edward was paying their farmers $3.75 for what was called number one string. I don't know what the other companies were paying, but I know they were paying $3.75. But this Candela number one wrapper we were contracting it for $6.00 a pound and it was really a life saver. It really didn't cost all that much more to do it. Everything was the same way except the curing. That was the only difference. To modify the barns we had to take corrugated paper and go all the way through and seal it airtight. All the workers had to do was go in once in a while to check it and get out as quick as they could. Since we had it in those sections we'd fill one full section in a day and got out and then they started to firing. Then we'd fill up the other end the next day the same way. There were no workers in there when it was being fired.

In the center section, when I was telling you about mulling it, you took that tobacco down after it was cured and hung it in that center section just as close as you could get it. Then I had to watch it real close and keep it to a certain case, or degree of moisture. And that is what's called mulling -- it would change the color of it to that olive drab color. Then when it was through mulling, we'd send it to the packing house. The packing house that we packed it in was right up town there in Greensboro. That packing house right near the caution light. We did business with Ed Fletcher and his brother Max and there was another Mr. Fletcher that lived at Providence that grew for Culbro.

I have a lot of kinfolks. I have three aunts that lived in the Greensboro community. My Aunt Florence Cumbie who lived right up town. My Aunt Susie who married Horace Clark. There was Uncle Horace, Mr. Lonnie Clark and Mr. Spurgeon Clark -- those three brothers in a settlement south of Flat Creek. On up the road lived Adrian Fletcher, a short distance from them. Juniper was the community. The Van Landinghams lived there. My other Aunt Hannah married Lem Suber. They had a lot of children.

During harvesting season I think we had as high as 120 workers. It took a lot of hand labor to take care of it. So many of the families had their own homes and all. The men worked at the Attapulgus Clay Company at the mines. We were fortunate enough to get help from their families. Now we did have four families that lived on the farm there year around. We had one minor hail damage, it wasn't too much and the insurance company paid off. It wasn't a great amount. Good gracious, we fought blue mold all the time and other diseases, too, and insects.

One of the things that both of us are very proud of, in 1964, we were chosen as the Farm Family of the Year from Gadsden County. Now that was something, I think, that was initiated by the *Tallahassee Democrat*. The editor was Malcolm Johnson and I think he was the one that started it. I believe the nominating committee probably came out of Farm Bureau and the county agent. On that weekend we went to Tallahassee to the Floridin Hotel. It was the biggest hotel in Tallahassee at that time. It's gone now. All of the families came to that hotel for the weekend. On the banquet night Supreme Court Justice Millard Caldwell was our speaker. That is something we remember quite well. The most satisfying thing about growing tobacco was if you knew you had a good crop to put it in the packing house and then when we were sorting it you could go to the packing house and you could see your tobacco and you knew you that you had a real good crop and everything was going to come out real good. It was a very satisfying feeling after going through all that stress. There's no other stress in the world like it because if you had one real bad crop you probably wouldn't be able to overcome it.

The last crop that I grew in 1973 it cost $5,500 an acre just to get it ready for the packing house. It just got too expensive. About 1970, John Lewis Taylor who was my buddy and a tobacco farmer just across the Georgia line, he was the son of Mr. Jimmy Taylor who was a big tobacco farmer. John Lewis took over the farm from his father when he passed away. He and I, you remember Ish Allen who sold cheesecloth and twine, well he was selling cheesecloth and twine in Nicaragua and Honduras. So John Lewis and I took it on ourselves to go with him to Nicaragua just to see how it was. And we got to travel to those farms in Nicaragua and we saw they had all of our know-how. You drove up to those farms and you would think you were driving right up to a farm here in Gadsden County. Now they could produce it for a third or less than what it was costing us. Also, here at home, cigar companies were developing a synthetic wrapper for cheap cigars. Well, we saw the handwriting on the wall. There wasn't no way that we were going to be able to compete and stay in business so I told the company that '73 was going to be my last crop and it was one of the best moves that I ever made.

There was no further use for the barns, of course. One of the barns (people were wanting the lumber and all) was being torn down. I don't know if they dropped a cigarette or what, and it was one of the barns that had that corrugated paper in it and that particular barn burned up. But the others were all torn down except one. There's one right by my house.

We had a large herd of Black Angus cattle. We kept those cattle to make compost. Compost was a very necessary thing for shade tobacco. I kept the herd and then I went to trying with corn, wheat and some soybeans and I continued to farm on until 1980 and then I decided it was time to hang it up. That's when I did, in 1980.

We have three grandchildren and three great-grandchildren. Ed Gibson is our daughter Anita's husband. They had two girls, Joy and Amy. Our son Jimmy had one girl, Meghan. She is now going to TCC in her fourth year. April 11, Nita and I will celebrate our 64th wedding anniversary.

Discussing barn-building:

The barns that we built, just about all of them were 42' x 120'. Four of those five that Johnny Davis built for us, four of them were 42' x 160'. We'd have at least six or more for a crew. The pillars were laid. The first section under the barn, you built that one section to start with. You anchored it real good and the rest of it a section at the time. You would lay it right back down on the rafters and you would build that complete section. We had two sets of block and tackle. You'd hook one block and tackle on this side and one on this side and hook it to the stud that was going up. Course, two of us would get on that rope and pull it until you got it up right, and when you got it up right then you had men to go up and anchor it. Then you would brace it good enough that whenever you built the next section you could pull it up and you just continue to do that until got the barn framed. One stall at a time.

Now I was talking here at the barn the other day to Forrest, Jr. (your brother) and he said after that they got to where they would build all of those sections at one time, just lay them right on top of one another. Then whenever they got ready to raise it why they'd just go in there raise it up one at a time. Except that first section. That first section had to be built and anchored good so you would have something to anchor to pull it up. They had improved on the way to build barns from how we did it back in the 30s.

Back then, brick pillars were laid. All the sills were 6x6's. The studs were 4x4's. The weatherboard was either 1x6 or 1x8 pine, roughsawn. Tierpoles were 2x4 rough pine. Rafters and braces were 2x6's. Braces had to be out of long timber. Sheeting in the barn was 1x4's, rough. And the roof was cypress or pine. Later, Johnny Davis (the builder) went to aluminum roofing. But in the shingle days, shingles were put on from the bottom. Each shingler had a partner. We were given a 16-foot straight-edge (a 1x4). The shingle had to have overlap except for 4 inches. You'd go to the top. You had a "task" (a certain portion to finish) – if you got that done, you could go home. Roscoe Cumbie was good – give him a mouthful of nails and there was no way I could keep up with him!

Today, to build a shade tobacco barn, you would need real good timber to be able to do it like it ought to be. We never did paint the barns. Our farm was called Barineau and McCall Farm, Inc. The farm Nita is talking about just had that letter. All those farms were known by a letter. Mrs. Barnineau said she believes Mr. Cantey's farm was "R." She also said she was the only daughter and her daddy said she was not supposed to work in tobacco that "I had to help cook, so that's what I did."

The windlass was how we got our well water. It was made from a log and it had an axle in each end of it along with a handle. The chain wrapped around the log and the bucket was fastened to the end of the chain and you would unwind the windlass and let it down and then when your bucket got to the water and filled why then you'd draw it, wind it back up. You also got the pulley type with the ropes and all. And also we had the ones that had the long buckets. The well itself was narrow and it had a long bucket and the water would come in from the bottom and fill it up and it would trap itself in that bucket. {Mrs. Barineau: We had a bathroom. There was a barrel at the well and they'd fill it with well water and had pipes running to the house. It was almost like indoor plumbing.}

Discussing when the McCall House was moved to Nicholson Farmhouse Restaurant:

The McCall house was built in 1905. After I went to work for the lumber company we moved into the McCall house which was just down from where we built our house now. We lived in the new house and used the McCall house kind of as a store house. Mr. Paul Nicholson asked my cousin Tommy if he knew of any old houses he might could move to his set-up there. Tommy told him about this one. So Sunday morning he knocked on the door after he'd gone down and looked at it. He asked me if I would be willing to sell it to him. What I wanted to do was get rid of it because there was no way I could restore it. I told him if he would move it I'd give it to him. He said no I want to give you something for it. But he moved that house, and it was a large house, and I had no idea they could move it in one piece, but they did. He used it at the business. They added a 30-foot section to the back. The main dining room would seat 100 or more people.

When we quit farming we had seven mules. I got rid of all of them but one. I kept one to work my garden. That mule lived to be almost 30 years old and 20 years is old for a mule, but we took good care of her and she lived about that long. Anyway after she passed away all of her gear and everything was in this house. I gave it to him. All of her plows and sweeps and scooters and everything were on the wall. Not long after, Mr. Nicholson was killed in South America and some time after that, the McCall house burned. It was a real heartbreak all around.

I had three great uncles that were killed in the Civil War. All of them enlisted in Quincy.

Mr. Barineau adds a footnote: Sarrah McCall Glover (Mack McCall's sister) was the farm bookkeeper. Wesley Catledge & Co. was the CPA. During all those years, we never received one call from the IRS.

Louie and Nita Barineau in front of their one remaining barn, Barineau Road north of Quincy.   (Photo by son Jimmy)

Twenty-six
Max Fletcher
Fletcher Home in Greensboro
August 17, 2006

The associations I have of tobacco are a whole lot of tension, long hours and hard work. My first memory was setting tobacco and my back hurt so bad by the time I got to the end of the row. I must've been about five (or six or seven) years old, I guess.

I was born in Quincy, I believe. I've lived in Greensboro all my life, except for a couple of years in the Marine Corps, in the Korean conflict. My parents were Thomas Bertell and Elvira Hentz Fletcher.

Kay: So that's where the name "Elvira Farm" came from?

Yeah.

Kay: What about the "Susanna Farm"?

The Susanna Farm was my older brother Edward's. The Susanna Farm was out in Providence, where Fernlea Nursery is now. It formerly belonged to Mr. Lem Suber and he wanted to retire, I think, and when Edward came back out of the Service in WWII, he bought that farm from Mr. Lem. Edward and I were the main ones (to grow tobacco). Hal and Howard had farms, but neither one of them actively farmed. They had somebody else doing it for them – mainly Daddy.

Kay: Your Daddy grew shade tobacco in the early 20s – where would his farm have been?

We're sitting on part of it (Fletcher home, just west of Greensboro High School). It went north. Well, in this part of the farm, it would probably have been 120 acres or so. Then he had other land scattered in smaller parcels. He died in 1969, I believe.

I farmed before I went into the Service, for a year or so after I got out of the U. of Florida. I came back out of the Service in 1953. Married Kathryn (McFarlin) in 1951. She grew up on a tobacco farm. She still owns half of it – she and her sister Annette own it together. It's about three miles north of Quincy on the Attapulgus Hwy.

I grew my last crop in 1975. There were some people who grew a few more years after that.

My oldest sister (Louise) just died this year. (Tells that there were eight children in Bertell and Elvira's family.) All the children worked when they were growing up – stringing, waiting tables. Everybody worked. I don't think Helen worked so much in the field; she had an eye condition, worked mostly in the house.

Kay: Your work crew, I assume, were mostly black? And lived on the place?

Yes. There were Jacksons – a lot of Jacksons. Also, Preshas, which is really Porcher (P-o-r-c-h-e-r), but they call it Presha and some of 'em spell it "P-r-e-s-h-a." They were all from Sawdust, I think.

Kay: So you had those families, and they were a carry-over from the early days?

Yes. All of my workers lived on the farm. Later, I hauled in a few, but most of 'em were right on the farm. They got along pretty well until Saturday night. We had to go down and separate 'em every once in awhile. Well, they were people. They had disagreements at home and out on the job. The worst ones were right in the same family – brothers and sisters.

Kay: Did you have any major disasters, like fires?

Oh, several barns.

Kay: Your daddy, or you?

Well, both.

Kay: Full of tobacco?

Yes, we had one on Aunt Clara's place, that I was responsible for. I was a boy and I was firing it that day, and it burned that night. I think everybody has a barn (burning) story. John has one – my next-older brother. We had one to burn in a hurricane. That was probably in the 60s.

Kay: Now, that property where they're building the new school (West Gadsden High School) – was that part of yours?

No, my Grandfather Badger's brother, Daniel Fletcher, inherited that part of the original farm. And it belongs to his grandson, Charlie Macon, now.

Kay: So Mr. Macon is a Fletcher, too!

His mother and my father (Bertell) were first cousins.

Kay: Did you have any white workers?

Yes. I had school kids every summer. We had one or two white people who worked year-round. Mr. John Goodwin … I had one named Roy Cheshire, who figured out why the weather turned so sour. He said, well he lisped and he said, "Mr. Max, I know whath wrong with thith weather. It's cause they let thoth athronauts go up there and pith on the moon"!

Most of our white workers were neighbors. I remember Olivia Hiers worked with us. She was just a little older than me. She was the daughter of Mr. General Hiers. And some of the Crosby kids worked with us – Annis, I remember in particular. And Larry Crosby worked for me after I started farming on my own. We had Mr. Elmer Chester's boy. We had some of the Dykes to work for us – Edna, who married Lloyd White and her younger sister, Sally.

Kay: What about your and Kathryn's children?

My children all worked – yes! My oldest son is named Jack McFarlin Fletcher; my next child was a daughter, Elizabeth Curry Fletcher; the third child was Max, Jr. My fourth was Clara Frances.

Kay: Four children! Which one is going to carry on (farming) for you?

I told my boys they needed to find some way to make a living besides farming. Max, Jr. wanted to farm, I think. He's kinda got it in his blood. But he's a CPA – I don't think he would come back and give up the other and try to farm. I don't really see much future in farming, unless things turn around from what they are now. It looks like it's getting worse instead of better. Costs are going up. The farmer does not set the price on his products – he's really in a bind.

Kay: How much tobacco did you grow? How many acres?

Well, I was growing 60 acres on my farm here and about the same amount – another 60 acres on the Shaw Farm, north of Quincy, in partnership with the Oliva Tobacco Company.

Kay: Oliva – that would be Cuban. Did you have ties with Cuban tobacco?

Oh yes! We were good friends with the Olivas. Still are. They brought Cuban farmers in here to show us how to cure the green wrapper – which was called Candela. We grew a lot of it. And they would come in every summer in the harvest season. When we got into it, more than half of mine was the Candela. It brought a higher price, and we weren't limited to the big manufacturers' monopolies, like we had been dealing with.

Kay: You established your own company, didn't you? You were not with Wedeles, or any of them?

No, ours we started – Edward and myself and Maxwell Strom, Eddie Blake, Joe Laslie and my father-in-law, Jack McFarlin. We started a co-op, and in the late '50s, that was Florida Leaf. I stayed with them for several years until we started growing Candela partly and also we had the General Cigar Company and we had this warehouse in town here (Greensboro) and packed tobacco there for a year or two. We had Louie Barineau in that with us, and Edwin Clark and Audie Clark also packed some tobacco with us that year. Two years, altogether – in the '60s. After we closed this packing house with General Cigar, I grew Candela for another co-op, which was the Havana Candela, formed by Edward Fletcher, Thomas Smith, Cecil Butler and Mr. Oliva.

Kay: Did you ever visit any of the Central American farms?

I went down to Honduras one time with Mr. Oliva. I was supposedly down there to advise his growers, but that was a whole different universe down there. I learned a whole lot more than I advised!

Kay: And Honduras is who primarily grows it now? Along with Connecticut and Cuba?

Well, they grow it all over the place now. Honduras, Nicaragua, I think they even grow some in Bolivia now. I'm not sure.

Kay: Do they use shades?

Yes, they have shades. But in Honduras in place of sewing the cloth on the wire like we did, they use barbed wire, and just hook the cloth on the barbed wire.

Kay: That's pretty smart. How come we didn't think of that?

I don't know. It wouldn't have been any more expensive. But I think with the winds we have it wouldn't have worked too well.

Kay: Someone said that in Mexico or Ecuador, I'm not sure which, the clouds are there so much they make a natural shade. Is that true?

I don't know. They grow a lot of tobacco in the sun in Honduras. But the really good wrapper they grow under shade.

Kay: Did you ever have any troubles packing? You packed your own, but sent it somewhere else to make the cigars?

It was John H. Swisher, originally. Then with the Florida Leaf, it was the Bayuk Cigar Company. They were headquartered in Philadelphia and didn't make any cigars down here. But then General Cigar Co. took our tobacco from up there. And we sold our Candela to a number of different companies. Our biggest customer was probably Mr. Eloy Vega – from Tampa.

Kay: So some of our tobacco did go to Tampa. I'm always saying that to people – that we helped make Tampa, and then I think, Boy, I bet they didn't use any of our tobacco!

They did. They used our wrappers on their Candela cigars – a lot of it.

Kay: What would some of their brand names have been?

I couldn't say.

Kay: Are you a smoker? A cigar smoker?

I have smoked. But not since the mid-'60s. I don't use tobacco now. I stopped using it 40 years ago.

Kay: Your wife Kathryn told me an interesting story. She said that when Mr. Joseph Fletcher, who was your great-great grandfather came here, with his wife who was a Tomberlin, someone's parents had been struck by lightning in a boat. Did I hear her right?

Little Joe's wife was a Tomberlin. And Kathryn's great-grandmother was Frances Ann Tomberlin. Frances Ann's parents died (Kathryn confirms that the lightning story is true). They were raised by Little Joe and his wife. Frances Ann Tomberlin grew up with Badger and the rest of the Fletcher children. That was Kathryn's father's grandmother.

Kay: So y'all are somewhat related!

Distant cousins. Our children always say, "Incest is best"! But they all married out of Gadsden County. They weren't taking any chances.

Kay: So it wasn't Little Joe's parents who were struck by lightning?

No, it was Little Joe's wife's sister (in-law) and brother.

Kay: Where did the Fletchers come from?

I think they were in Virginia, originally, and then they came to Irwin Co., GA and then to Quincy – to Greensboro—about 1843, I think.

Kay: In looking back on the tobacco, was there any unusual or special experience you could tell about?

They were all like that. When the fertilizer plant burned, and then later when the Fletcher Company itself burned, I was the Volunteer Fire Chief then, and I couldn't save either of them. Quite depressing.

Kay: Fletcher Company was such a landmark. Everybody talks about it.

Well, another interesting little episode was when the armed robbery took place at the Fletcher Company. That was in the '60s, I guess. Edward had offered this fellow (or I guess the fellow wrote to Edward, because he was coming up for parole and he needed some kind of "sponsor" and a job). So Edward said, "Well, I'll take a chance on him."

So he gave him a job and put him to work as a mechanic. And he was really a genius mechanic. He could do wonderful things with those old wrecks we were running then. He courted a very sweet, nice girl we had working in the office there and I think she became pregnant and one day he went in the office with a gun and held his own wife up and ran to the river swamp – the Apalachicola River Swamp. And we all went down there and hunted him for several weeks. But he lived in that river swamp and part of the time I think he was supplying himself by going into the store at night and helping himself to what he needed.

He didn't have a key, but we had an old man in there for a night watchman. The story is that he came in there one night and frightened the old man so much he couldn't say anything (laughing). I don't know whether that's true or not. But anyway, they didn't catch him until he came out and stole a boat down near Panama City. They caught him there and put him in prison. He broke out several times – I don't know what finally became of him.

Kay: He had such a promising thing. What happened about his wife and the baby?

Well, of course, she divorced him. I think she later married again and had a good life. Don't know what became of her to tell you the truth.

Kay: Those were hairy experiences. Did you have any bright spots? Like being a Century Pioneer Farm Family? Weren't you and Kathryn one of those?

Everyday's a bright spot when you wake up and nothing else hurts!

Kay: You did sorta like it, or you wouldn't have stayed (in tobacco) so long?!

Well, I enjoyed growing things. I didn't enjoy dealing with all the people – I still enjoy growing things.

Kay: You grow sod and pine trees now?

Yeah, they don't have so many people. I enjoyed growing tomatoes a whole lot and grew tomatoes for 20 years.

Kay: And then retired? Or do you consider yourself retired?

I guess I consider myself retired. I still work all day everyday. But the pressure's a whole lot less now.

Kay: One last opportunity – do you have anything that's in your heart or mind to say about the tobacco?

Well, I'm glad I don't have to grow it anymore – I'll tell you that much.

Kay: Did you celebrate the 4th of July in the barn? We didn't, but some farms did.

Well, when we got through with the tobacco, we had a fish fry every year, when we sent it to the packing house.

Kay: You know that was my favorite part – taking it down.

Evidently, a stick never hit you in the head then.

Kay: No, but I saw my brother fall out of the tip-top. He did that twice.

Oh, that's one thing I did not mention. I was renting a barn from Thomas Smith one year out on Flat Creek. A hanger up in the top of the barn was on a tierpole that gave way. He fell out of the barn, it crippled him and he landed on another man; it killed him. A terrible time. The hanger was Griff Boyd. He recovered enough that he was able to work, but he limped the rest of his life.

Kay: Did you have the barn – there was one where Thad White's brother was killed when lightning struck in it?

That was Jimmy Smith's barn. I don't know the particulars, but I think he was up in the barn.

Kay: There must have been two incidents. Somebody told me about a little black girl, who just went to the door of the barn, and was struck.

Adrian Fletcher had one or two killed by lightning striking them. I think they were sitting on the outside sill of the barn – the sill that ran along the outside. (they were sitting along the outside wall of the barn). They were inside. So if lightning struck the barn it would hit them.

Kay: There were some close calls with lightning on ours. But nobody ever got killed. But you had the fish fry. All the Fletchers, or just your farm?

Just our farm. Just for the hands. I think they enjoyed it. We used to have a fishing trip, too. Down on the Florida River, or New River. It was more for the farm superintendents. I didn't mention that my father had several farms out in Sycamore, too. We had the Bentleys there and the McPhersons. I think some of them would go on the fishing trips.

None of the black people wanted to work on the 20th of May. That was their Emancipation Day. And they were all off on the 20th of May. But the rest of us worked! My father was a firm believer in that. I remember we had Senior Skip Day. I went to him, and I said, "Daddy, can I have the car to go to Senior Skip Day"? He said, "You don't have to go to school"? I said, "No sir." He said, "I need you in the tobacco patch"! (Laughs) All my classmates went to Glenn Julia and had a good time and I sweated it out in the tobacco field.

Kay: Somehow that was one of the things about being the farmer's children.

I can tell you another anecdote about the tobacco business you may not want to hear.

Kay: Oh I want to hear 'em all!

There was a young boy – Marion Conner. He would do anything for a nickel. So all my devilish older brothers offered him a nickel to bite the head off a hornworm. So he popped it in his mouth and bit it!

On that note, Max and I closed the interview. But he and Kathryn gave me a tour of their home. Over their mantel is a lovely painting of a shade, with several primers and toters. They told me the painting is by Carol Davis Pallister. ("She is Bill Davis' daughter, and Amos Davis' granddaughter.")

About the land across the road:

Miss Clara Fletcher (Max' aunt) inherited the land from her father, Edward Badger Fletcher. I had two aunts, who were my father's sisters – Clara and Myrtice. Myrtice married, but Aunt Clara never married. She was a spinster at 102, when she died.

About the Fletcher Trading Company:

I worked there, and I owned a small part of it.

Twenty-seven
Trudy (Grubb) Wheeler and Jo-Ann (Grubb) Anderson
Visit at the Barn
September 13, 2006

(For this "barn tour," Kay's sister Saradee Davis Bowen is on hand to share her experiences. She and the Grubb sisters who grew up in Mt. Pleasant have been longtime friends. Farmer brother Johnny also checks in.)

Jo-Ann: We worked for the Hubbards — Rachel's daddy (Mr. Arch Hubbard). I can't remember what we were paid. He had a little Austin car and he would come pick us up. Come around the neighborhood and pick up all the children. We'd all cram into this little Austin and it looked like the clowns that get out of the car at the Circus. We were packed in there!

Trudy's husband Jake: They couldn't have made a living at this, not at the rate they worked.

Jo-Ann: The black men would step up on these rafters and climb way up to the top and work their way down …

Jake: How long did it take to dry?

Jo-Ann: Several weeks, wasn't it? And it had to be "in case." They'd tell me they couldn't do anything with the tobacco until it was "in case," and that would mean it had gotten soft and pliable. It wouldn't break or be brittle when they handled it. So if it was in case they would push it together on that string and take that string off the stick and wrap the string around the ends of the tobacco. And they would pack it away to send to the warehouse (packing house).

Kay: How many years did you work?

Jo-Ann: I imagine three summers I might have done that.

Kay: How old were you?

Jo-Ann: Oh my, eight, nine, ten, maybe.

Kay: What was your job?

Jo-Ann: I was a stringer! My sister, Edna Gertrude, was so slow and poor at it they promoted her. (Edna Gertrude laughing behind us.) She didn't have to stand there and string tobacco all day. They made her a toter. You know what a toter is, Kay?

Kay: Out in the field. She worked out in the field?

Jo-Ann: No, she worked inside.

Trudy: I did, though (work outside). Picking bugs off. Underneath the shade, which was not shady at all. It was hot as could be! And

I picked the bugs off. You'd pick 'em off and throw 'em on the ground and step on 'em.

Saradee: Were they worms? We got a penny apiece for every hornworm that we got. And we'd have to show em. We'd put 'em in a jar and show 'em to whoever was the Barn Superintendent (like Mr. Phillips).

Trudy: Ooh, I wish I had talked to you then. They took advantage of me! We got a weekly wage or something.

Kay: I think we have a class action suit here!

Saradee: I didn't know we were so well off!

Jo-Ann: We'd take our little lunches with us, and Mrs. Hubbard would say, "Now you all come up to my house for lunch." And she'd sit us on the back porch, because we were pretty dirty. And we'd wash out on the porch in her basin. She started feeding us because we always went to her house to wash our hands, and one day we left our lunch on the front porch and the dog ate our lunch. She felt sorry for us and invited us to come in and eat with them. Then she just decided to feed us everyday!

Kay: Well, see, it evened out!

Jo-Ann: I was telling about Trudy's job. See, they would bring these barges. The mules would bring the barges in, loaded with the fresh green tobacco. And women would be standing there stringing tobacco. And when they'd get out, they'd say, "Bowcka"! And that was Trudy's job to run to the barge and get a load of tobacco and put it on their table and keep them in tobacco all day long.

Saradee: Well, I was a step above you! Because I not only did that (and I can prove it because I just saw a picture of me over there), but I also carried the punchers in my pocket and I was the Barn Lady; every time they got a bundle of 50 sticks I gave them a punch on their card, and they got a penny a stick.

Kay: There's a punch card up there, over Hester's table.

Trudy: Why was she your favorite person?

Kay: There's no way to describe ... unless you knew Hester. Saradee might could tell you.

Saradee: She was a beautiful, Christian lady who put her God first, and her family. She had a sweet, lovely family that she would bring them and they would have little pallets (behind her) and she sang ... she would sing. Other people did, too. But Kay remembers Hester more than others. But sometimes we would have a whole thing going, and in the field you could hear 'em singing. And I loved that.

Kay: And all Hester's family worked and grew up here. They came from Jackson County – over around Two Egg.

Trudy: I remember when some of the women had such small babies. They'd nurse 'em in the barn. And then they'd put 'em right back on that pallet and go right back to stringing!

Saradee: And they were so good. But here, one of the things – we'd rush home to eat and I'd rush back out to work. I didn't know that you ever said you were sick or you didn't feel good or this was not a day to go to work. We had a show every day at lunch-time nearly. There'd be a black preacher – J.C. Simms was the black preacher and another one – Rabbit Rumlin. And they would preach and we had some that sang on the radio – had a quartet and sang on the radio on Sunday morning. And then there was Ed (Chambers) could do the buck dance and there was a little boy that could do the buck dance. And different ones. And they'd sing. And to me this was just heaven.

Kay: This was the social center of our life, really.

Discussing tobacco artifacts:

Kay: This is a "Brown's Mule" – and you had one at your daddy's store (Mr. Dan Grubb's Store in Mt. Pleasant, FL!)?

Jo-Ann: Yes. Tobacco came in what seems like a long twist (chewing tobacco). People couldn't afford the whole length. So they would buy what they could afford. And you'd put it in there (the Brown's Mule cutter), press it down and cut off the amount that they want – a couple of inches, or whatever.

Trudy: I remember those being a bar instead of a twist.

Saradee: How much did it cost?

Trudy: I wish I could remember that, but I don't.

Saradee: You didn't have a sign up there that said, "A Nickel a Short Plug" or something like that?

Trudy: People knew how much it was.

Discussing how to string tobacco:

Jo-Ann: The leaves have a definite front and a definite back, as most leaves do. And you would just string 'em, front to front, back to back. Or, as Kay said, "belly to belly" and "back to back." And you would space 'em, too. You'd have about a finger's space between each one.

Kay: Did you get many holes or pricks in your fingers?

Jo-Ann: Oh yeah! We would bandage our hands with adhesive tape. And it would get just as black and gummy and yucky – but you would occasionally stick a hole in your finger, too.

We would have to thread our sticks before we strung the leaves. And we didn't have but one needle. So we'd have to keep up with our needle.

Discussing Hubbard Farm:

Jo-Ann: I don't think Arch Hubbard had any tractors, do you, Trudy?

Trudy: Not when we were working for him.

Jo-Ann: But he was Superintendent for someone else. (Not sure who.) Isn't that funny we didn't know who. You know, there was

Archie B. and Billy and Jean and Rachel (the Hubbard children). Now you wouldn't have known any of them except Rachel. Billy's still alive.

Discussing seeing the barns disappear:

Jo-Ann: I was telling Kay about Max Herrin's farm. It was on the road into Mt. Pleasant, and there were at least three tobacco barns you could see as you rode along. And all of a sudden they were gone, and it just broke my heart ... that I hadn't taken the time to do my video-camera pictures of 'em or some stills, or something.

Discussing hanging the tobacco:

Saradee: So everybody had a different color string?

Johnny (Davis): Yeah, so they could tell it apart at the packing house.

Kay: That (that we were looking at) is Owens string (donated to the Barn by Jerry Owens, from his father Maurice Owens' farm).

Johnny: Mine was green and red and (white).

Kay: Now, why would they have the different string? So they wouldn't swap it with somebody else's in the packing house?

Johnny: Yeah.

Kay: Johnny, do you remember when you fell out of the top of the barn, several days later, your watch was found up there dangling from a tobacco stick?

Johnny: What I did, I had my arm coming down and dragging on it. But I was so sore the next morning I couldn't get up.

Discussing tobacco artifacts (cigar-mold and press):

Johnny: That's where, at a cigar factory, when they hand-rolled the cigars in those molds, they'd set the molds under there and press that down where the cigar would be shaped right.

Jo-Ann: You know our Aunt Mary worked for the Budd Cigar Factory for years, in the Office. And that was very interesting when I was a child to go there and see the women sitting there rolling and also, cutting the leaves.

Johnny demonstrates how the cigar mold was clamped down by the press. This served to make the cigars tightly-packed and uniform.

Johnny: Jeff (his son) went down to Tampa to the Bering Cigar Factory when he was working for King Edward Tobacco Co. and those molds were piled up. They sent him and a man to get some fans to bring back to the packing house up here. King Edward had bought Bering out and they had shut down the hand-rolling operation. They were one of those factories that made the high-priced cigars down in Tampa. When he got down there, those molds were just piled up – just hundreds of 'em. He brought some back and come to find out they had those dry termites in them. And so they went and bromide-gassed 'em, that's about the only way to kill 'em. They'll get in furniture and everything and eat it up. He could have brought a bunch of those things back.

Ladies: And sold 'em at Antique Stores!

Johnny: Yeah.

Jo-Ann: She collects tobacco boxes, and all kinds of old things.

Discussing tobacco artifacts
(wire-stretchers and wire-reel, for building a shade):

Kay: What is this thing that looks like claws?

Johnny: Well, you had a chain and you'd hook the claw in and then pull on the handle and pull the stretch and you would put the other one on there; when you pulled that back, that would loosen the other one up and you'd keep doing it – it was slow. It wasn't near as fast as what we could do with these other stretchers.

Kay: The ones like you and Nathaniel built our little model shade with?

Johnny: Yeah.

Kay: This big thing is just a wire …

Johnny: Reel – see, you'd push that in the dirt there. It'll come out ayonder and you just drive it down and set the wire on it and then you'd pull the wire off.

Kay: And you used it more for fences than for shades?

Johnny: Well, I mean that's what it was originally used for, but then you could use a fence stretcher to stretch shade wire. And we'd use a come-a-long thing instead of a clamp.

Jo-Ann: When you got your cloth, how did it come? Uncut and just miles and miles of it?

Johnny: No, it was in bales – pads inside bales. And so many feet. It'd be about five pads to a bale. It'd take about two bales, I believe what we used, to the acre. It was about half-an-acre in one of those bales.

Jo-Ann: And then you sewed it together?

Johnny: Yeah, and if you run out at the end, and it was out there in the middle somewhere, you could splice it together. Sew it together.

Kay: I learned how hard it is to make a shade. Because that's what he helped me do …

Johnny: Yeah, but I could make a bigger one a heap easier than I could make a little one.

Kay: Ha, but that was an education for me. See, this is our shade right there …

As we're looking out, Johnny realizes he's left his truck running the whole time. He says: I gotta go anyway, I gotta go pick scuppernongs!

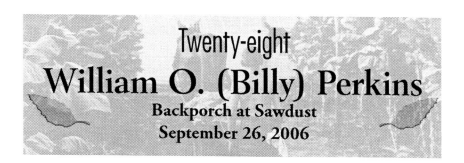

Twenty-eight
William O. (Billy) Perkins
Backporch at Sawdust
September 26, 2006

(Billy's brother Malcolm Perkins is the subject with which Billy began his memories of shade tobacco.)

I was a very small boy, and my older brother Malcolm was hanging tobacco the day he got his draft notice to go to the Army.

That was in 1945. Mama brought the notice out, saying he had been drafted and had to go to Camp Blanding for eight weeks of training, after which he then went to France. That's where he gave his life – he was in Service about three months before he got killed.

Our oldest brother Jack was in the Army Air Corps in France. But he was out on a mission when Malcolm came through and they missed seeing each other by about three hours. Malcolm went on to the front line and Jack couldn't locate him anywhere. So they didn't see each other.

But, anyhow, on to the tobacco, when we were all little we'd go to school and when we got home from school we'd change clothes and go out to the tobacco field. We'd put a bud poison pack on us, and we'd poison tobacco in the afternoons till it got dark. Then we'd come in, do our chores and get our homework. And that's basically it – we grew up that way.

And (brother) Ralph was with Embry Tobacco Co., and Daddy (Marvin Perkins) was working for them growing tobacco. Ralph became Superintendent of what they called the C&E Farm. They grew tobacco there and Daddy also raised it on the farm where we lived. I worked in it – all of us worked in tobacco. Besides poisoning, we helped gather and harvest it. Then when we got grown, Ralph stayed in the tobacco. I did, too. Pete finally got back in it, running the packing house. Ralph ran the packing house and I worked on the farm during the harvesting/curing season. Then I went to the packing house and worked there during Fall and winter. I'd come back out around February to start the crop again, putting up cheesecloth, planting seed beds, all this. So I started raising tobacco on my own in 1965, growing it on my own though still with Embry. Then from Embry Tobacco Co. to King Edward. I grew tobacco and worked on the farm through the harvest season until 1976. That was the last year that King Edward operated, with the shade tobacco.

Daddy farmed for awhile and then they hired him as a carpenter. He would go from farm to farm and keep the barns and tenant houses repaired. He did that until he passed away in 1959. Ralph, Pete and I stayed in the tobacco till it went out of business.
Daddy had started tobacco in 1935. We moved from Jacksonville when I was two years old. When we got big enough to work, we worked in tobacco in the afternoons when school was out. The

school timed it so that most of the kids would be out when it was time to start harvesting tobacco. There were a lot of kids that worked in tobacco.

As for Mama's family (the Stricklands), I really don't know when they got started. Earlier. I figure maybe '27. Because when we moved here, the tobacco company was in business. Embry Tobacco Co. sold out to King Edward in the middle '50s. But the personnel didn't change. That's where we sold our tobacco.

Embry's headquarters were located in Quincy. It was one block from the Leaf Theater, take a right – it sat on the corner of … I can't remember the street. It's been destroyed and homes all built in the area now.

The Strickland brothers that were involved in tobacco were Pasco and Roy. Guy operated a filling station in Tallahassee. Pasco was the head of Embry Tobacco Co. and Roy was the "Riding Boss." He checked tobacco on all the farms and kept the Superintendents hired and kept up the farms. And they stayed in the tobacco business until they retired.

My parents were Ada Strickland and Marvin Perkins. He was raised in Coonbottom -- but jobs were scarce there in the 30s. So Daddy went to Jacksonville to work for Love & Haire Trucking Co, hauling, I think, gas and diesel fuel and stuff.

When we came back, my sister Ann was born. We called her the "C.O.D. Girl." That was 'cause she was born in the front room of the house that used to be a Post Office a long time ago. We told her she came C.O.D. (cash on delivery)!*

*(It wasn't too bad having her, Billy said, because she was the inside worker in the tobacco operation, learning to be a "pretty good cook" at a very young age and helping their mother run the house.)

The place we came back to was called the Edwards Community. It's not called that now, but that's where I still live, and where I continued growing tobacco after Daddy. I grew 10 acres every year. The labor we hired – some of them lived on the place and a lot of 'em came out of Quincy. My land joined Embry Tobacco Company's land. Tobacco was grown on my place. Daddy had grown it there. So we just worked it all together, and we paid a per cent of the payroll.

Most of our help were people we'd work year to year to year. We had Fred Edwards and his family. One of the biggest families we had was five boys and four or five girls. Arch Lumpkin had three boys and two girls that worked there. Oscar Gaines had, I think, a couple of girls and a couple of boys and his wife. Mae Belle Harrison was a lady that worked. We hired her as a straw boss (kind of a foreman) in the field when we had kids that'd tie the tobacco up (looping young plants to the row-wire). We'd put her in charge of the kids that would come in and put the first wrap on tobacco to make sure they slipped the loop down around the plant to start the wrap off right. Then she'd move to inside the barn when we started the harvesting. She would wait the tables, keep the rack-toters straight, all like that. We had a good crew.

Most of our help was black. All of 'em, I'd say. They were good workers. Some of 'em when their kids got up older would either work on the farm or they'd move to another part of the county. They'd be working on one of the other farms. They were pretty well tied in with tobacco growing. It was a good thing. It taught a lot of people how to work. Kids used the money they'd make to buy their school clothes. It helped the families out. And all the families that lived on the farm would have a garden spot around the house that they could raise stuff, they could use the mules out of the lot and use the fertilizer and all. So it benefited them some. Helped with their grocery bill and all.

We had eight mules on the farm, and on one of the bigger farms they had about 16 mules. You can't find a single mule in Gadsden County now!

Farming has basically gone. We used to grow a lot of pole beans, turnip greens and collards during the off-season in tobacco. We used to raise just about everything on our farm. I mean we'd go buy stuff like sugar and flour – but all the meat was raised. Sweet potatoes, all our vegetables … raised most everything we ate on the farm.

As for fertilizer, we had one farm that had about 300 head of cows and that farm would furnish their own fertilizer. But ours, and most of the other farms, had to buy it out of Georgia. They would haul their stable fertilizer down and we would scatter it out on the mound. We'd put about 10-12 tons per acre. Then we'd side-dress – had a tobacco special that we had made up, put about 5,000 lbs. to the acre of that. We'd put about 3,000 lbs. to the acre just before we got ready to plant and then we got a good stand going, before we'd tie it up. We'd go out there and side-dress with 1,000 lbs. more. We'd tie it up and when it got up about knee high, we'd apply about another 1,000 lbs. to the acre. It was really fertilized!

For irrigation, we first had what we called "flood irrigation." That's where we had a pipe that you'd run in the field. We'd pump the water out of the pond through that pipe and have it ditched inside the field. We'd have some sandbags and run water down two or three rows at a time. We'd sandbag it up so the water couldn't keep going down the ditch and would turn down the rows. When those rows were done, we'd move those sandbags down and catch another three or four rows. It would take some time. It would take all day and all night and maybe another day to get over irrigation. If you got over it and it hadn't rained, you'd start over – doing it again. I think it was in the late 40s, they came out with where you had a big pipeline and put sprinklers in. Then you had two lines of those that went all the way through the field and while we'd irrigate one line, then we'd move the other line, move it over and set it up. Then when we got through irrigating that line we cut one line on and cut the other one off, move that pipe over and then repeat it.

Then I think it was the late 50s – that they came out with what they called "overhead irrigation." We had a main line that ran across the end of the shade and through the middle of it, and we had two inch lateral lines that went off both ways. You could turn the valve on that main line and shoot the water. So it really helped out when we went to the overhead. You had to make sure the sprinklers were turning and kept unstopped.

I would irrigate my tobacco and when we got it in the barns, I was fireman. I had to build fires. I remember building fires one time when they used wood to cure the tobacco. There'd be so much smoke. I used dry green oak wood, so it wouldn't blaze up too much. But there was so much smoke coming out of the barn, you'd think it was on fire!

We fired many years with charcoal. And then they came out with gas heaters, where you'd put a line of heaters in the barn and have a gas tank outside. We'd have a 500-gallon tank and it would probably take two or three of those tanks a week to get the tobacco cured. Once you got it cured, nothing but just some kinda green stems, you wouldn't have to fire it all night. You'd just more or less fire it until the tobacco got kinda dry and then you cut the fire off. And in the mornings it'd be what they called "in case." The tobacco would be kinda soft.

You could open the windows and let it air a little while and that would help cure those green stems. Then when it got completely cured, you would have to bring it in and out of case. You wanted it "in case," where it would be soft and pliable to handle so as not to break it. Didn't want any holes in the tobacco 'cause it was wrapper tobacco. That was to wrap on the outside of the cigar.

When you got it into case you could bulk it down and tie it up and send it to the packing house. There, it'd be bulked in big ole bulks, kind of oval-shaped bulks – about 5 feet tall, about six or eight feet wide and about 18 or 20 feet long. You bulked it so you could put a pipe about halfway inside with a thermometer in it. We'd read those thermometers every afternoon and every morning. When it got up to about 100 or 105 degrees, you'd have to start taking the tobacco and shaking it by hand. Shaking it out and turning it – what we called "turning the bulk."

We'd take the top layers, start shaking it out and giving it to the men over at an empty place to bulk it down three, and they'd take the tobacco that was on the inside and they'd put it on the outside, on the rim and that way they kept the air circulating. It would usually make the tobacco cure out and the color be pretty well the same. And like I say, it got *real* hot, if the tobacco was in real high case when it came in. When we bulked it, it it would go up to about 110 – 112 degrees, so we had to turn that in a hurry. Get it moved around so it could lose some moisture, bulk it back down, so when they got the tobacco – it was sweated enough.

The womenfolk off the farms would take this tobacco and would look at every leaf of it. If there were discolored leaves they would pull them out and if it was a smooth color they would put them in one stack and if it was a dark color they'd put it in another stack and if it was a leaf that, say, had "brokes" on one side (like the left side), they would make a pile on the table (left-handed brokes) and if it was broke on the righthand side they would pull it out and put it on that stack.

So we had lefthanded brokes and righthanded brokes and we had off-color. And the #1 would be the smooth tobacco that was a real smooth brown. And then if you had some that was really torn up bad they'd pull it out – what they called the "strippers." They'd use that and grind it up to help make a mix. They'd mix that with a finer tobacco in the North and make the filler for the inside of the cigar.

It was a complicated process. But it gave people a year-round job, because once they got through delivering tobacco out of all the farms there wouldn't be but just two or three weeks and they would start in the packing house. And that would run to Christmas or sometimes, over to the latter part of January. And then most of the time, they would get about two or three weeks off before they'd go back out on the farm and they'd start putting up cheesecloth and getting everything ready for the next year's crop.

And when they got the cheesecloth up, it wouldn't be just maybe a week when the plants would be big enough to start planting and usually in February or March (by the latter or middle part of March), we'd start the tobacco in the shade and when we got through hoeing the tobacco it was about time to tie it up.

We got away from bud poisoning. They came in with blow guns – hand-blow guns that you had to walk up and down every row. Then we had the mule blow-guns that you could blow two rows at one time, and then, after they got up so big they came in with the airplane and blowed the poison in a spray over the top of the shade. That pretty well took the insects that way. It was, to me, really an interesting crop.

There were a lot of furnishings and tools (not to mention the barns and shades) you had to build that weren't like any other farm-style things. It used to be when it was harvest season and the tobacco leaves were strung by hand, we built the stringing tables. They were about 4 feet wide and probably about 18 or 20-22 feet long, whatever you could get your lumber in. You'd put the tables in the side of a barn and we had the ladies that would take so many stringers and keep tobacco on the table for them to string and they'd string it and put it on a stick, tie the end of the thread to the stick, and hang it on the rack.

The toters would get the strung tobacco off the rack and take it down to the end of the barn. It would take three or four men up in the barn to reach up in the top of the barn and then as they would hang three to four tiers of tobacco across as they went. They would usually top out about what they figured they were gonna fill in a day. Might be about 12 or 15 stalls (what we called them) and the stalls were about four feet wide. When you did that, it would cut a lot of heat out of the barn because that green tobacco would be between the roof and down under and it'd make the barn cooler. It'd take really probably about three or three-and-a-half days (according to how much you had) of stringing to fill a barn. Maybe four days.

From the time we first hung and fired the tobacco, it would take about five to six weeks to take it down. You started your temperature off real low to wilt the tobacco down so the heat could get all the way to the top. Then you'd fire a little bit every day. For about the first three or four days you just wanta' keep the heat round about 90 degrees. Hard to do when you got the temperature outside that's 95 degrees! But it was what you wanted to keep it at, because you didn't want to cook the tobacco and have that greenish tint to it.

The color you wanted was a good smooth brown. And, of course, a lot of factors would work into that. If you had rain that washed a lot of your fertilizer out you would get different colors of tobacco. If you had that, you wouldn't have as much of what we called #1 String. The off-grade that was closest to the #1 String was the FC-1. It was a light off-colored and you had your dark and medium dark grades, along with your "brokes" and "strippers," that I told about earlier.

Did I ever have any crops that were flops? Well, a storm would come up and blow the cheesecloth and we'd have hail come along. On some farms it would flatten the shades and we'd have to pick the shades up off the tobacco.

I had it where I had to split the cheesecloth with a butcher knife so the ice on top would fall on the ground and it'd keep it from tearing the shade down. But hail'd get it. You'd have storms come through and it'd blow and tangle it if wasn't wrapped up good.

Sometimes the weeds would get so bad if it went to raining you couldn't get in there to plow like you really needed to plow. And sometimes you'd have to go in there and pull out some of the bigger weeds by hand so they wouldn't grow up into the tobacco. It was a challenge. Everything didn't run smooth.

One thing ... you had to refill some of your barns on the farm because you didn't have enough barns – couldn't afford to build enough barns to hold the whole crop. You'd have to tie up tobacco out of maybe two or three of 'em so you could go back and refill 'em. There'd be times there'd be no humidity in the air. You needed barn room and you couldn't get your tobacco in case to where you could take it down and get barn room. If it stayed too long in the field and didn't get primed, it could go to specking on you.

So, I mean, it was something. We'd haul water into the barn, pour it on the ground, try to get the humidity up so the tobacco would come in case to where you could take it down and get barn room. We'd even put sprinklers around the barns and turn the pump on and let the water sprinkle on the barn on the outside, and open the doors and windows at night to feel that moisture, to case it up. If you worked with it, you could get it. But it was slow.

Where did we get our seed? When they first started growing, they'd just save seed from some of the tobacco. And then they came out either in the 50s or 60s with hybrid tobacco. So then we had certain farms throughout the county where they'd grow hybrid tobacco way off from other tobacco. They could save those seeds. And then they had hothouses. They had some in Havana on the May Tobacco Company Farm. They had three hothouses to grow the seed. When they went into the hybrid, Dr. Clayton came in and set up the hothouses – the seed then cost $100 an ounce.

Yes, it was called Gold Dust! That was all hybrid tobacco. It was a *good* tobacco. That was basically where we got our seed till the tobacco business went out.

How did I feel when that happened? Well, I thought it was really a blow to the county. Tobacco, to me, was a good crop – it employed a lot of people and a lot of people learned how to work. Now you don't have all these jobs for kids that're in school so you got more kids in trouble. Nothing to do in the summer, 'cause there's not that much for them to do. So, I think it was a loss to the economy, to the country and to the county. I know smoking is a bad thing, but very few people that smoked cigars inhaled, so it wasn't as dangerous smoking cigars as it is cigarettes.

When growing tobacco phased out, I thought of going in with my brother Ralph and Jimmy Bowen and Douglas Poppell. They were gonna lease land and plant soybeans and corn and wheat. But I decided I didn't want to go that route. There wasn't all that kind of money in those crops. And if you didn't have rain to make the corn, it could be a disaster. Then the wheat and soybeans – it was all so dicy. So I decided to go with Flint Hardware, which was family-operated. Even there the business had dropped off after the tobacco economy left. With the three family members besides me, we didn't sell enough to stay busy all day. That's the reason I only worked there for a year. So I went to work for the Farm Service Agency. I retired from there.

Mae Wilcox Perkins
Experience in Tobacco

I was 10 years old when I started working in the tobacco barn (on one of Tom Maxwell's farms). My first job was picking up tobacco leaves that fell on the ground when the needles the stringers used did not go through the middle of the tobacco stems. Sometimes I would get tobacco out of the wagons that came out of the shades and put it on the tables so the stringers would constantly have tobacco on their tables. I remember getting my first paycheck after having worked five days -- $12.50. I thought I was rich. I also remember when the tobacco was cured I counted the sticks the tobacco had been strung on and tied them in bundles – 50 sticks to a bundle. When I was older, I strung tobacco on machines, and, of course, made more money which I used to buy clothes, school supplies and even had a little spending money.

(Note: Mae's grandfather, Dempsey Phillips, was Superintendent of the barn when I was a child. We all loved and looked up to him. He carried the box with the punchers and a watch on a fob to let us know time to knock off. Mae's mother, Cora Lee Phillips, and her husband Coy Lee Wilcox, moved to Havana so that Mae's later working years were on the May Tobacco Company farm. -- Author)

Twenty-nine
M. E. Smith Howell
Conversation in the "Copy Shop," Quincy Square
October 26, 2006

When I was a small, tiny child, my daddy worked for the AST Company, and he would take me and throw me up on top of the shade – the top of the tobacco shade! I didn't weigh much so I didn't pull the shade down and I could walk up there. I was probably the only one of us who ever did, because I was so small. And I can remember doing that, and it was a lot of fun. You know kids – that would be a memory they would always have.

Kay: And where was the shade?

It was on the Dixon Farm. Our first tobacco farm was the Dixon Farm and we lived there for five years. It was in Gadsden Co., just south of Edgar Blake's farm on the Watson Road, at Douglas City. I think Daddy had something like from two to five acres of shade tobacco – back in the '40s and '50s. His name was Monroe Smith. He was a Superintendent for 14 years for the AST Company. I was 14 years old when they closed their doors and he was the last Superintendent to be let go – about 1957.

Kay: And you also lived on another tobacco farm (between Gretna and Sawdust)?

Right. That was later. Bill Middleton owned that farm and then C.W. Harbin. When my father died, Dewey Johnson owned it. Each time the farm was sold they wanted Daddy to keep working for 'em, so he went – like selling a mule! – to the new owners. He died in 1966. Dewey Johnson still owned the farm then.

Kay: And it was close to the present-day Gretna Prison? (Gadsden Correctional Institute is located at what we called "Rock Comfort," when I was growing up.)

It was right across from what we called Parker's Store. Of course, my daddy called it a few other things – but we won't go into that!

Kay: It *was* a jook joint at one time! But a Bible Store later on. Well, did you work in tobacco?

ALL my life! I didn't sow the seed, but I have done almost everything else. I helped my daddy spray it with an old tobacco sprayer (poison-duster) that I carried on my back and it would be so heavy. Now I was a teen-ager but I'd be waddling down those rows with my daddy. It would be heavy but I'd help him spray that tobacco. I'd go up and down those rows with him – you know what a tobacco bed looked like? They're just like a tobacco shade.

Kay: You're talking about the seed bed. But they'd be little plants.

The little, little plants – before they were ever planted. I've done that all the way to working in it when it left the tobacco barn to go to the warehouse. I've worn out many a pair of shorts up in the top of the barn.

Kay: You were hanging it? You hung?

Yes, I was the "second hanger." I didn't hang it. But I'd be right under him (the top hanger). There would be three people

Kay: But girls didn't hang!

When you were my daddy's child, you did! Well, my legs weren't long enough to go from one to the other tierpole. But I had to sit on a tierpole, wrap my legs around that tierpole and brace on the one underneath me and hold onto the one above me with my free hand. I couldn't lift more than two tobacco sticks at the time. But we got the job done.

And I also strung tobacco. Some, by hand. But mostly, I did my stringing when the machines came in – the electric machines.

Kay: How many could you string a day?

Four hundred and fifty!

Kay: Did you get paid?

I did get paid. I don't remember how much. But you were making money when you made $4.50! And then, I wasn't working for

Daddy 'cause when I was working for Daddy I didn't get anything! (Chuckles)

Kay: So you worked for other farmers, too?

Well, yeah. I was in the tobacco barn helping Daddy when he was the Superintendent. I was there every summer and made spending money. But when Daddy was growing tobacco on his own, that's when you worked for nothing.

Kay: Were there other white children?

Oh yes. All my brothers and sisters. All of us worked out there. My mother ran the barn (is what she called it) and my daddy operated the field. You know, he took care of the field. But she saw to it that all the tobacco was strung and hung and marked – you know, you had to mark 'em by primings – first priming, second priming, third priming and on up the stalk. First, though, it comes "sand-leaves" – that's when you get all the dirt in your hair! I toted a many a turn of tobacco, chased rabbits and all those kinds of good things!

Kay: You mean like totin' in the field?

Yeah. They called 'em "luggers." Have you ever heard 'em called luggers before?

Kay: Recently. We just called 'em toters. Who were your sisters and brothers?

James Smith, which was "Pete" Smith. After he grew up and married and raised a family, he was City Building Inspector. Bernice Smith was my sister – she married a painter, Virgil Hemanes and they lived in Tallahassee. He was a painting contractor. My brother Alvin Smith went to the Army, retired, came back and worked at Mo-Trim. And Shirley, my sister, was a beautician. She married Sidney Yawn. He was a barber and they had a barber/beauty shop in Quincy for years and years. Then they moved to Venice where he had a barber shop and she had a beauty shop. They're thinking about coming back. My brother Wilmer Smith was a barber and lived in Venice, and has retired in Perry. And then there's M.E. That's me! I retired from Sykes' and now I work for my daughter (Gay Steffen) at the Copy Shop two days a week!

The name "M.E." comes from my mother, M.E. Chason Smith. My mother's father was James Chason, from Spring Creek, GA. He died in 1904 – he was a school teacher. He died with pneumonia. He had two children – Mama and Gola Mae Chason Anthony. Mama can't remember him because she was only three years old when he died. My grandmother, Minnie Johnson Chason, was pregnant with my Aunt Gola Mae when he died (of pneumonia in 1904). I still have his teacher's certificates. They were dated 1895.

"Haunted House Story"

M.E. adds: We lived on the Dixon Farm five years, which was as long as anybody ever lived there, because it was supposed to be haunted. One time my family and I were sitting around a table and all of a sudden, a shingle started working its way down through the ceiling. Just as my mother climbed up and tried to grab it, it was yanked back up in the attic. We went up there to see what was pushing it. Nothing! No shingle in sight. Odder yet, the boards above that spot in the attic were criss-crossed in such a way nothing could be slid between them.

Another time, everybody was sitting in the living room. We heard a big commotion, like every pot and pan in the kitchen was crashing together. But we went in and everything was in perfect order!

Thirty
Robert M. (Bobby) Hollingsworth
Kitchen at Sawdust
November 8, 2006

My earliest memory of shade tobacco was when I used to come to Quincy and go out to my Uncle Carl Spooner's place – which I must have been eight or nine years old. And in the tobacco deal I was what you call a "lugger" or a "toter." This is when the small kids followed the primers and went back and forth and back and forth through the tobacco on the row, carrying the tobacco in what we called "pads" out to the end of the row where there was usually a lady that put the tobacco in a "barge" (or a "slide") and this is what we did … that's my earliest recollections of me being in shade tobacco.

I also remember a little bit about how they used to irrigate, and that was gravity flow, at first. I can remember them pulling up the rocks and the dirt to turn the water down a row and it would go all the way down to the other end and after it had done that awhile they moved it into another row and that was the way irrigation was done in my earliest recollection.

From there, until earliest teens, I was a small child so I was still a lugger up until I was maybe 12 or 13. I didn't come to Quincy every year but the years I did that's where I stayed – with Uncle Carl and Aunt Vera. And we worked the tobacco.

The last year time I really worked in tobacco was the year I got out of high school, came to Quincy and by then Uncle Carl, Murray Spooner and Carl Spooner, Jr. all had farms. Well, they made me "stick man." Well, that was a job that would work you to death with one farm, but we had three farms, in which time we just went around and around.

The three farms that we had – one was in Greensboro (that was Murray's); Uncle Carl's was over on the Glory Road, three miles out of Quincy. Junior's farm was in Jamison. So, counting 50 sticks, bundling 50 sticks with a barn-full of people stringing tobacco, and you had to carry 'em and punch the card each and every time you could not hardly get back and count 50 sticks before somebody else needed sticks and there you go again. And you did it over and over and over.

So, that was really the ending of my days on the farm in the tobacco.

Later, I got a job with Southern Chemical Sales & Service. We were in the fumigation business – fumigated seed beds first, which consisted of a plastic cloth being stretched over irrigation pipe in order to make a small tent-like effect -- we put oil cans down along the row of pipe; we put hose with a dispenser on the end for methyl bromide. Methyl bromide would sterilize the soil. It had a 2% tear gas in it where you could tell when you were too close to it. And it would burn your eyes so you would kinda move back. But anyway, we put the methyl bromide through the hose into the cans and it sterilized the soil and you came back a few days later and took the cover off and flipped it over and did some more. That was part of my first job at Southern Chemical.

After I went into Service and came back in 1955, I got into the field fumigation. That's where we used a product known as Telon, and that killed nematodes in the big fields. We had two tractors, and we went out and worked from about daylight till dark in the wintertime -- with treating these tobacco shades.

Well, and I formulated poisons. All different kinds – parathion, DDT, all of that stuff that's real bad for you now. I guess it wasn't then – I'm still here. Anyway, that's what we did in that part, as I worked for Southern Chemical 12 years.

After that, I went with L.I. Allen Company. (Ish Allen). We were in the shade cloth business. All of the tobacco was grown under a shade. Shade cloth was like a gauze. It would be fields of as much as ten and 20 acres under shade. So that's one of the things we sold along with the twine that they used to sew the cloth on the shade, along with the twines each and every plant had to have – this was a small string at the base of the plant up to the top of the shade, because shade tobacco was a spindly plant and you would have to wrap around and around to help hold it up. So that was one of the things we did with the L.I. Allen Company. I was there for another 13 years.

We also sold the twine that you strung the tobacco on the stick with. A different color string for every farm was something we came up with. Everybody in all the years before had white twine.

Toward the end of the tobacco-growing, before it went out, we figured out you could put one strand – it was nine strands in a piece of twine, you could put one strand of any color … say somebody'd have red … somebody'd have green … somebody 'd have yellow until you ran out of colors, then you would put two colors, then you could put three colors. When we ordered it, we had to have it special-made. So each and every farm, unless you wanted to stay with white, had a different color and could follow their tobacco all the way through the process of it going through the packing houses.

Packing houses were all over Quincy – we treated packing houses with this same methyl bromide gas I was talking about before. They would put tobaccos in a big bulk – some 12 or 15 feet long and about 6 feet wide and sometimes up as high as 5 feet, and that would be what they called a bulk of tobacco. This methyl bromide gas would penetrate all the way through a bulk of tobacco. Also, it would penetrate through one foot square of wood because there were a lot of big posts in these old packing houses, so if they did have a termite he couldn't get away! They didn't bother the tobacco, but they did have bugs in tobacco.

So that's another thing we did when I was with Southern Chemical was fumigate tobacco warehouses. We had quite a few in Quincy (I couldn't even think about how many) and also in Madison. Madison grew shade tobacco, also. We carried the soil fumigants that we used in the fields – we carried that down there and we carried the plastic and the methyl bromide with the tear gas to Madison. We also fumigated the warehouses, sold them cheesecloth – I'm putting everything together in one I did.

Madison was a pretty big grower down there. We did only a very little business in Georgia. It (shade tobacco) went up as far as Calvary, maybe a little but further than Calvary there were some farms. Over at Amsterdam at one time had been real big. AST Company had had some big warehouses up there.

We were not the only supplier of shade cloth – but we were the bigger supplier. Another man that came in from out of the North – he sold a lot of cheesecloth in Connecticut. That was the next place that they grew shade tobacco (Connecticut). He sold most of his wares up there, but he did come into Gadsden Co. and sell some here.

Tell a little about Ish? Well, Ish was a talker, and everybody knew that and he talked loud, he talked too much, and a lot of other things about Ish. But people used to ask me, "How do you put up with it"? and I said, "I don't listen to him"! But anyway, he was a great guy – I never worked a day *for* Ish Allen, I worked *with* Ish Allen. There's a whole lot of difference in working for and working with. I was like a partner in the business and I had nothing invested. I did well, we'll say!

Ish was a good guy, and he also, I don't know, he treated me real, real good over the years.

I don't really know how many farms or farmers we came in contact with. In the area there were some five to six thousand acres of tobacco grown but back then in those years I probably did, well, I *did* know every farmer. But Ish knew the farmer, he knew the farmer's wife, he knew the children, he knew everything about 'em. And one amazing thing about Ish. Most people if they see you in a place and they see you again in a place, they know you. But him! If he saw you on the other side of the street in New York City, he was gonna holler at you and call you by your name, because you were never out of place wherever you were with him. He was just good with names. He took this Dale Carnegie Course and he did *not* need it! He took it twice!

He just did it for … I don't know. You'd have to ask him. And you can't now.

Let me say something about cheesecloth. There were two kinds, for a long time, of cheesecloth. One was just plain white cheesecloth. And another was the yellow cheesecloth that was treated with chromate – bad for you again! Well, anyway, later before it was all over we did have a synthetic material weaved into the cotton cloth trying to make it last a little longer. When we went out of the tobacco business in and around Gadsden Co. there were some of the farmers that went to Nicaragua and Honduras to grow. That's where all of the business went to when it left Gadsden Co., but there were a few farmers like Cecil Butler and Edward Fletcher and one or two others that had farms down there – for just a little while. It didn't last long. They did keep growing in that area.
The cloth was made in Kanapolis, North Carolina, at Cannon Mills, which everybody's heard of, that makes the towels, sheets and stuff like that. I did have opportunity to go through that mill. It's just amazing to watch those spindles shoot back and forth in the process of making this cheesecloth. It was a big, big factory. We probably sold, out of the six thousand acres we might have sold five thousand acres of that cloth. It took a lot of cloth to cover an acre, let alone five thousand acres.

When we got the cloth in at first, we would get it in by railroad car. And we'd get quite a few railroad cars and start storing it and delivering it. We delivered a lot of that shade cloth to the packing houses where the farmer would be carrying his product after he made it. We'd just go ahead and deliver it there. And a lot of places, we just brought it out to the farm and put it in the barn – whatever needed to be done with it.

And then after the "cloth season" came down, we would start getting it by semi-trucks. The volume coming in at one time was less, but it was still a lot of it. Volume-wise, it was quite a bit of shade cloth. Quite a bit of twine. We would get boxcar loads of twine, and if you can imagine how much twine that would entail, between the twine that you sewed the cloth on, the twine that you put the tobacco on in the shade where you tied it up to the overhead wire, and then the volume of twine you used to string this tobacco on the stick with – it was quite a bit.

Also, at the packing houses, we sold the cardboard boxes. After they processed it, repacked it, got it ready for shipping, they used quite a few cardboard boxes and we sold cardboard products. At one time I went to Monroe, LA, where they made the cardboard boxes and stenciled the names and everything on them that had to be done. That was a big place, too.

It took quite a volume of stuff. Then, and this was very odd in a way, we could use the white cheesecloth one year and the ultra-violet rays and acid rains and everything we had would weaken it to the point we could only use it around the edge of the shade in what we called "walls," and then only if we put the cloth up in four or five or six thicknesses. But we could take the same cloth, bale it and ship it down to the other countries and they could use it for three more years. Because they did not have the ultra-violet rays and acid rains and their air didn't break it down like it did here.

So we bought shade cloth back, went out and got it, reprocessed it, cut out sections of it that were damaged, rebaled it and send it down to Central America.

About me? I grew up in a little town of Pinetta, which is between Madison and Valdosta (GA). I say "grew up" – I'm not quite grown up yet!

As far as my childhood years, I always had a pretty good time. Everything in tobacco went smooth. Nothing ever really happened that was bad. Regular good times.

There were, of course, other children (boys) working. Wayne Brockman, a cousin of mine – I'd worry about him a little bit because he used to drive the mule that pulled the barge down to the barn. And he'd have to get back there between that barge with that singletree and hook it up, and that ole mule would be stompin' around a little bit but Wayne never seemed to be afraid of it.

Uncle Carl and Murray and Junior didn't have any girls old enough to work. So there weren't any girls in our operation. We just all did what we were supposed to do (blacks and whites, old and young) and it never changed.

I could come over here (from Pinetta) and work a summer in tobacco and then go home and when I got home, Mama and Dad would take me to Valdosta where I could buy my school clothes for the next year. That left a bad taste in a way, because sometimes it took all I had made to buy two pairs of pants and a pair of shoes and a shirt!

In 1950, we moved to Gadsden County permanently. From Feb., 1953 to Jan.,1955, Uncle Sam sent me on a paid vacation to Japan. And from Japan we went to Korea. It was 19 months to the day from the time I got on a plane in Tallahassee until I stepped back in my Dad's service station out on Jefferson Street – the Gulf Oak Service Station, which today looks almost as it did when he opened it in 1951 or '52.

And I married a Madison County girl, Clara Nell Wells. She hates "Clara," so when she left Madison she left Clara there. And now she's just Nell. She and I had gone to school together, but we never dated in high school. But when she came to Tallahassee and started college, for some reason or other I looked her up. And down!

But anyway, we've been together 53 years now, plus tax. We have a son, Robert Randall Hollingsworth – who lives in Gainesville. Randy – he and his wife have given us two grandchildren, David and Aubrey. Randy is about 52 years old, David about six and Aubrey about four. Send 'em your prayers!

We have a daughter Debra. She's married to Rusty Ivey. Rusty has the NAPA store in Havana. At this time, they live about a half mile from the store. Debra is a dental assistant. Younger daughter Lynn lives in Tallahassee, and she works for the VA as a lab tech. That's our kids and the two grandkids.

My mom was born and raised in Gadsden County. It's an odd thing – there was quite a bit of marriage between Madison Co.

and Gadsden Co. I don't know how this came about unless maybe some kind of connection through the old tobacco industry. Dad's brother, Tom Hollingsworth, married Fannie McPherson from Gretna. My dad married Cornelia Brockman from off the Glory Road – three miles out of Quincy. There were some others – Mr. Fraleigh married a lady from Gadsden Co., Miss Hinson. There was a lot of intermarriage, and as I said, after I moved here, I married a Madison Co. girl.

My dad was Robert Franklin Hollingsworth, and I'm Robert Marshall. Where did the Hollingsworths come from? The way I like to tell it after the Civil War, my great-grandfather, Timothy, was on his way back home. His people's home was down in Lakeland. I don't know that this is a fact, but this is the way I've got it figured. In those days, they probably rode the rivers. Because after the Civil War, there was no way to travel other than the rivers, and they came down the Withlacoochee River that would take 'em on down the state toward Lakeland. He looked over on the bank there, and there stood Great-Grandma! He got off of his log or raft, or whatever he might have been on, and so that started the Hollingsworths in Madison County!

(Before all that) Timothy joined the Army and went into the Civil War and was captured for a second time and he was in Maryland. So all they did was turn him loose. Can you imagine how long it would take walking or following the rivers to come? I figure it took the better part of a year to get down to Madison County, on one side and Lowndes Co. (GA) on the other. Anyway, it happened. And we happened!

One of the stories I like better is that my cousin and his wife, Jack and Charlotte went on this genealogy deal and they wanted to find out this, that and the other. They went to Lakeland and found the old Hollingsworth Family. And in talking to the old family, they said, "Well, you know we lost Timothy in the Civil War." My cousin said, "I don't think so"!

For some reason, he never ever contacted his family in Lakeland. From the Georgia line, which the Withlacoochee River was, down to Lakeland was a long, long way in the 1860s. And there was no telephone and no E-mail!

I guess he could have written 'em, but apparently he saw no reason to.

Judy Hollingsworth Barnett
(Bobby's Sister)

Well, my experiences in tobacco aren't very much. I do remember working for Uncle Carl Spooner, probably just one summer. Might have been two. But anyway I was a toter in the barn. After the stringers had strung up, I had to carry the sticks of tobacco over to the ones who put it up in the barn – the hangers. And I walked many a mile, I think!

Then one summer, the other thing I really remember, we had a big storm. The storm came through and knocked down a lot of Charles and Grace Brinks' tobacco. So my mother volunteered me and Ann Jackson to go help for two weeks, so they could get their tobacco in. I'm sure we had a hilarious time. They probably were glad when we all left! I remember Ann and I both drank so much lemonade that we both broke out in hives. I think that kinda ended our tobacco days!

Other tobacco experiences Bobby shared:

About "turning leaves": After a little windstorm, the leaves – they were so big – they would kind of fold over or flip part of the way over. You would have to go through the field and turn the leaf back over in its rightful position, because this tobacco leaf was gonna be made into the outside wrapper on a cigar. And it had to be perfect. No holes, no creases, no tears, no anything …

I'm gonna tell this, you may not like it, but I'm gonna tell it anyway. In the barn, after the tobacco was cured my Uncle Carl told me that how you knew when the tobacco was ripe and ready to come down, it felt just like a lady's silk panties. Well, I didn't know how it felt so, therefore, I could not say when it was ready!

Well now, I've got to tell you about the "rocky shades": The fields we were talking about before, where you used to use the gravity feed for irrigation – the consistency in them was rock and a little clay. That was supposed to be the best land for growing shade tobacco. I don't know what made it so, but it did make it so.

What the rocks did as far as the irrigation – I guess it let the water seep into the ground better if it was a little rocky. And if you pulled up a berm of dirt with a hoe, it would have some rocks – not big ones -- they'd be about marble size.

If the water was going in this row and you wanted it to go in this one, you put a little dirt across this row and then it came down and you could put a berm there and turn it down the one you wanted. I can remember up there (at Uncle Carl's) all the rows ran with the main road because that was downhill in that shade. Most of that water would run back down into the pond.

About "crop-dusting": The funniest story that I have … well, a tobacco shade was made of poles to hold up the wire and everything. The poles were about 16 feet apart. And you could raise the walls on the end of the shade in the daytime – lift it up to let it air out and whatever. But anyway, John Boggs would always go to Connecticut, where they used to get a lot of people in from the Dutch Indies and places like that where they grew a lot of tobacco. And then up there, there was enough room for John to land the plane close to the shade to load it up with the tobacco poison.

One day, this guy was looking at the airplane and he was looking at the shade. And he'd look at the airplane and he'd look at the shade. He said, "You know, it's gonna be real close you going down those rows in that airplane."

And John said, "Well, that's not the bad part. The bad part is when they let that wall down and you have to turn around and come back out"!

More about "crop-dusting": Well, this is about when I had a chance to be a crop-duster, flying a Stearman Airplane. Bob Hayes told me I could learn to fly – he'd teach me if I would work for him for two years. Well, I never learned to fly because I did *not* want to be a crop-duster. A young guy that I knew had taken him up on the deal, and when they went to Louisiana or Texas or somewhere out there dusting cotton at the end of our tobacco season his plane came down and he got killed. So that turned me against any kind of deal with crop-dusting.

About "dust-guns": The dust-guns were hand-operated, and they walked down through the fields, turning this little hand-operated dust-gun and dusting the tobacco for the insects. And of course, it started at the first when you wore a little apron with the poison in the apron sack and you'd walk along and put a little poison in the bud by hand. No gloves. Paris green and again, that stuff'll kill you! (No gloves, just your hands to sprinkle a little in the buds). And then they went to that hand blow-gun. At Southern Chemical, we also sold mule-drawn dust guns. And the mule would pull it along and it had a fan in it and a big hopper on it and we would go down the row and dust the tobacco. Also, we had the airplanes – most of 'em were Stearman, the double-winged plane that could fly kind of slow, over the top of the shade and drop the dust out from under it. Meter it out and dust the shade. The dust would float through the shade, because the threads in the shade was eight strands going one way, and ten going the other in what we called 8 x 10. And so it was porous enough the dust from the airplane and the blast would scatter it inside the shade. They tried helicopters at one time, because that blade would really blast it down under there and make it come under the leaf. But it would mess up the tobacco too bad, so they only tried it a year or two.

When they were doing with the helicopters, at Southern Chemical, in one of our cabinets, we had a watch that had a stainless steel band – a solid band -- that had been burned. This helicopter did not see the big electrical wires, flew into it, crashed and burned and we still had the guy's watch when I was at Southern Chemical – back in the '50s.

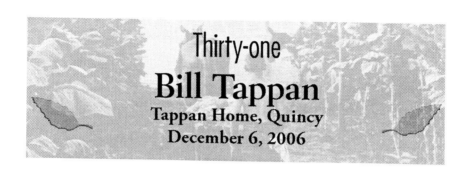

Thirty-one
Bill Tappan
Tappan Home, Quincy
December 6, 2006

(Bill was an entomologist with the North Florida Experiment Station, Quincy)

The Experiment Station was set up in 1921. They had a blackshank problem, a disease of the stalk of the tobacco. Dr. W.D. Tisdale was assigned by the Main Station Director at the University of Florida in Gainesville to study the disease. As a result of this problem, the North Florida Experiment Station was established. The shade tobacco farmers bought and gave to the University 42 acres of land where research could be conducted. The land was located where the Gadsden County School Board Office building, the Vocational School, bus maintenance and parking lot, and Carter-Parramore Academy track presently are located.

Then by about 1928, Dr. Randall R. Kincaid came and took over the work for Dr. Tisdale. Then in 1946, they had the green peach aphid problem which almost wiped out the crop so they brought in an entomologist so we had a pathologist and an entomologist working on tobacco. The entomologist was Kelvin Dorward and he didn't stay here but about a year and he went with the USDA in Washington. Then they brought in Dr. Winfred C. Rhoades and he worked for a couple of years and they made him Director of the Experiment Station. So then they brought in Frank E. Guthrie and he was the entomologist for a year or two. And he went to North Carolina State. And then they brought me in, and I've been in here until I retired in 1988.

But the green peach aphid is primarily why they brought in an entomologist. Blackshank was the primary reason they brought in a pathologist. But the blackshank almost decimated the crop. Over on the Gregory Farm, which is on Pat Thomas Blvd. South, they grew some experimental tobacco and they found one stalk in there that didn't die. That's how they got the resistance to the blackshank. One stalk! And they called it Rg, for Round-tip Cuban on the Gregory Farm. So that pretty well established the Experiment Station here then.

I did insect control work primarily on shade tobacco, because the tobacco leaf when it was wrapped on the cigar had to be almost perfect. Couldn't have any holes in it or any blemishes. If you did, then you had a lower grade tobacco and you didn't get the maximum price which was about $1.85 a pound when I came here. And you could grow a crop of tobacco then for about $1,500 an acre. When I retired it was up to about $8500 an acre. So the margin of profit had been squeezed down. And the crop began to diminish as far as acreage because of the pressure on the margin of profit. Because the banks and lenders didn't care to lend money on a crop you might lose and it take you four or five years to pay it back whereas when I came here they were growing an acre of shade tobacco for about $1,500 an acre were the expenses and then if they lost the crop the next year they could make it back.

But with time, as expenses got more and more, the margin of profit was squeezed down. But we worked on – I don't know – probably 25 species of insects that attacked tobacco: the tobacco hornworm, the budworm, the flea beetles and the wireworm, which got in the root system. There were just a number of them.

Kay: They really liked that nicotine, didn't they?!

The thing of it was the nicotine didn't really bother the insects. Evidently, they had resistance to it.

Kay: What were some of the steps you took to control them?

Well, what I did primarily was experimental. They brought in different chemicals from companies that manufactured insecticides. They had 'em in experimental stage. They'd bring 'em in here. We'd test 'em on the tobacco. Whenever we found out we had no problems with it, they'd go through the process of getting it registered with the USDA. It'd probably take 'em, oh with a numbered compound which would be an experimental compound, it would probably take 'em 10 to 15 years – get it to the stage that they were going to market it. Then, oh, it would require about 1 billion dollars to get an insecticide registered for commercial use. And it wasn't an easy process. But that's what I did primarily. I tested insecticides on insects that were a pest on tobacco. And later on, when shade tobacco went out, I did work on flue-cured, which is cigarette tobacco -- what people call sun tobacco or bright tobacco.

This research on flue-cured tobacco was conducted at the Suwannee Valley Station in Live Oak, FL. Also, I did research on peanut insect control at the Marianna Unit, a branch of the North Florida Experiment Station.

When I came, Dr. Kincaid was the only one here working on tobacco. The rest of 'em, Frank Guthrie was the last entomologist before I came, and he quit and went to a better position with North Carolina State University in a program on flue-cured tobacco up there. That's what they primarily grow up there.

Looking at pictures:

This is me and Dr. Kincaid and Dr. Charles E. Dean. Dr. Dean came here about 1959 to work on genetics of shade tobacco, as a plant breeder. Trying to develop a more stable tobacco, because the one that had been developed that most of the farmers were using was Dixie Shade, and it had so many different varieties mixed into that thing – you had early-blooming, late-blooming, mid-blooming, all kinds of varieties. And what Dr. Dean was trying to do was develop a variety that was stable and produced good quality cigar wrappers. And he died several years ago, but he went to the University as head of the Dept. of Agronomy down there, at Gainesville.

But the tobacco went out here, as far as our research, about 1972. Then the last crop that was grown was on the Violetta Farm by Denny Hutchinson in 1978. Now they had so-called experiments, but they never amounted to anything.

Kay: What about Mr. Adrian Garland? I understood that he grew the last crop.

No, Denny Hutchinson. He grew it for Hav-A-Tampa, and the packing house was down there across from the high school on the corner, across from Corry Field.

Kay: Was that the Wedeles Packing House – originally?

That was it.

Kay: And that was Hav-A-Tampa? I remember. The school bus would go right by it.

Garland may have grown one of those little, small experimental things. But I didn't know anything about it. Denny Hutchinson was the last one to grow it commercially.

Kay: Then tell me about Dr. Kincaid. He was the one who developed the Rg variety (the blackshank-resistant one)?

He didn't develop it. You see, it was accidental. They just found that one stalk in the field.

Kay: But he was the pathologist?

Yeah, plant pathologist. He studied diseases. Blue mold, blackshank, virus diseases, so forth.

Kay: Which you have to treat differently from insects?

Oh yeah, quite a bit. See, you have some diseases that are soil-borne and other diseases are air-borne. Like blue mold. Blue mold travels through the air. If they're growing a crop up there in Georgia, early, then our blue mold that's spawned down here may blow in the wind and go all the way up into Georgia and North Carolina, into that area. It's a small spore that's spread by wind and it can travel miles and miles and miles.

Kay: The same thing was true of ozone, too, wasn't it? There wasn't anything you could do about it, though, could you?

See, ozone is produced by sunshine acting on oxygen. Oxygen is one atom of oxygen, whereas carbon dioxide contains two atoms, and ozone contains three atoms. You got three atoms of oxygen, and the sunshine acting on the oxygen in the air will form ozone.

Kay: What about those factories that were emitting ozone, up North?

But you see, the factories produced carbon dioxide. The sunshine acting on that would produce ozone, and it would drift in here with thunderstorms and lightning in the storms would act on the carbon dioxide thereby producing ozone. And black light like they used to use for light traps would produce ozone. Washing machines or dryers that used to have the black light lamp inside to purify the clothes that you were drying produced ozone.

Kay: Good gracious! That's why a tobacco farmer was jinxed then!

That's right.

Kay: Let me ask you a dumb question. You went to the University of Florida (I could tell by the Gator theme), and you majored in entomology? Let's see, what are you trying to show me?!

Records! The last crop was 25 acres.

Kay: Let's see, back in 1964, the total number of acres was 4,100. Now was this shade tobacco? Does it include what they were growing in Georgia?

Yep, yep. This was the whole thing excluding 1,300 acres in Georgia, making a total of 5,400 acres in both states – from when it started in 1921. And it went down to 1963, and I carried it on from there. Dr. Kincaid compiled all this stuff.

Kay: And the total crop value went from $1,881,000 in 1921.

Yep, and it got down here in 1963, we had a drop. This is about the highest year – 1969 ($21,744,000). Then, when it finished, in 1978, it was $255,000.

Kay: Good gracious. Went from $21 million in 1969, down to $255,000.

Yeah, well see it started back here around a million and it gradually kept increasing, until 1969, it had increased to a little over $21 million. And then it started its decline. That was about the time that AST Company (American Sumatra) was beginning to decline. And it kept going downhill from then on.

Kay: The individual farmers couldn't quite hack it. Against Central America. And everything.

That's true. The expense of growing an acre of shade tobacco was too costly.

This is a speech that James J. Love gave, before the Florida Historical Society. And he was talking about years and years ago, before they had the shades, they grew this tobacco in the open and the price of tobacco went down about $.25 a pound and it just about went out for this area. And it goes back to the first shade was about 1899, I think. And you know where King Edward Packing House is on Lillian Springs Road? That's where the first shades were set up.

Kay: Was it D.A. Shaw, who did it?

I don't know just who it was, but it says he was one of them.

Kay: Is that packing house still there?

Yeah, supposed to be both of them. Last time I saw it. You know where Mr. Morris lives, that used to work on TVs. You go down Lillian Springs Road and turn down there until you come to the first street to the left. The packing houses are right there.

Kay: And that's where the first shade was? And it was a slat shade?

Yep.

Kay: 1899?

Yep.

(Here Bill shows me a copy of the Love Speech, from his extensive collection).

Kay: "History of Tobacco-Growing in Florida" … Talk before the Florida Historical Society, Quincy, FL, March 28, 1940, by James J. Love.

Well, you see, the tobacco farmers came in here with the Presbyterian people out of North Carolina, Virginia and South Carolina. They'd moved down here in the 1800s, about 1820 (somewhere in there) and they brought the tobacco with 'em. But it wasn't shade tobacco. I've got a picture in here somewhere. Slat shades. I don't know whether you knew Mr. Frank S. Chamberlin. He lived on King Street. He was the USDA entomologist, and he worked here for a good while. And Mr. Lucian L.M. May worked under him. Where Dr. J.M. Griffin's office used to be across from Stewart's, well the next house was the USDA Lab. Next was the King Edward Packing House, across from the First Baptist Church. You don't remember that?

Kay: All those packing houses were such a part of the landscape, I didn't think about which was which!

There's Mr. May out there blowing the tobacco …

Kay: He's using the blow-gun. I've had a lot of people tell me they used that.

The Power Pack Duster. This is the hand-cranked one. Later, they had the Power Pack driven by a gasoline engine.

(Showing more pictures): Now, see that's one of the old slat shades. See, when it first started, the posts were on 16-foot centers. Then later on, they changed it to where it was 32-foot centers. But in the post row, they were 16-feet apart. But they eliminated that one post row that was in the middle, so they could get tractors in there. And primarily, cultivation was done by mules to start with. And as expenses began to build up (it became more and more expensive to produce it), they went to tractors as much as they could, but they still had to have mules to plow that post row.

Kay: He's telling about John "Virginia" Smith in this.

Yep.

Kay, reading: Tobacco history in this county began in the early 1820s when Florida was ceded to the United States. Coming here at that time was John Smith, from Lunenberg Co., VA. Since there was already a man of that name here, he was called "Virginia" Smith.

There's Mr. May, when he was young. Lucian Lawrence Mitchell May!

Kay: You called him Luke!

What he's doing there he's pinching cornmeal bait into the bud of the tobacco plant. They used cornmeal or cottonseed meal. Most of the poison back then was arsenic – lead arsenate or calcium arsenate mixed with the cornmeal or cottonseed meal.

Kay: They wouldn't approve of us doing it now, would they?

Wonder people hadn't died from it! But that's what he's doing ... pinching it in the bud.

Kay: We're all here. Would Paris Green be the name of that arsenic? I think I remember that's what we called it.

Paris Green was lead arsenate. But you see that later on they found out that the arsenic compounds mixed with the meal caused plant damage. I don't know if you know what plasmolysis is, but if the concentration of salts (or something) on the leaf is greater than it is on the inside of the cell it pulls the sap out of the cell. And so it would cause spots and burn the leaf. So they got away from that and when DDT was developed during WWII – after the War they began to go to it, because it did a better job with the insects. And they didn't have that tedious labor of putting it in the bud. Just go in there and dust it over the plants.

Kay: And then DDTeeee ....was found to be ... a No-No.

Propaganda. You see, right now they're squawking about malaria. Because DDT has been banned, and you've got malaria problems in tropical countries. DDT is less toxic than some of the organic phosphates they came up with later on that they approved to be used. So DDT is almost non-toxic. LD-50 is the lethal dose in milligrams per kilogram of body-weight required to kill 50% of all animals or insects being treated. On DDT it was so low, it didn't hurt anybody. In fact, during WWII, they used it for lice-control on troops. They'd dust 'em with DDT.

Kay: Well, what about ... the big fuss about it was with the food chain. The birds eating the insects.

What they primarily started off with was the Peregrine Falcon. Something was causing thinness in the eggshell of the Peregrine Falcon. Well, they did research later on, and when they found out what caused it, they didn't publish it. The people going up there, bothering the nest were causing the Peregrine Falcon to have psychosis, or whatever you call it! Making thin eggshells.

The same thing with the Brown Pelican. Environmentalists (like Common Cause) say:
"I don't have to prove anything I say – you've got to disprove it."

And that was their attitude. But if you go and study the chemistry of the insecticides, you'll find that some of the organic phosphate like parathion and malathion are even more dangerous than DDT.

Kay: That's real interesting! Now, tell me about Mr. Love, who gave this great speech.

James J. Love was Chairman of the Board of Control at one time. The Universities – all the Universities in the State of Florida used to be under the Board of Control. And he was chairman of it.

Kay (acknowleging his gift of a copy of the speech, from his private collection): You're still as interested in all this as you once were, aren't you? Were you raised here?

No, I was born and reared in DeFuniak Springs.

Kay: That's where my Daddy was from. Or real close -- he was born in Eucheanna.

Yep. You see, my granddad and my daddy and my uncle and great-uncles were all brickmasons – and they did everything: plastering, setting tombstones, pouring concrete, whatever. And they used to go down to Euchee Valley (in Walton County) and they built these concrete burial vaults and they'd bury people, and I've been down there. There was a Presbyterian Church – a frame church. And they used to tell us, "Don't go up there in that church. There's a ghost in it"! We'd stay clear of that church! But you'd go look in the front door, and there'd just be a goat up at the pulpit.

The Tappans came out of New Carlyle, IN. They came down to Florida in 1894. My daddy was Walter LeBaron Tappan.

Kay: The old Davis Cemetery that I'm trying to protect in Freeport has a really beautiful headstone. It's black marble. That's the Great-Grandpa Davis' headstone. They may have made his!

Granddad made concrete headstones. They set the marble stones at the head of the graves.

Kay (looking at 1946 Walton High School Yearbook): Were you Burgess?! And they called you …

Brutus! Old Perry Curtis Rutherford hung that thing on me!

Kay: You were the Sports Editor of the *War Whoop* and the *Waltonian* and the Manager of the Football Team, Key Club secretary … president of Junior Homeroom, "Who's Who," Library Society and Vice-President of the Senior Class! My goodness! But you hadn't ever worked in shade tobacco, or known anything about it till you got here?

Yeah. I *smoked* cigars!

Kay: Oh, you did? Well, that qualifies.

When I was in the Service, down there on those islands in the South Pacific with nothing to do, you had to find something to keep you occupied. So I started – down there you'd get a supply ship come in once a month, one time you'd get chewing tobacco, the next time it'd be cigars and the next time cigarettes …

Kay: Was it free?

No! It was cheap, but not free.

Kay: Dr. Kincaid was kind of a legend, wasn't he?

He worked 42 years and was the only one working on tobacco when I came here. Then there was Dr. Dean. He was from Monticello, but he graduated from North Carolina State with a PhD. in Genetics. Here, he developed a stable variety.

Kay: Did Dr. Clayton work with you all, too?

E. E. Clayton was with USDA. He retired from the USDA and he had an Experimental Greenhouse over here, you know where the May Tobacco Company is, going into Havana – after you pass that road that goes over into Dogtown, going into Havana, then a road turns to the left – there a store at the corner where May Nursery is.

Dr. Clayton was a USDA pathologist breeder -- plant breeder, briefly. And he retired, then he went over there, and developed some of those hybrid varieties of tobacco.

But the hybrids, see, you had to produce the seed every year because they wouldn't breed true. You could plant the seed, but it wouldn't come up to be the plant you thought it would be. It had to be grown on the plant and then planted. If you tried to take a plant and produce seed from it, you didn't get the same plant.

Kay: So he was independent from you all?

Yeah, he was private when he came here, but he had worked for the USDA for years.

Kay: Was it true that when he died, his wife had all of his seed destroyed.

Yeah, she destroyed all of his genetic material.

(Showing an article that Dr. Clayton wrote)

Kay: So he wrote, too?

Yeah, he was in research – like I was, and Dr. Kincaid and Dr. Dean. We called Dr. Dean "Charlie" – his name was Charles Edgar Dean and when he came here, Dr. Clayton would not give him background information on the genetics of the tobacco he was developing, so Charlie had to do …

Kay: He was possessive of his research! Like Coca-Cola. Did you come up with a book?

No, I published articles in various professional journals. There are some of them there.

(Here Bill shows a bibliography of some of his articles).

Kay, reading them: W.B. Tappan, "Insecticides for the Control of the Green Peach Aphid on Shade Tobacco" in *Journal of Economic Entomology*. And he did one on "Mole Cricket Control in Shade Tobacco Plant Beds" in the *Florida Entomologist*. And he did one: "Insecticides for Flea Beatle Control on Cigar Wrapper Tobacco," *Journal of Economic Entomologist*. Oh, W.B. Tappan did a lot! Here's one on the hornworm even.

You see, on a tobacco hornworm, when tobacco was in its earlier stages in Florida they planted their tobacco later in the year. The tobacco hornworm's peak population came along at the time the crop was in the field. But as time progressed and they began to use irrigation and stuff like that, their season was earlier. Because the weather conditions were right, too. So it missed that peak population. So you had a decline in damage. If the crop was growing when you had that peak population, you would have a lot of damage from it. But as the crop progressed over the years and they began planting earlier and earlier, you missed that.

One year, I remember they planted in February. They transplanted from the plant bed because conditions were right. So when they plant that early you almost have no hornworms.

Kay: Were there any big, monumental things that happened while you were here? Some disaster that swept the county?

No, not necessarily. We kept it under control. Well, see I used to dabble a little bit in nematode control. Dr. Kincaid used to call it "coarse root" on tobacco (cigar wrapper tobacco), because the nematodes would damage all the feeder roots and they'd slough off. And so all you'd have was the coarse root of the root system, because all the feeder roots would be gone. So the plant would wilt, go down. They found out, working with nematologists out of the University of Florida, that the Meadow Nematode which normally occurs in the grasslands was attacking the root system. It was causing the "coarse root." So we began using the nematocides and that eliminated the nematodes in the tobacco fields, and that more or less eliminated the problem.

Kay: You said developing these insectides would take ten years?

It'd depend on the insecticide.

Kay: Well, what would the poor farmers be doing all this time?

Well, they had materials they were using. But as these newer materials became available on the market, then they would start using those.

Kay: But they might be having some poor tobacco in between, mightn't they?

Well, not necessarily. We had 'em under control. But we developed better insecticides, fungicides and nematocides – just like drugs for humans.

But anyhow, the Root Knot Nematode was a different nematode altogether, a different species that caused the roots to be knotty, big lumps on the roots and that would prevent the uptake of nutrients out of the soil. In doing the work with the Meadow Nematode, that same nematocide they used for that would control the root knot. So you could get double control with just one material, and the material we were using – ethylene dibromide in the field and methyl bromide in the plant beds.

Kay: Are all these things in use in crops now, or have they been forbidden?

You see, ethylene dibromide – your bromine compounds like it – have been banned just like DDT. But the problems they conjured up to eliminate those materials were a bunch of hot air.

Kay: Well, there was one other "animal" you had an article on, and that was the wireworm. Tell about him!

Yeah, the wireworm … was different from those other insects because it feeds on the root system. Primarily in the ground. Unless you know what you're looking for, you never see it. But you see the plant go down and the Potato Wireworm was one of the primary ones that attacked tobacco. Let's see if I can find a picture. Well, there's another one we dealt with – thrips. They had rasping mouth parts and they'd just rasp off the top of the cells of the leaves. Then that cell would die and you' get blotches on the leaves. That insect was probably about 1/25 inch in length. Teeny-tiny. If you've ever been out in the woods in the Spring of the year, they attack flowers, too. Thrips do. You get a handkerchief and knock it on the flower – those things you can see all over the handkerchief. It's a real small insect, and it's hard to see.

Kay: Was your wife Barbara from Gadsden County?

Barbara was born in Dublin, GA. They moved to Bradenton – I don't know how old she was, probably about six months – well, her sister's husband was working for a fish and tackle outfit and he came up here (well, first he was working at Independent Insurance), and her sister was working for Dr. Gray as a Dental Hygienist. And so Barbara came up here to stay for awhile -- and that's how I met her. Audley Manning's wife set up a blind date.

(Telling about wife Barbara's career with State Senator Dewey Johnson, also a shade tobacco farmer):

He was a lawyer, he and Tracy Riddle. They were practicing there by the Leaf Theater (where it used to be). She worked for him, then when he got elected Representative and later on as State Senator in the Legislature, she went over there. Then when he was appointed Appellate Judge, she kept working with him.

Kay: But she didn't do anything with regard to the farm?

Well, maybe some of the legal work. I was looking for a picture of a wireworm. They're about a half-inch long, about one-sixteenth of an inch in diameter.

Thirty-two
Katie Williams Bell
Bell Home, Hester Lane, Gretna
June 20, 2006

I was born in Jackson County, FL, at a place called Two Egg, and my parents were Hester and Johnny Williams.

My oldest brother was Jack. James was his name, but we called him Jack. And then I.C. after me, then Johnny B. And the twins, Lendell and Wendell. And after them was Ella Reese, then Bessie, and then the baby was a boy, Josh.

One of the things I remember best about growing up was walking from my mama's house to my grandmama's house. She was Jenny C. Hartsfield. Oh, we played a lot from one house to the other. But we also had to help with the work, and walk to where we worked. We'd have to clean up new ground. That's what we called it – new ground. Clean up a place like clean all the trees and things off of it. This was when I was home with my mama and them. And then we shucked peanuts, picked cotton, picked field peas and corn … and we stripped cane, pulled corn (you know what that is, take all the fodder on the corn, when they strip it and put it together and tie it in bundles). We had to tote water to wash, all that … the housekeeping chores, as well as the field chores.

Of the field chores I liked to shake peanuts. I liked that the best. And I liked to pick cotton. This was on my granddaddy's farm. His name was James Williams. He and my daddy grew cane, too. My daddy made cane syrup, they had potatoes, hogs, all that …

When I was grown up, we did all those things, but when I was down little, we played games. One of the games I remember was:

> *Merry-go-round-the-moon*
> *Merry-go-round-the-sun*
> *Merry-go-round-the-sunshine*
> *Every afternoon!*

And then they'd go *kaboom*! And when you say that you drop down behind somebody and take off and run. The school I went to was called Cook's Seminary. It was the same school my mother (Hester) went to. I met my husband Will when I was going there, but he went to another school – Callishaw. I don't know how to spell it. He was about 17, and I was 16.

Kay: When you got married, did you "jump the broom"?

Katie: What's that mean? (Katie laughs, then grows quiet.)

Katie's granddaughter Chelsea: Jumping the broom is after they announce that they're husband and wife, and everybody claps. Then they put the broom down on the floor … and then they jump over it.

Kay: You hadn't ever heard of that, Katie?

I never heard of that. (Laughs.)

Kay: Did you get married at church?

No, we got married at Bainbridge, GA at the Courthouse. It must have been about '45.

Kay: And then you had your first little chick, Iristeen. How did you arrive at that name?

Katie: Will named all of 'em.

Kay: Well, he came up with some pretty names. So Iristeen was the oldest. And you came to Gadsden County with your parents.

Katie: When she was 3 months old.

Kay: Did you live with Johnny and Hester?

Katie: We were living back of them (on the Arthur and Thelma Bowen Place). The one we were living in was right behind Mr. Arthur's, and the one they were living in was above them. About where I-10 is now. Then we moved up to your daddy's – the Forrest Davis Place, where the grapevines are now. It was to work in tobacco that we moved from Two Egg for. Mr. Johnny was in charge.

At the start of the crop, they pulled the plants and then we (I haven't ever pulled any plants) but I always would wrap 'em when they got up big enough. Then I tied 'em to the wire, got up on the bench.

Kay: You climbed up on the bench?

Katie: And tied the string to the wire. I loved to do that! That's the main thing I loved to do in tobacco. Tie the string to the wire and jump up on the bench.

Kay: How many of you would there be on a bench?

Katie: Just me on the bench, and one on the ground – the one handing the string up to me. You know there would be more than one bench.

Kay: How long would it take y'all to do that?

Katie: I don't know. It'd go so fast.

Kay: So it wouldn't take you more than a week to get the whole shade done – if that long?

Katie: I hadn't thought – according to how many people were in there.

Kay: How many years did you work in tobacco? '47 until '75. Thirty years?

Katie: Yes.

Kay: Can you remember Johnny when you first came?

Katie: Yeah (laughing).

Kay: He wasn't anything but a boy, but he was all business, wasn't he? From the very beginning … and he and our brother Hal were exact opposites!

Katie: Yeah! I remember he was standing there right by where we were tying the tobacco (to the wire) and he said, 'Katie, that's not tight up there.' And I said, "Yes, it is.' And I started doing some feeling to show it was tight. And he pulled on the string and he said, 'Well, it is tight'!

Kay: He's such a perfectionist. I can't ever do anything to suit him. Now how many children did you have?

Katie: Nine.

Kay: But you lost some.

Katie: Four. Geraldine was the first one. After Iristeen. And then Ethel (still living). And Lonnie (still living). Then Mitzi Ann (on the day she was born they took her to the hospital and she passed the next day).

Kay: I remember Mitzi. She was born on Johnny's birthday, and you sent and asked if he would like to name her. And there was a girl he thought a lot of – she was married to his friend Ben Duncan, they were both classmates. And he said, 'Well, Mitzi…" (for her). And we were all hoping Mitzi would grow up and live happily ever after. We're never promised tomorrow, though, are we?

Katie: No, sure not. Then, I had Annie Lou. She was 15, when she passed away.

Kay: I remember Johnny (her granddaddy) telling me. (I was walking along by the shade when I met him and he said she had died and told me how. He had such a loving, good face. That moment touched me, because I was so fond of both him and Annie Lou.)

Katie: Barbara was after Annie, and then Alice (naming her remaining children). And then we had Will, Jr., that was stillborn. We were down at Mama's (Hester's). I.C. and his wife were up here from Miami. I come back, went to bed feeling good, but before daylight, I was having convulsions. They took me off to the hospital …

Kay: So you would have had a boy. I wonder what Will, Jr. would have been like! (Katie laughs.) So your daughter Alice is the baby, and she's Chelsea's mother. (Chelsea tells that her mother and daddy are Darrell and Alice Horn. She has a sister Shirelle, who goes to college, and she is going into fourth grade at Gadsden Elementary Magnet.)

We digress for Katie to tell a story about a night of horror we both remember from the tobacco years, when her children were small:

The "Empty" Box on the Sawdust Pile (A Near Tragedy)

There were some big boxes up on the sawdust pile. Ethel and Bobbie, they were two of the little ones, they were down there hiding from some more children. They got in a box and called themselves hid. But my brother Lendell and your father come by with a load of poles on the truck and run over the box. It went over 'em, the right wheel did. Ethel had her arm around Bobbie, the baby. They hollered. Well, your daddy stopped cold and started throwing stuff off the truck and Lendell went up under that truck and brought them out. I got there and I just reached down and got the baby. She was limp as a doll. I just went to shaking and shaking her. I dropped down on my knees so I could blow, blow, blow into her mouth. I said, "Somebody take me to the doctor"!

It all turned out well. The baby completely revived, and Ethel suffered only a broken arm. When she came to the barn with a cast the next morning, she was a big celebrity!

But the incident was a terrifying one for Forrest Davis (Papa). He came in that night, deeply shaken, saying, "I think I've killed Katie's children"! My mother and I were horrified. Mama went to Katie and Will's house and brought the other children to stay with us. Late that night, the relieved parents and grandparents came home – saying everything was "gonna be okay." Papa said it taught him an "empty" box isn't always empty!

Katie ended by telling about her brothers and sisters. The twins Lendell and Wendell grew up to become lifetime city bus drivers in Miami. The oldest, Jack, a carpenter (deceased), and I. C. who was a welder, as well as Johnny B., all lived in Miami. Johnny B. worked for the City of West Palm Beach. Katie's sister, Ella Reese Williams Baker, too, lived in Miami, until her death. Her two other siblings live closeby, as do a number of Williams/Bell grand and great-grandchildren and even one great-great grandchild! Bessie retired from Scandia Draperies in Tallahassee after a long career there. Youngest brother Josh retired from driving a Gadsden County school bus to enjoy his real love, barbering. He has his own barber shop next door to Katie on "Hester Lane," and a very loyal clientele. The Williams hold a Family Reunion every May to honor their parents, Johnny and Hester Williams. A key component is singing! Beautiful music is a Williams trademark.

Thirty-three
Edna Dykes White
Edna's Kitchen, Sawdust
January 2, 2007

I worked at Joe Budd's (Cigar Factory) in Quincy, when I was about 17, and then I went to Frieder's (Cigar Factory) in Greensboro. I was about 37 when I stopped rolling cigars. Between that time, I worked in the tobacco fields and then in the barns, stringing.

At the cigar factory, there was a big old machine. Two people operated one machine. We had a wrapper layer and a bunch-maker. I was the one making the bunches. It was only shade tobacco they used for the wrapper. But they used scrap (or cut-up) tobacco for the inside (called the binder, or filler). It was thicker tobacco. We put that in the "buncher." The machine would put the piece of tobacco on a slat-thing and roll it up and put it in a mold and it went on down and the wrapper was put on it.

From there, they sent it back to a room to be boxed. I never went back there. We worked rolling cigars in the factory year-round. But it's like everything else. It got where they could do it cheaper in one of those islands. They didn't have to pay as high wages. If you look at that, though, they weren't paying very much then. (Shows a slip of yellow paper, a prized record of her last paycheck – from "S. Frieder & Sons Co., 3rd and Spruce St., Phila., Pa." -- April 2, 1954, Gross pay was $35.62 for the week; the employer withheld $4.10 for federal income tax and $.71 for f.o.a.b. So her actual take-home pay was $30.81.)

I left at that time, because that's when the factory closed. It was that big old brick building as you come into Greensboro (across from where that 7-11 store and gas station is now). It's still there. At the time, there may have been over 100 people working there over that whole building. Charlie Macon was the supervisor. My brother David (Dykes) worked there, too. And my sister-in-law.

Rolling the cigars was like stringing tobacco in that the more you did the more you got paid. If you had a good partner and a good machine, it was easier to do more. There were 50 machines in the room where I was working. That was Frieder's. They'd have big rooms with nothing but those machines in 'em. Then they had the stripping department and they had the packing department. The stripping department was where they cut out the veins. I don't remember Joe Budd's too much.

Now, as for sorting the leaves, you know that was done at the packing house. And that's where it went when it left the barn. I don't know where it went from the packing house. Just that when it got to us it was ready to be put on the cigars. And that was all by machine. Of course, when they first started off, which was before my time, at Budd's Factory, they rolled 'em by hand. Mr. Brandon (Clarence's father) was the one in charge of that at Budd's. He was even there when I first got there.

The reason I left Budd's was that my brother (David) got a chance at a better job in Greensboro and he took it. That was at Frieder's and I could ride with him. When I was working in Quincy, Budd's had a bus that came around and picked you up.

At Frieder's, we worked from 8 to 4. (They gave us more than five minutes off for lunch!) Still, we didn't have time to associate much. You had to work. But I made some good friends.

The only thing I really didn't like was the scent. Oh, gol! It's make you sick nearly 'bout till you got used to it. My house, everything smelt like a cigar. Your pillow, even. That scent, you know, would get all in your hair.

But it was food on the table. I tried to save every dollar I could. That's how I got this house. I saved all I could and bought this little piece of land. It was five acres until the State came in and took some for the road. I bought it about '52, because I was living in it by '54, when the factory closed. I got the Kevers (from Greensboro) to build it. It seems like a Mr. Potter put the frame up, but I don't remember. A lot of these things you forget. But such as it is, I'm proud of it. It's what I scuffled for and saved for. That's what can make me so aggravated with modern folks. They all believe in spending, and I believe in saving!

Too, I worked in the field a many a day and spent it all on Sally and Bo – the ones that were younger than I was – to go to school. My parents were William Henry Dykes and Bessie Edwards. There were five boys and four girls: Evelyn, Jay, Beatrice, Lloyd, Edna (me), Bill, David, Sally and Bo. I married another Lloyd – Lloyd White. He grew up in Greensboro, in the old White house that's still there (Thad White's home). I was born in Sawdust, right up the road there – it was then Alma and Edna Chester's place. She's who I was named for. I called her "Big Mama." My daddy built houses, and he built one for us on your daddy's farm. It was way down in the field there, close to the cemetery. We lived several places in Sawdust, then moved to Greensboro.

Lloyd White had a tobacco farm, and it was on Lloyd's farm that my brother Jay (J.Z. Dykes) sharecropped after we left to live over there. That was when I did my first tobacco work – about when I was 16. Stringing the tobacco in the barn was one part. I could string about 500 sticks a day. We got $.10 a hundred! After my brother Jay was killed in WWII, I went to work for Fletcher Company (Mr. Bertell Fletcher's farm), working there and from there to Hubert Clark's. That's where I did my last tobacco work.

Working for Mr. Bertell in his shade or barn was quite an experience. He meant working. He said, "Anybody shouldn't take over five minutes to eat lunch"! He put you out, he'd be back before you could get a sandwich made to pick you up. His children all worked, too. He worked everything! Tobacco was more important that anything.

It was all hard work to me. Nothing extra. I was glad anytime I didn't have to be out in the hot sun. Before I went to the cigar factory, I did a lot of that – working out in the field. You had to get out there and hoe that tobacco. You had to tie it up, you had to wrap it every so many days – once a week, I believe, it was. Sew cheesecloth. That was the first thing you did, then you pulled the plants from the seedbed and planted them. It was work, work, work – until you took the last leaf out of the barn!

Just a footnote: Later, I realized I hadn't asked Edna if she'd ever worked for Papa in tobacco when the Dykes lived in Sawdust. She said, "No, but I hoed many a row of pinders (peanuts) in those fields around there."

Her brother, J.Z. (Jay) Dykes, sharecropped for Cousin Betty Edwards (Aunt Bet, they called her) before he went to Greensboro and sharecropped for Lloyd White. J.Z. was drafted during World War II and was killed in service in the Philippines. He was only 18 years old when he was drafted – it's hard to imagine that someone so young had already farmed and done so much to shape the life of his younger siblings. Not all heroes are recognized.

At the Frieder Cigar Factory, Edna remembered working with Ernest Chester and Lonnie (or Lottie) Rowan. Ruth Sansom and Ruth Willis both worked in the office.

Thirty-Four
Nathaniel McNealy
Kitchen at Sawdust
January 6, 2007

(Nathaniel and his brother John were almost solely responsible for the entire project of restoring the Barn on our place. Here, Nathaniel is kindly reprising an earlier interview – as that tape has been temporarily misplaced.)

When I met your father, Jeff was a little boy. You know that was a long time ago. Jeff was a little ole bitty fellow trying to drive your Papa's truck around here – you know, that El Camino. But you know, now he's grown up. Made a fine fellow – you know there's nobody any better than Jeff. He's a good guy.

I learned to love carpentry when I was a small boy in Alabama. By the time I was 16 and was living here, I learned it as a trade – a lot of it I learned from Mr. T.J. Lambert, over there in Havana. (We lived in Quincy, but a neighbor, Mr. Ralph Ray, was working for Mr. Lambert and he took John and me with him to help out on jobs.), Also, we were going to school and afternoons we were working in tobacco. When the school year let out, we'd be working in the tobacco all day.

I didn't grow up working in tobacco, because we moved here from Headland, AL (near Dothan). I think I was 11 years old when I left there. My daddy brought me here in 1954. Mr. Joe Adams moved all of us down here to his tobacco farm. We stayed with Mr. Joe for about seven years. Both he and his wife, Miss Peggy, were fine people.

When I was working at Mr. Joe's, mostly what I did was blowing the tobacco. Using the blow-gun. And another thing was plowing the mules. That would be a sight, me trying to hitch Old Becky. That was a crazy mule. It was kinda rough, but we made it!

I helped load the barges, but I never did haul tobacco too much to the barn. We primed tobacco, leaf by leaf by leaf. About the time I got used to everything, it went out of business.

It really gave the kids something to do, in Gadsden County. They don't have anything to do at the time now. They don't have any work. Once they get out of school they just run wild. I'm glad I don't have any kids right now – my kids didn't get a whole lot of work on the tobacco farm, but some of 'em did it. By the time they got here it was all over.

Going back to when I first learned carpentry as a small boy, there was a man named Nathaniel Stringfield. I was named for him. So I never will forget his name. He thought the world and all of me – he was a white fellow. Everyday at lunch-time, when he'd be working near our house, I'd go out there, 'cause I knew he was gonna give me something to eat. And so, from there on … he was an old man, so I know he's gone now. But he was a wonderful fellow. I watched him drive nails day after day. Basically, that's how I got started. I wasn't much more than five or six years old.

We couldn't get a whole lot to eat back in those times. You know how that was. He'd bring a little lunch, and it would be something good.

The day I was born my daddy had one buffalo nickel. He didn't know where he was going to get the next one from. He made it, though. Also, back when I was born, there was midwives. So I wasn't born in a hospital.

My brother John was three years older than I was. Altogether, there were eleven of us. I was next to the youngest. My daddy was Jim Henry McNealy, and my mama was Lealia (Lee) Acker. Mama died in 1971, and Dad died in '73. They lived to see their children get grown. We were proud of that.

About 1967. John and I helped your daddy build a room addition on to your sister Miss Saradee's house in Chipley, with Mr. Ray. Then, we went to Panama City and helped build some houses for your Papa. We did a lot of house building work down there. We stayed there for six months. I had met and married Ruby by then – she was Ruby Everett from the Attapulgus and Bainbridge area. She was going to school and using the car. We were having a time, because she couldn't get the hang of the standard shift! And I just came home once a week. But anyway she got that over with and she finished college. Now she's the Supervisor of the Child Care Center at Carter-Parramore School.

Ruby and I have been married 43 years, and we have five children that are living – Alicia Renee, Torriscello (Torris), Shama, Dupheslo (Dee), and Kendra is my baby. (A son Everett died in 1988, while a student at FAMU.) I guess I got a lot of my dad's drive. Even though he just had that buffalo nickel when I was born, he kept on and on, even though they weren't paying that much back then – but he bought about two acres of land (near the High Bridge Road). He and John were alike about being saving with their money and all. I didn't ever have any to save! Because, of course, I had so many problems -- bills you know, children coming up and, man! I had to pay those hospital bills without any insurance.

It took a long time before I got it paid. The children were 25 years old. My son that was premature, he's now taller than I am, about to finish college. My baby's already finished – she's a nurse.

My son Shama went to college but then pitched in helping me at Willis Builders, after my brother John died. Now that the Willises don't do construction work anymore, we work with the youngest Willis daughter. She has a business doing yards.

John and I started working for Mr. Willis in 1973, I believe. We were with them till 2005. How we got to know Mr. Willis was we were working for the Commonwealth – the young man's name was William Lambert (me and him were about the same age). Before it went out of business, they sent us over there to set some pre-fab houses for Mr. Willis. So Mr. Willis saw how we worked, and he liked it. Well, we were off a couple of weeks, and I was running around all over Tallahassee, trying to find a job. I was out there talking to him, Ruby was with me at the time and I had an old green 1966 Chevrolet pickup.

He was working there by himself. Guess he wasn't much older than 30 years old when I went out there to work. I said, "Mr. Willis, we don't have a job. You think you could use us for anything out here"?

"Yeah, I think maybe I can, Nathan," he said. He always called me Nathan.

And I said, "Okay, Mr. Willis."

And he said, "Well, I'll tell you what I'll do. You come on Monday." – I think it was a Tuesday or Wednesday when I went out there looking for a job, John and I went to work for him and were there from then on.

(John McNealy died January 19, 2005, shortly after his retirement.)

A typical day for us was getting up about the crack of dawn, driving over to Centerville Road in Tallahassee. It seemed like it got longer every day! That was a long ways. The houses that are on that road, we started the business. Every house you see down there, we built. As the job'd get bigger and bigger, he hired a couple of guys to come in and do this and that for us. Starting off, we had to do it all – dig the foundations, everything. But he wanted to speed up. We started off slow, but he wanted to get faster. We never did the plumbing or electricity. But we hung the sheetrock, poured the cement (after awhile, he got somebody to come in and pour the cement for us); and we'd frame 'em up and trim 'em out.

Then we helped with the maintenance and the landscaping. We mowed 'em and cut the bushes. He always tried to keep us something to do. Then we'd start building another house. He kept us something to do – we never did run out of work! I can't believe he did it for 30 years – that's a long time!

Going back to Mr. Joe Adams, I don't how he knew about us. Some fellow that had moved down here must have told him about my daddy, what kind of man he was. One thing I know -- I didn't like it too much when I first got here. It looked like water everywhere. I thought the shades were water! (It was dark when we moved. And all I could see was big ole white fields everywhere. I had never seen anything like that before. It looked so funny! After I got used to it, it came just like that.)

I never did help build a shade, except that little one out there by your barn. Mr. Joe had me driving the tractor. I'd do anything he put me to doing. He always depended on me to do things like that. We had a lot of men out there, but I guess most of 'em's dead and gone. He had some of the prettiest mules you'd ever want to see. They weren't as pretty as those mules your Mama fed out there in that lot, though. Hot dog! Those were some fat mules. I never will forget them!

When I first had to plow one, I didn't know how. And that mule was stepping all over the tobacco! Man, that was the craziest mule. Nobody else would mess with him. I had to run him down to catch him. He was all over that lot. Two of the mules were Slim and Ada – can't remember the others. John didn't plow so much, 'cause he was hanging tobacco. That was something I never did care too much for. It hurt my back to lean over that thing – you know how wide those tierpoles were. I was just a young boy. Them things were four feet wide! The way he did it, he got in between. If I did it, I did it standing straddle just one tierpole. But it was a hassle, keeping up with all those women stringing all those sticks. There'd be a line bringing it to you clear from the end of the barn!

Even with my back hurting, I could "stob" the tobacco (plant it in the ground). But you better not look down at that end. That back would go to hurting worse then! It looked like you were never gonna get to the end. I say, "Great goodness"! The lady ahead of you dropping it, and you putting it in the ground! A crew came behind us and watered it.

I never will forget, Mr. Joe had a 10-acre shade, and he had a 4-acre shade and an 8-acre shade. He had one more, but I can't remember how big it was. Those three I remember, that's for sure.

Mr. Joe sold his land, and the City owns it now. They've torn down all them tobacco barns and everything. They mighta left one down by that pond, but I can't see down there.

Just like Mr. Joe taught me all I know about tobacco work, Mr. T.J. Lambert (first) and your Papa (later on) taught me what I know about carpentry. John and I learned roofing from your daddy, because we were putting on two a day down in Panama City. That was a job – good gracious, great balls of fire!

Note: Nathaniel ended with that expression, because it was his theme words while we would all be working on "saving" the barn. Or, when we planned the next project, he would always say, "If the Good Lord's willing, and life lasts."

Thirty-five
Frances Lester Butler
Kitchen at Sawdust
February 7, 2007

My parents were Robert Lester and Myrtle Hall. I grew up in Quincy – was born and raised in Quincy. To tell you an interesting story, my children were all born in the Thomas Memorial Baptist Church. It was the old hospital, and it was converted and annexed to the Baptist Church and both my children were born there.

My mother, Myrtle Hall, was Oliver Hall's daughter. And Oliver Hall established the first Academy in this area, in Concord.

I met my husband, Cecil Butler, when I was visiting my cousin, Sarah Smith – Mrs. Virginius Smith -- in Havana. And we were downtown, sitting in front of the drugstore. They had curb service, and we had ordered Cokes and crackers and Cecil walked up to the car. I was quite young (he was seven years older than I was). And he walked up and said, "What are you girls doing"? And we said we were having a Coke and talking. And he asked me if I would go to the movies with him the next night. I was quite flattered, because he was an "older man."

We dated for several years, then we separated, got interested in other people. Then I met him again at a reception for an elderly couple in Havana. He asked me for another date, and that led to a beautiful romance. We married Sept. 7, 1937. We had 48 beautiful years together ... and two fine children. Betty (Frances Elizabeth) and Victor (Cecil Victor). I have four grandchildren. Ten great-granddaughters, and one great-grandson.

All my life, up to marrying Cecil, I'd worked in tobacco. I did several different jobs, but my main job was waiting on tables. Carrying the tobacco from the barge to the table to be strung. Daddy was a tobacco grower for the American Sumatra Tobacco Company. We were on Floradora Farm, two miles north of Quincy – on the Attapulgus Road.

I just loved the people. They were loyal and I loved to hear them sing. Daddy would walk in the barn and he would say, "Aunt Belle, heist me a tune"! And she would start humming, and then she'd say, "You men up in the barn, bass this thing"! And they would sing and sing. It was gorgeous. The harmony was just unreal.

At the time I was working in the barn ('20s and '30s), I made 50 cents a day. At the end of the week, I was so rich. I had $2.50.

Cecil was born in Whigham, GA., and his father (Arthur Butler) moved to Gadsden County, to become farm superintendent for Mr. C.R. Shaw. His father was growing shade tobacco when Cecil was six years old and they were newly-moved to Havana.

His father died when he was a sophomore in college. Cecil came home and just took over the farm and started raising tobacco.

(The college he was attending was Palmer College, in DeFuniak Springs, FL. It was a Presbyterian Church-affiliated college. Said he didn't learn much, but he had a good time!)

He was growing tobacco here from then (early '30s), until it went out in the '70s. At one time, we had up to 125 acres. It was a very specialized crop. And we had, I would say, 20 families that lived on the farm year-round. In the summer, we would transport young black people from Quincy and surrounding areas. We would have as many as four or five hundred working in the summer.

His barns had been built by his father. I don't ever remember him building one. Of course, the shades had to be alternated every year – couldn't grow a crop on the same land two years in a row. Our farm didn't have any official name, although in later years, he became associated with Edward Fletcher from Greensboro, and they called it Fletcher-Butler Growers. When the tobacco industry went out in Gadsden County, for about five or six years, they grew it in Central America.

Shade tobacco was his livelihood. He didn't know anything else! From it, we went into the tomato packing business, growing tomatoes for the market. But that didn't last very long. It was a different ballgame.

Victor (our son) began working in the tobacco when he was about seven years old. He had a job called "Gate Boy." The gates had to be opened and closed for the barges to go through, hauling the tobacco. You couldn't leave them open because of the cattle. He would sit at the gate, and every time a wagon would come, he'd open the gate, then close it. He grew up and advanced to being "Stick Boy" in the barn.

For the farm in Central America there was a superintendent, so Cecil never had to stay there. But he would go back and forth quite often. The farmhouse was a very ordinary little house. It wasn't sealed. One time we went down with Cecil's brother and his wife and Ed and Betty Fletcher. That night, Ed and Betty drew the living room with cots in it. And the farm superintendent came in real early and left the door open. The chickens came in the house and got up on Miss Betty's chest. She woke up with chickens on her chest!

She didn't think it was funny then, but later she enjoyed telling the story. That was in San Pedros, Honduras. And then he grew tobacco in Belize. But the economy got so unstable and we were kind of afraid to be there. It wasn't because of the chickens!

Back to our farm in Havana, we had a unique couple – Albert and Millie Butler. Albert's grandfather had been a slave. He took the name Butler. And Albert, from a young age, was assigned to Cecil's father. He taught him to hunt and fish, and he was who taught my son Victor to hunt and fish. His wife, Millie, was in my kitchen for 42 years. She told me what to do, I didn't tell her!

She was a real Southern cook -- did all Southern cooking. And she gave us the benefit of her old-time "health remedies." When I was pregnant, she told me not to raise my arms above my head. And she would always say the first rain in May go out and get your head wet 'cause that was good luck!

When I was growing up, we had a black woman named Belle. I had a wart on my knee, and Aunt Belle said, "I can cure that wart." One afternoon she was keeping us while my mother was uptown at a meeting. She said, "Go in the house and get me one of those little gold safety pins." I went and got the pin, and she said, "See that oak tree out there. Go and get one of the dry limbs off that oak tree and get me a piece of newspaper." She took the little pin and pricked the water till it bled and dabbed that stick in the blood and wrapped that newspaper and handed it to me. She said, "Go down that road until I tell you to stop. When you stop, turn around and throw that stick over your left shoulder. Don't look back – come straight back to me. And the wart'll go away." And do you know, it went away.

Another time, Mother lost a diamond stone out of her engagement ring. And there was a black woman named Beanie, and somebody told Mama Nina to go see Beanie and she could tell her where the stone was. Of course, Mama Nina had no faith in that at all, but she went out of curiosity. Beanie took her cards and she shuffled them, and she said, "Now, Mrs. Lester, that diamond is in your house. It's between two rooms." Daddy had already taken a turkey feather and swept under all the thresholds in that big old farmhouse with the rough flooring in it. But he went back and did it again. When he got to the threshold between the bathroom and the bedroom, out rolled the diamond!

That was at Floradora. It was a big old house with an 8' wide hall down the middle of it, two bedrooms on either side, the kitchen off from the back. Somebody now has bought it and moved it to another location.

I was born in town. Daddy had a dry cleaning place for awhile. Something I didn't mention was that my mother died when I was about five years old. Daddy married again – a Nina Weatherly. She came to live with us, and she brought her father and her younger brother and sister to live with us. We called her Mama Nina. She and Daddy had three children. Plus I had an older sister and two older brothers! And there were a few more relatives Daddy "adopted." We had from eight to 10 every meal three times a day!

But I grew up in tobacco. From childhood on, I knew that tobacco crop had to be taken care of. When it was over, it was always a happy time because we (Cecil and I and the children) did a few things we didn't have time to do while the tobacco was growing. It was good to us for many years, and we did very well on it. But we had our share of disasters. Barns to burn, hail … sometimes hail would completely destroy a field of tobacco. But they would pull those shades back up and cut those stalks off, and grow what they would call a "sucker crop." It was never the same quality it would have been if it had been the natural plant. But we would break even.

We sold to Swisher in Jacksonville, and we also sold to American Tobacco. Our tobacco broker was a Mr. Oliva from Tampa. He would come up and buy the crop and it would go to Hav-A-Tampa – some of it. We also had a broker in New York and he would come down and buy the tobacco.

Tobacco was bought before it was ever grown in the field. They knew from the crop before what kind of farmer you were. So they would depend on you raising another good crop. The price range in the tobacco went from 8 cents a pound to the highest price was somewhere in the neighborhood of $6 to $8 a pound. But prices varied depending on the quality of the tobacco.

Something Gold

In the end when Cecil and I grew it, we went to firing it the Candela way. We had a man come from Tampa and show us how. We sealed the barns with sheets of corrugated paper and then they were heated with gas heat. Where it originally took us two to three weeks to cure it, we could cure tobacco in 72 hours. We modified most of our barns.

I didn't personally work in the barns after I was married, except if a superintendent was out I would go down and supervise the barn that day. We never had any trouble with our workers. They worked beautifully together. We had a few incidents to happen, but not related to the work. We even had a murder.

One Sunday morning, one of the boys on the farm came up to the house, rang the back doorbell and my son Victor went to the door. There was Johnny Lee, standing with a butcher knife in his hand with blood all over it. He said, "Tell Mr. Cecil to come and help me. I've done killed Roy. I killed him dead"! He had killed his friend. And he died in jail, I guess. These things would happen on a farm sometimes. Usually, it was with a knife, not a gun.

Moonshining wasn't anything we had going on on our farm (to our knowledge!), but once Cecil and I were fishing on Dead Lakes, and I said, "I smell candy cooking"! Cecil said, "No, you don't"! I said, "Yes, I do." He said, "Not down here in Dead Lakes, you don't! And don't you ever say you smelled candy cooking on Dead Lakes, 'cause somebody'll be knocking on our door and knocking us in the head"!

When I was a child, I had a very close call. I was about three, and I was standing near the fireplace – the only way you could heat those big old houses. I was standing too close and had on my little flannel gown and it caught on fire. Daddy said (I don't remember this), my mother grabbed the rug that was in front of the fireplace, wrapped me in it and put the flames out. I still have scars from that. My older sister was Ruby, and she was lucky enough to have two years of college. At that time, they would give you what they called a "life certificate," to teach in elementary school. Her first year of teaching, she went to Concord School (the Academy our grandfather had established). I remember going with her to it. I thought it was real unusual (and neat) for her to teach there at "Granddaddy Hall's school."

Thirty-six
Suzanne Davis Powell
Backporch at Sawdust
2007

I have fond memories of tobacco farming in Gadsden County. As a little girl, I was always told to stay at the house and not go out to the tobacco barns or fields, but it was always so intriguing – I just had to go see what all was going on. I can remember going out to the seed bed with my daddy and brothers to check on the plants. The seed bed was across the creek. Daddy would plant the seeds and then when the plants got big enough, they would be transplanted in the tobacco shades. The transplanter-machine was cool. I loved sitting on it and pretending to be planting. Daddy let me ride on it and actually plant some tobacco once. That was fun! Riding the tobacco buggies was fun, also. Jeff and Gary usually drove the tractors.

When I would sneak out to the tobacco barns, I would deliver bundles of tobacco to the women stringing the tobacco. Hester had her own special table because she always strung the tobacco by hand. Everyone else used the stringing machines. Hester was just as fast or faster than those using the machines. After the tobacco was strung, it would be taken to the men hanging it in the barn. There would be an assembly line of men in the rafters passing the tobacco up to be hung.

A recurring scene happened every day. I felt sorry for a boy named Horace, because every day Daddy would fire Horace! I can't remember why. But the next day Horace would be back!

Another special memory for me was when Daddy would let us go with him to the barns in the evening to light the fires. To this day, I could probably recognize the smell of a tobacco barn. It's one of those smells you don't forget and if you smell it, memories come flowing back to your mind. These were always special times with Daddy.

I can remember that I was upset when tobacco farming left Gadsden County. The main reason was because that was Gadsden County and what I had grown up knowing. I believe it was the year that I turned 13 because it was the year I was finally going to get to start working for real.

Suzanne Davis serving as a "collector" of tobacco after it's been cured, taken off the stick and ready to be pressed down in large wooden boxes and hauled to the packing house.

"Loose" Leaves

"Leaf girl" or "leaf boy" was a job the smallest child could do. It involved picking up good leaves that sometimes fell on the dirt floor of the barn. Every leaf without holes was considered valuable. A classmate, Lynda Brinks Pfeiffer, has called it the "entry-level job"!

So the following section is devoted to tobacco tales that I've heard off the tape these past 20+ years – either from visitors to the Barn or at meetings or whenever I have button-holed people about their memories.

Bill Munroe describes being a small boy and gazing up at his daddy holding a tobacco plant with a gory-looking long black stalk: the dreaded blackshank disease! It almost wiped out our shade tobacco industry in the 1920s. (Luckily, as Bill Tappan tells earlier, one single tobacco plant that had resistance revived the industry and set in motion the North Florida Experiment Station.)

Sarah Lines Munroe (Bill's wife) grew up on the Lines Farm (present Sawdust Road) and remembers not just the tobacco but the night of the "Whale Light"! Everybody in Quincy saw an eerie light bathing the countryside and all were prepared for the End of the World. It turned out just to be the giant oscillating lights accompanying a touring attraction for a dead whale exhibit!

Max Herrin told me "farmers that survived in the '70s and '80s, after tobacco went out, were those that fixed up or adapted *what they had* (reinvented their business)." He also told of a family he admired that had worked for him, Ben and Pearl Miller – and their daughter, Barbara.

Peggy Ann Oliver & Valerie Oates strung tobacco at the Lee Parramore Farm, Mt. Pleasant (near Hooty's Scrap Military Yard). They remembered climbing up in the barn to play as children. (Their mothers had come with them to the Barn. I think they had strung tobacco even in the days before their daughters.). All four expressed the view: "This is part of our history … it was our living."

Chip Gray worked on the Violetta Farm. Told the story of a black man who was hanging tobacco and happened to rest his arm on one of the upper tierpoles and there was a snake! He was so surprised he literally slung down through the tierpoles and out the front door! (And he was at least five or six stalls from the front door.) Chip also told about a barn or field superintendent who was pretty taciturn, hardly ever said a word – he brought his lunch everyday. One day somebody stole it. He let loose a lot of words that day! It was the crew's turn to be tight-lipped. But on the bus on the way home (Chip was a little boy riding with them), the poker-faced crew got to singing: "Who stole Mmm – mmm's lunch Hoom-da"? Etc. Chip can parody it to a tee! He also reminded me how eerie-quiet it got when it was raining and thundering and we were all marooned in the barn together. "You remember how nobody would say a word"!

Irene Luttrell told of working with the Gadsden County Commission at the time her boss was helping sponsor the Young Black Artists program. In this promising group was one Dean Mitchell, whose paintings (some of which reflect the Gadsden County landscape) are today recognized all over the art world.

John Shaw Curry remembered the year the hail was so heavy on top of a shade at the May-Ball Farm that it could have sagged the whole shade down. He and another boy were put to scooping the ice in buckets or tubs. John Shaw said that in his experience as a "toter" or "lugger," they used baskets on runners to pull the tobacco from the primer to the tractor-drawn carrier. A different system from most farms.

Ray Lester worked at the Bobby D. Woodward Farm. He hung in the top of the barn, called it "topping out." He also supervised the packing at the Wedeles Packing House (under Denny Hutchinson). It was at the stage after it had been sorted – when they put it in plain cardboard boxes, marked it and shipped it to Hav-A-Tampa. He said there were about 300 black women there, and they filled the place with music. Ray's mother, Sunny Lester, said her husband Nick, who went into the military and missed out on tobacco-growing, always said the singing was what he remembered most. Nick's great-uncle Tom Lester is credited by one source as being the "fellow who started shade tobacco" when he grew some under an arbor.

Jack Freeman (I think) had packing house supervising experience, too. If I am telling this right, he said that always on the last day everybody celebrated with singing. "It was a glorious sound"!

Darlene Frost remembered a terrible lightning storm, with everyone cooped up in the barn. There came a sudden violent crash, and one worker headed to the other end down that long, dark hall. Everybody followed just like the FAMU Marching 100! But then there came another violent crash from that end. Darlene says they all wheeled around as if on cue and came hotfooting it back!

Shirley Green Knight told of stringing on the Winton (Squint) Laslie Farm, just over the Georgia line. She grew up in Robertsville.

Reginald James rode on a cut-down semi-truck with other hands (a chief memory in his tobacco-working days) as a boy.

Benny Peacock grew up beside the "Sunshine Farm" and tells that Mr. Sam Woodbery was the Superintendent. (It was an AST Farm, on both sides of Hwy. 90 near the present-day Bradwell Mortuary). Benny worked there from age five, up. His first job was running to open the gate for the barge driver or take him water or lunch. That way, he got to con the driver into letting him drive the barge a little piece. He told about Mr. LaDucca, who was Mr. Woodbury's son-in-law. He was from New York and had never seen a cow before. Was terrified to cross a pasture with one in it! Mr. LaDucca taught at the high school in Quincy.

Geraldine Black worked on Miles Womack's father's farm. She said her tobacco work helped pay her way through college. Her husband, Henry, best-known by all for his longtime barbecue catering, worked on the Sunnyside Farm, owned by George Munroe. Melvin Jowers, the superintendent at Sunnyside, was her friend Geri Jowers Coggin's dad. When Mr. Jowers started growing a crop of tobacco on his own, he had the children pour cement mix in bean hampers, and thus he had the pillars to build the barn!

Hentz Fletcher once told me of working on his Granddaddy Bertell's farm in Greensboro. According to Hentz, there were 12 mules to pull the drags (barges). His mule was named "Sneaky

Pete," because "every time anybody'd go to hitch him up, if you weren't looking, he'd bite you." Said one of the delights of his working days was sometimes the 12 barge drivers would head their mules over to Clark's Pond (up the road by the Sonny Suber Place where Hackney's Nursery is today) and all jump in "buck naked" to swim (white and black). Apparently, though, the mules weren't pulling the tobacco in fast enough to suit Mr. Bertell because he decided to try hitching up his 1954 Chevrolet to one of the drags. "Burned the Fletcher out of his motor"! Hentz remembered. He added that his granddad was a dynamo at farming, though. Along with everything else, he ran four sugar mills. One was at Sycamore, and Mr. Bentley ran it for him. One cold December day, 10-year-old Hentz watched as Mr. Bentley fired a 30-foot long furnace with oak kindling. Even though the weather was freezing, Mr. Bentley was sweating down in the hole under the furnace and evaporator. "His overalls could've stood by themselves!" It taught young Hentz to respect hard work.

Dr. Scott Gregory found a way to take a catnap at his Uncle Cecil Butler's farm in Havana while waiting for the sticks to be handed up (when he was a boy hanging tobacco in the barn). Luckily, he never fell out!

Emily Clark Rowan recalled the struggle it was for her father, Worth Clark, when he first started in tobacco. "Didn't even have any land. He farmed his brother's land and gave his brother half of what the crop brought in – which was a good thing and a bad thing, but it worked out for both of them. He put up a barn. He had to pay the cost of that. And then a tobacco shade. Had to pay for the cost of that. With our weather, he had to have water. So then he had to put in a pond. More money. So for about five years we had a struggle. Some years, he didn't make very much money.

But I owe what I became and what my children became to my father, growing tobacco. It made me a better person, a stronger person, a person who loved other people, because in a tobacco barn everybody's your buddy … (you spend lots of time together). We'd get there early, we'd leave late and we'd come back later to fire the barn. We have a wonderful heritage – those of us fortunate enough to be born in this era (at the time we may not have thought so) – and to grow up doing what we did and working together to make this the county it became, and still is.

Russell Smith of Flat Creek, also mentioned the struggle. He had just gone through "some old stuff of my daddy's between the years of '41 and '50. And quite frankly, some times they hardly made it from one year to the next. You had all kinds of things to deal with – blue mold and a whole host of other stuff. They would sometimes mortgage an entire place to make it that year, and if they didn't they would lose their place eventually. And as much as there were lots of people who gained from tobacco, there were lots of people who didn't. They'd lose everything they had. But they still tried. They had the heart and soul. And kept pushing forward every year. Go in debt, grow it, go in debt and grow it again."

Jeannie Evans, like so many, told about the music. She said her mom (Betty Jean Cross) used to love to get the black women to sing. So she would pretend she didn't know how a song went – that would get everybody going. "And they would rock the barn"! Her own memory was when her grandfather had to sell – he couldn't keep the farm anymore. "My brother and I cried because we loved playing in the tobacco barn. He would put ropes up the rafters and we'd swing and play …"

Ralph Perkins shared that at the end of tobacco-growing in Gadsden County, he became manager of the Swisher Stripping Factory on Porro Street in Quincy. It processed tobacco from Central America for shipment to the King Edward (Swisher) Factory in Waycross, GA well into the early 1990s. His wife Rachel partnered in this operation. Women at machines cut and de-stemmed leaves, tobacco was swirled and fanned, some of it was even colored black. Black cigars were marketed under the name "Maudura." He said what makes cigars expensive ($2 to $5 apiece) is if they're "all tobacco." Many of today's less expensive ones have "paper" wrappers (as explained by Ernst & Barbara Bietenholz earlier). "Invincible" is the King Edward brand that is all tobacco.

Somehow, we all thought the cigars being produced in Quincy, FL were the "gold standard" – the most deluxe of all. Now I know they weren't, even though most of the cigars being made in America were being made from our efforts. I have a feeling there is a lesson in this somewhere. I think it is what Kahlil Gibran said in *The Prophet*: "Work is love made visible." Gadsden County, a place of billowing Springtime beauty and a youthful work ethic, instilled in each of us love and pride. Those things bely the market.

There are 1,000s more memories. Just as it took galaxies of thread to supply our industry (with all the hand-sewn shades and leaves), the tobacco itself tied *us* together, and continues to do so. Not long ago, I was in the Flowers Bread Store, and **Joann (Shepard) Wells**, the clerk, warmly greeted a customer with an allusion to the "tobacco times." She and the customer's daughter had strung tobacco together on Charlie Macon's farm in Greensboro.

A word of thanks to all who have helped with this "project"

There've been so many, there isn't space. But I do want to mention several, for sure: Harriett Strickland, who first "took on" the daunting task of transcribing tapes. She didn't grow up here, but she has a farm-girl spirit, as evidenced by the nature preserve she and her husband Don created on their reclaimed former Flat Creek tobacco farmplace. She's often sustained my flagging will with her homemade bread or black-eyed susan treats. (For a hint of her heart, imagine someone who over the years had made some 20 Cabbage Patch dolls and, without blinking, donated them all to worthwhile causes -- mostly to brighten less-fortunate children this past Christmas.)

The *whole* Gadsden County McGill Public Library staff, just with their patience and good humor, eased me into the computer age – never once buying into my certainty that I was a nuisance and wearing them out. Through them, I enrolled in Robbie Bullock's course. With Robbie's guidance, the final scary stages of scanning photos and other technical aspects the printer had insisted on were accomplished.

Also, there was Jan Summerford, Florida Dept. of Agriculture marketing specialist, with her overall support and faith, not only in this book effort, but in the Jamestown 2007 Barn Day (June 2nd), which the book helps celebrate. Thanks, too, to the Jamestown 2007 Committee and their Statewide Program Manager, Amy Ritchie, for recognizing Gadsden County as "somewhere special" – deserving to be honored even though it's outside Virginia.

And, naturally, I wish to thank each "participant" – or subject who was recorded. As obvious, these interviews took place over a long period of time. Just as heartening as they were – were the reconnections with the subject or family member who checked and gave permission to use these beloved spiels.

Last, I hope my family and friends, who've borne with this as with all my "tangents" in the cause of preserving history, especially Southern and Sawdust and Old Florida history, will feel this work has not unduly bared their souls (in the baring of mine). They have all been my props, always. Beginning with Olean and Forrest – my parents.

Kay (Shuler) Davis Lay

If the previous chapters (or leaves) didn't "bang any drums" about it, it's no secret anymore that many modest Gadsden County shade tobacco farmers were a breed apart. (Some of those in this book could be, or also have been featured, in the *Gadsden County Times.* Another article told that one community, Providence, gave eleven sons – farm boys – in WWII) While H.M. Butler was not someone I got to interview, he was always "on my list." I didn't know this about him. (As Tom Brokaw has pointed out, WWII heroes didn't brag a lot.) Maybe this next beautiful article tells his part best.

Gadsden County Times   February 9, 2006

A young man went to war; a hero came home

H.M. Butler won the Bronze Star for his heroism, but now faces another battle

By BYRON SPIRES
Times Staff Writer

You would think it is just a book, you might even confuse it with an old high school annual. Its blue cover and gold lettering, however, ring of a different kind of school.

A school that took America's brightest and best and thrust them into a world of war. Its classroom was a time turned upside down with tyranny and threats of world domination.

The book is the history of the Fourth Infantry Division, 12th Infantry Regiment during World War Two in Europe.

Its pages are full of pictures of America at war. From the 12th's landing at Utah Beach on D-day to the final occupation of Germany.

This is the story of one of those men from here in Gadsden County.

Henry M. Butler, now 80, was one of those bright faces with a kid smile that makes you realize how young these men were when they were asked to go to war for their country.

This is his story.

H.M. as his friends and family know him, entered the service at 19. He was inducted at Camp Blanding in August 1944. Instead of the usual 16 weeks of training Butler would get an expedited infantry training and be out in 12 weeks. He would finish his training in Fort Meade, Maryland. It would be in Fort Meade. Butler would remember receiving all of his equipment, including his M-1 rifle.

His entering the Army coincided with the Allied force's push into the Hurtgen Forest on Germany's doorstep.

Replacements were needed soon and it would cut his training by four weeks.

Called Hurtgen's Bloody Forest, the 12th suffered considerable losses in the battle of the Hurtgen Forest. It is said that it was the most grueling battle of the war between D-Day and V-E day.

Butler arrived in Metz France at about the same time that the famous "Battle of the Bulge" started.

He was assigned to the 12th Infantry Regiment Company F. Butler was with the 12th when it entered Germany at the Siegfried Line. The weather was horrendous with freezing rain and snow. The 12th had to cross open fields in knee deep snow. The 12th plowed ahead into Germany, taking such towns as Basan and Schweiler.

Shortly after these battles the 12th was relieved for some much needed rest in Verriere de Porticux, France. Then it was back on the path to roast the Germans. The regiment moved forward into Germany on March 21, crossing the Rhine River at Worms on March 30. By April 4 the regiment had turned south toward the Alps.

It was in this push that Butler received his Bronze Star Medal.

Near the city of Ellerbach, Germany, on April 26, Butler and his platoon would come under heavy fire from a German machine gun nest.

One of his comrades who happened to be carrying a Browning Automatic Rifle (B.A.R. is a one man machine gun) panicked.

Butler took the B.A.R. from the man and crawled out in front of the platoon to gain a better view of the machine gun. By doing this he came under direct fire from the machine gun. Through this heroic act Butler was able to destroy the machine gun nest.

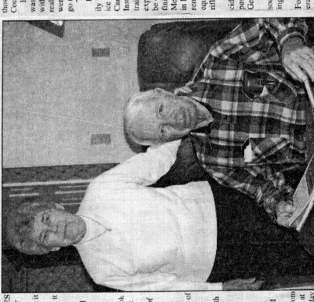

H.M. Butler and his wife, Janice, spend a few minutes looking at the blue book that traces Butler's 12th Infantry Regiment's exploits in World War Two.

But that was not where his heroism would end. He then crawled further forward and placed a murderous fire on enemy riflemen who had been delaying the advance of an adjacent platoon.

Butler's citation reads, "With the assistance of Private Butler's automatic rifle fire, the company was able to drive the enemy from the area. Private Butler's courageous actions and unswerving devotion to duty reflect great credit upon himself and the military service." Approved by command of Major General Hays.

During his travels he met two other Gadsden Countians: Malcolm Perkins and Mac Blount. Both men were from the Providence area. They were two of the eleven men from that area who died serving their country.

The war ended in May of 1945 and Butler stayed in service until October 1946.

He came back to Gadsden County and then went on to Chipola Junior College.

Butler then spent the next 23 years raising shade tobacco, corn, soybeans and beef cattle.

After farming, Butler joined the extension service and retired in 1990. Butler has been a director of the Gadsden County Farm Bureau and is a member of the First Baptist Church in Quincy.

He married Janice Betts in 1952 and the couple has three children and five grandchildren.

It has been a little over 60 years since the war ended. As time moves forward many of those who lived through those days are slowly slipping away from us. With them are memories of one of our finest hours. A time some say that the greatest generation stepped up to the plate and served their country.

As a reminder of his heroism of 60 years ago, US Represenitive Allen Boyd had an American flag flown over the US capital for Butler last year on the anniversary of his heroic act that earned him the Bronz

Star.

Although he faced enemy fire in World War Two, he now faces an even greater foe, dementia and Parkinson's disease.

These diseases not only attack your body, they attack your memory as well. He has good days and bad days, his wife said. His memory is slowly slipping away and as it does so does another one of those heroes to whom we all owe so much.

WWII hero story

Other Books and Other Resources

(To know and understand more about our county – once known as the Shade Tobacco Capital of Florida)

<u>WFSU & Gadsden County Historical Society Shade Tobacco Story</u>, video available from Gadsden Arts Center, downtown Quincy, $20.

<u>Shade Tobacco Days in Gadsden County</u>, an honors thesis by Harbert Scott Gregory, Jr., St. Andrews Presbyterian College, May 1, 1991.

<u>Gadsden A Florida County in Word and Picture</u>. Miles Kenan Womack, Jr. Gadsden County Historical Commission, 1976.

"Agriculture in the Southern U.S. to 1860," Lewis Carol Gray, Carnegie Institute of Washington.

"Gadsden County: 150 Years Young," *Tallahassee Democrat* Special Supplement, April 29, 1973.

"Tylear Sanders: Big Bend Success Story," Clarence Bizet, *Tallahassee Democrat*, July 23, 1967. (Story of black shade tobacco farmer in Quincy.)

"Memories of Hardaway," by J.C. Campbell, *Twin City News* Chattahoochee, FL June 2004 (Series of glimpses into a tobacco-growing community)

Uncertain Seasons, by Betty Shelfer Morgan. (A memoir of a shade tobacco childhood in Havana, FL during WWII – impacted in later life by reading letters from a soldier uncle who did not return home).

Also, of interest:

"It Took Special Men To Grow Shade Tobacco," series by Mayo Livingston, Bainbridge Post-Searchlight

American Beauty, by Edna Ferber. (A novel set in the Connecticut River Valley shade tobacco-growing country).

History of Decatur County, GA. by Frank S. Jones.

"The Story of John Rolfe who Saved a Colony and Planted the Seeds of a Nation," 350th Anniversary of Jamestown booklet.

In Memory

Forrest Davis, Sr. 1977
Byron Suber 1998
Isabelle Suber 1993
Newton Edwards 1995
Arch Hubbard 1992
Joe Cantey 1998
Nellie Cantey 1998
Jimmy Bowen 2006
Harbert Gregory 1998
Marjorie Gregory 2005
Lynn Betts 1990
Herschel Edwards 1998
Pat Carman 2000
Ernst Bietenholz 1998
Rev. Louis Mims 1996
Robert Parramore 2000
Hal Davis 1998
Maidee Barnett 1994
Fain Embry
Olean Davis 2005
Hester Williams 1996
Audrey Bassett Peavy 2004
Bob Lay 1996
John Henry McNealy 2005

(Their part in this effort was inestimable.)

Also, in memory: John Shaw Vaughan 2006 – killed in action
Mosul, Iraq
(grandson of shade tobacco's C.R. "Dick" Shaw Family)

Note: The Canteys (Joe and Nellie) died in February and April, respectively. They would have been married 80 years on May 8, 1998. They had their 75th Anniversary at the McLaughlin House (Nellie's girlhood home, that had then only recently been moved to Havana to be the Community Center – it was where they had been married "at high noon" and from which they had "taken the train on a honeymoon to St. Augustine.")

Printed in the United States
83256LV00003B